Addresses on
THE FIRST EPISTLE TO THE
CORINTHIANS

Addresses on

THE FIRST EPISTLE TO THE

CORINTHIANS

By H. A. IRONSIDE, Litt. D.

Expository Sermons Preached in the
MOODY MEMORIAL CHURCH, CHICAGO, ILL.

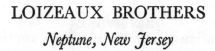

LOIZEAUX BROTHERS
Neptune, New Jersey

FIRST EDITION, OCTOBER 1938
FOURTEENTH PRINTING, SEPTEMBER 1979

Published by LOIZEAUX BROTHERS, INC.

*A Nonprofit Organization, Devoted to the Lord's Work
and to the Spread of His Truth*

ISBN 0-87213-354-0
PRINTED IN THE UNITED STATES OF AMERICA

PREFATORY NOTE

For nearly two years, 1934 and 1935, it was my privilege to attempt to expound the Corinthian epistles at the regular Sunday morning gatherings, numbering from 2500 to 3500 people, in the Auditorium of the Moody Memorial Church in Chicago. With Radio equipment these addresses were broadcast over a large stretch of territory, thus reaching many thousands more. So insistent has been the demand for their publication in printed form that I have decided to send them out in this way. The original messages were taken down by a competent reporter and have been considerably revised and shortened, as otherwise it would have taken several volumes to reproduce them. I am more firmly convinced than ever that there is need to emphasize the fundamental principles set forth in these letters given by inspiration through the apostle to the Gentiles, in order that Christians generally may be called back to the simplicity of early days. In First Corinthians we have the order that should prevail in Christian assemblies, while the second epistle deals more particularly with the ministry of the Church. If it please God, the addresses on that letter will be published later.

I hope my readers will not come to this book looking for a critical analysis of the epistle. If so, they will be disappointed. The object I had in view was to expound the Word as simply as possible for the edification and instruction of plain people who have neither the time nor the learning to follow heavy and erudite comments. If any such are helped to a greater appreciation of the value of this portion of the Word of God I shall be abundantly repaid for the time and labor required to reproduce the spoken messages.

H. A. IRONSIDE.

Chicago, 1938.

CONTENTS

SANCTIFIED IN CHRIST JESUS

✓ ✓ ✓

"Paul, called an apostle of Jesus Christ through the will of God, and Sosthenes our brother, unto the church of God which is at Corinth, to them that are sanctified in Christ Jesus, called saints, with all that in every place call upon the name of Jesus Christ our Lord, both theirs and ours: Grace be unto you, and peace, from God our Father, and from the Lord Jesus Christ" (1 Cor. 1: 1-3).

✓ ✓ ✓

THE two letters to the Corinthians, the letter to the Romans, and that to the Galatians form a quartet of epistles which were apparently written during Paul's third missionary journey and bear a very intimate relationship each to the other. In Romans we have set forth the great fundamental doctrine of justification by faith alone. In Galatians that doctrine is defended after having been called in question by legal teachers. These two epistles, Romans and Galatians, form therefore the very foundation of Christian teaching. Then in the two letters to the Corinthians we have instruction as to the Church.

9

In the first epistle we have the ordering, the calling, and the discipline of the Church. In the second we have the ministry of the Church. If we should lose all the rest of the New Testament—which God forbid we should—and have only these four letters preserved, they would be sufficient to show us the way of salvation and how to conduct ourselves as Christian people coming together in church relationship. Therefore, we can get some idea of the importance of being thoroughly familiar with them.

How the gospel reached Corinth we learn from Acts 18, where we are told that the apostle Paul after his visit to Athens passed on to Corinth and at first began the work in a very quiet way. He did not enter the city with any blare of trumpets; he was not advertised as a great evangelist or Bible teacher; but he simply went in quietly as an unknown craftsman. He was a tent-maker, and in association with two friends of his, Aquila and Priscilla, who were engaged in the same business, an establishment was opened up where they wrought, we are told, night and day. We learn elsewhere that in this way the apostle was able to support not only himself but all who labored with him when the churches forgot their responsibility to them. He was a great foreign missionary and when the churches of God did recognize their responsibility and sent gifts, as in the

case of the Philippian church, he gladly received
them and used the money for the glory of God.
But if he were neglected, he did not sit down and
pine and whimper because of the cold-heartedness
of Christians elsewhere, but simply created a job
for himself and went to work making tents and
providing the wherewithal to carry on his testimony. This in a way was a real help, for sometimes a preacher or a missionary goes into a field
where he is looked upon as a well-supported individual bearing an official title and relationship to
the church, and the people often are not as interested in him and his message as if he came among
them working with his own hands as they have
to do.

Having established his business the apostle began to move among the Jews. There was a synagogue in the city, which he attended and where
he doubtless listened to the regular services, and
then when opportunity was given, he presented
the gospel there. There was a great deal of free-
dom in a Jewish synagogue. Jewish visitors, particularly if attired in the teacher's garb, were
permitted to take part in the service. Undoubtedly when Paul went there he wore the garments
that showed that he was a graduate of the school
of Gamaliel and therefore he was recognized as
a teacher. On one occasion as he and Barnabas
sat in a synagogue, the rulers, having completed

the first part of the service, recognized these two
men as teachers and said, "Ye men and brethren.
if ye have any word of exhortation for the people, say on." And we read, "Then Paul stood up,
and beckoning with his hand said, Men of Israel,
and ye that fear God, give audience" (Acts 13:
15, 16). This would be the customary procedure
in the Jewish synagogue. There was nothing
irregular and nothing disorderly about it. Paul
was simply availing himself of a privilege. So
from Sabbath to Sabbath, that is, on Saturday of
course, he reasoned with the Jews and any Gentiles who might be present. It was a common
thing for inquiring Gentiles to attend the Jewish services. Tired and weary of the customary
recurring heathen festivities, finding nothing in
paganism to answer the yearning desires of their
hearts, they sought there what they could not
find elsewhere. When they in a measure at least
accepted the Jewish doctrines, they were recognized as "Proselytes of the Gate." To these people the apostle presented the message; he reasoned with them on the Sabbath Day.

Some of our present-day legalistic friends who
have never known the blessedness of deliverance
from law say, "We read in the book of Acts that
Paul preached on the Sabbath Day, and that day
is Saturday and so we are in duty bound to recognize that day rather than Sunday as the Lord's

Day." The fact is that the apostle was simply accommodating himself to the Jews who met on their Sabbath. If he wished to reach them, he had to reach them on that day. The Christians themselves met together on the first day of the week to break bread and for prayer. The earliest Christian testimony along that line confirms that very thing. One of those early writers says, "On the first day of the week, the day after the Jewish Sabbath, the day which we Christians call the Lord's Day, we come together for worship, etc." This was the custom of Christians from the beginning, but on the Jewish Sabbath they found opportunity to minister to the Jews, and so used that day for that purpose. We learn that Paul at first simply dealt with them from the standpoint of the Old Testament, but "when Silas and Timotheus were come from Macedonia, Paul was pressed in the spirit and testified to the Jews that Jesus was Christ" (Acts 18:5). His work up to this time was preparation, but now, with the backing of other helpers, he feels the time has come to give a clear ringing testimony, to show that all these Old Testament scriptures pointed to the One who had been crucified at Jerusalem, had been raised from the dead, and ascended into heaven. And now many of the Jews turned from them, they opposed the message, and the apostle did a very significant thing. He wore the long eastern robes, and he shook his garments and said, "Your blood be upon your own heads; I am clean: from henceforth I will go unto the Gentiles" (Acts 18: 6). And so he left the synagogue, never to enter it again as far as this particular city was concerned. He found a preaching place in the house of a man named Justus.

Justus was evidently a Gentile, but one who was a proselyte; he had accepted the Jewish revelation as to God, and his house adjoined the synagogue. Paul began preaching in his house, and one of the first converts was the chief ruler of the synagogue, Crispus, who believed with all his house; and the work went on for a year and a half, and many of the Corinthians having heard the Word believed and were baptized.

Notice the order. They heard the message, they believed the gospel, and then they were publicly baptized, thus confessing that they had received the crucified One as their own personal Saviour. I emphasize that because some people imagine that in his epistles the apostle seems to minimize the importance of Christian baptism. He did not ordinarily do the baptizing himself, but he was always insistent to see that it was done. The fact that Paul himself was generally not the baptizer does not indicate that he slighted the Christian ordinance of baptism.

As we go on in that eighteenth chapter of Acts

we read of the insurrection stirred up against
Paul in the days of Gallio, and we are told that
the Greeks caught Sosthenes, who had become the
chief ruler of the synagogue, and beat him for his
attempt to foment a riot. It would seem that the
beating did him good because we next find his
name linked with the apostle Paul in Corinthians
as a Christian. Of course we have no positive
proof that this is the same man, but I take it for
granted that it is. It brought him at last to accept the Lord Jesus Christ as his Saviour.

A mighty work of God was accomplished during the year and a half that Paul was in Corinth.
It was not a likely field for missionary service; it
was one of the metropolises of the ancient world.
Its population numbered at this time between six
and seven hundred thousand people and it was
given over to the worship of the goddess Aphrodite, the Greek name for the one whom the
Romans worshipped as Venus, the goddess of lust,
or carnal love, and in celebrating the rites of
Aphrodite, the Corinthians gave themselves up to
the most shameful licentiousness. So notorious
was this that, in all parts of the Greek-speaking
world, if men or women were found behaving in
an unclean way, the worst that anybody could say
of them was that they acted like Corinthians.
Just as, for instance, the names of those two
cities of the plains have come down to our day,

linked with such wickedness that if one says of a person, he is like the people of Sodom and Gomorrah, you at once understand that he lives a life of vilest uncleanness. So to say one behaved like a Corinthian, or was Corinthianized, intimated that he was a man totally lost to all sense of morality or decency. Such was the city into which Paul went to preach the gospel of the grace of God, and in this city that gospel won many to the knowledge of Christ. It was the means of delivering people from their lives of wickedness, of making saints out of those who had been vicious and utterly lost to all sense of decency.

When we have this background before us, what interest it gives to these opening verses, "Paul, called an apostle of Jesus Christ through the will of God, and Sosthenes our brother." I leave out the italicized words, "to be," because I want to convey to you the fact that they should be left out in the second verse also. Paul was not called *to be* an apostle, he *was* an apostle, but he was a *called* apostle, an apostle by divine call. And so you and I are not called *to be* saints, if we have trusted the Lord Jesus; we *are* saints, we are saints by calling. Notice then that Paul's apostleship, as he tells us in the letter to the Galatians, was not of man, neither by man. No one had anything to do with putting him into the apostolate except the risen Lord. An apostle was one who had seen the Lord and went forth to proclaim His message. Paul, as Saul, saw the Lord that day on the Damascus turnpike and went forth to proclaim Christ to the Jews and Gentiles. It was the will of God that made him what he was.

Notice how he links with himself, "Sosthenes our brother." I take it for granted that this must have been the Corinthian Sosthenes, because those receiving the letter would at once recognize his name, and a thrill would go through their hearts as they exclaimed, "Yes, Sosthenes, once the persecutor, converted here in our own city, is still with the apostle Paul, and is sending his greetings to us." We value the greetings of those we love and esteem in the Lord, and when they go elsewhere we are always pleased to hear from them, and so the Corinthians would get a special thrill of pleasure as they found his name linked with that of the apostle Paul.

"Unto the church of God which is at Corinth." What a change had taken place since the years when this very man as Saul of Tarsus persecuted the Church of God and wasted it. There is a strange teaching going around today that the Church of the book of Acts is not the Church of our day, that the Church, the Body of Christ, did not begin until after Paul was put in prison in Rome. Paul persecuted the Church of God when

still unconverted. How could he have persecuted
that which had not existence? The Church had
its birthday on the day of Pentecost; and after
that, churches of God were established in local
communities. Here it was one composed of those
who were once legalistic Jews or blind Gentiles,
but now all one in Christ Jesus. And the apostle
speaks of them as, "the sanctified." "Unto the
church of God which is at Corinth, to them that
are sanctified in Christ Jesus, called saints, with
all that in every place call upon the name of Jesus
Christ our Lord, both theirs and ours." Our idea
of a saint or a sanctified one is often a sinless person. We see someone in whom the grace of God
shines out most wonderfully and we say, "Well,
certainly there is a saint." Or, perhaps some one
has just gone Home, and we speak of "The
sainted So-and-so," because they have gotten beyond the reach of sin. But that is not the way
Scripture uses these terms. "The sanctified," not
the sinless; "saints," not those absolutely holy.
The saints are the separated, the sanctified are
those set apart to God in Christ Jesus. These are
two words that come from the same root, meaning separated, set apart, devoted to a holy purpose. Are you saved, have you put your trust in
the Lord Jesus Christ? The moment you did so
God separated you from a world under judgment
and set you apart unto Himself in Christ Jesus,

and that instant you became a saint, that moment
you were sanctified, and that sanctification is a
perfect one.

We read in Hebrews, "He hath perfected forever them that are sanctified." I used to be
taught, and perhaps some of you have been told,
that a man has first to be justified, and then perhaps sometime afterward he goes on to receive
what they call the second blessing and he becomes
sanctified. When I turn to the Book of God, I
find the very opposite. I find that in the first
place a man is sanctified by the work of the Spirit
in his heart even before he comes to the knowledge of Christ. It is the sanctifying, separating
work of the Spirit of God that leads him to faith
in the Lord Jesus Christ. But the moment he
puts his faith in Christ, that moment God sees
him as sanctified in Christ Jesus, set apart to God
from the old life, the old ways, the world, that to
which he once belonged, set apart to God and
counted clean in His sight because of the infinite
value of the atoning work of His beloved Son.
Have you trusted Christ? Are you sanctified?
Do you say to me, "I would hardly dare say that.
I know I am a Christian, I trust I am justified,
but I am afraid I am not good enough yet to say
that I am sanctified." Just as your goodness had
nothing to do with your justification, so it is not
your goodness that entitles you to take your place

among the sanctified. You were justified by faith
in the Lord Jesus Christ and all the past put
away forever, and God gave you a new standing
before Him. But sin makes men not only guilty
but unclean. Because we are guilty we need to
be justified, because we are unclean we need to be
sanctified. But we are cleansed by the blessed
atoning blood through which we are justified. So
we read of being sanctified by the blood of His
covenant. "Wherefore Jesus also, that He might
sanctify the people with His own blood, suffered
without the gate" (Heb. 13: 12). "And for their
sakes I sanctify Myself, that they also might be
sanctified through the truth" (John 17: 19). The
moment He rose from the dead God saw all believers as linked with Him. In Hebrews we read,
"He that sanctifieth and they who are sanctified
are all of one: for which cause He is not ashamed
to call them brethren" (Heb. 2: 11). So if you
are a Christian and have any doubt about your
sanctification, put it away and thank God that
you are in Christ and therefore sanctified.

As we go on in this epistle we find the apostle
had to bring a great many things before these
Corinthians that needed correction. He told them
that they were carnal, going to law with one another, tolerating all kinds of unholy things in
their midst. Some had wrong ideas about the
marriage relationship, some were very ignorant

about their relation to their past idolatry, but the
apostle speaks of them all as the sanctified in
Christ Jesus. But observe, he not only addresses
this letter to, "The church of God which is at
Corinth, to them that are sanctified in Christ
Jesus, called saints," but widens out the address
so that it takes in every Christian to the end of
the dispensation, "With all that in every place
call upon the name of Jesus Christ our Lord, both
theirs and ours." Do you see the importance of
that? There are many things in this epistle that
some Christians today try to dodge and get away
from, and very often you will hear, as the epistle
is read, "Oh, well, that was for that age and that
day, or for folks living in Corinth, but not for
people today." Now notice the address is, "To all
that in every place call upon the name of Jesus
Christ our Lord, both theirs and ours." This
letter then is addressed to each one who seeks to
own the Lordship of Christ; and therefore, as we
study it, I trust we will accept it as a personal
message from the Holy Spirit of God to each one
of us as Christian individuals.

We would not like to think that the great grace
passages in this epistle were only for the Corinthians. Let us not then attempt to put the responsibility passages upon the people of Corinth alone,
but remember that all is written for the whole
Church of God, clear down to the coming of our

Lord Jesus and our gathering together unto Him.

In the third verse we have the apostolic salutation, "Grace be unto you, and peace, from God our Father, and from the Lord Jesus Christ." We are saved by grace, but of course this is not the grace to which he here refers. He knows that is settled, these people who are sanctified in Christ Jesus are already justified by faith, saved by grace. It is not that which he is thinking of when he says, "Grace be unto you, and peace, from God our Father, and from the Lord Jesus Christ." And then again all Christians have peace with God through our Lord Jesus Christ. We read in Romans 5:1, "Therefore being justified by faith, we *have* peace with God"—it is a settled thing— "through our Lord Jesus Christ." He is not praying that these Christians may obtain that grace of which he speaks here. First of all, it is grace to sustain in all the trials of the way, grace to enable us to overcome in every hour of temptation. In Hebrews we are bidden to "come boldly unto the throne of grace"—upon which our great High Priest sits—"that we may obtain mercy, and find grace for seasonable help" (Heb. 4:16). We need grace every day of our lives. The grace of yesterday will not suffice for today. We need to go to God morning by morning, to draw down from above by meditation and prayer supplies of grace to start the day aright. But throughout the

day we need to learn to "Pray without ceasing"
that our hearts may continually be reaching out
to Him that new supplies of grace may come
down to us constantly. We cannot keep ourselves, not for one moment, therefore the need of
the grace that is in Christ Jesus. And the peace,
I repeat, is not peace *with* God, but that peace *of*
God of which we read in Philippians 4: 6, 7: "Be
careful for nothing; but in everything, by prayer
and supplication, with thanksgiving, let your requests be made known unto God. And the peace
of God, which passeth all understanding, shall
keep your hearts and minds through Christ
Jesus." You see this has nothing to do with the
sin question. That is settled.

We have peace with God because our sins have
been forever put away, but this has to do with the
question of things that would keep us anxious, the
trials of life that press upon our hearts. How
blessed the privilege to go to God about them all.
I am afraid many dear Christians miss a great
deal here because they have never learned to go
to Him about their temporal affairs as well as
their spiritual needs. Christians have looked at
me aghast when I have told them of praying
about money and regarding family affairs. They
say, "You do not mean to say that God who created the world is concerned that I have money to
meet my rent and to pay for food, that He will

interfere in my family affairs?" "Be careful for nothing; but in everything"—that is all-inclusive —"by prayer and supplication, with thanksgiving, let your requests be made known unto God." My brother, my sister, not a trial ever comes to you, there is not a perplexity you are called upon to face, there is not a need you will have to meet, but God invites you to come to Him about it, and you have the promise, "My God shall supply all your need according to His riches in glory by Christ Jesus" (Phil. 4: 19).

LECTURE II.

THE FELLOWSHIP OF GOD'S SON

✓ ✓ ✓

"I thank my God always on your behalf, for the grace
of God which is given you by Jesus Christ; that in every
thing ye are enriched by Him, in all utterance, and in all
knowledge; even as the testimony of Christ was confirmed
in you: so that ye come behind in no gift; waiting for the
coming of our Lord Jesus Christ: who shall also confirm you
unto the end, that ye may be blameless in the day of our
Lord Jesus Christ. God is faithful by whom ye were called
unto the fellowship of His Son Jesus Christ our Lord"
(1 Cor. 1: 4-9).

✓ ✓ ✓

EVEN as we read these words we cannot but
notice how frequently the full name and
title of our Saviour is used, and throughout
this entire epistle we shall find this is characteristic. He who brought these Corinthians out of
darkness into His marvelous light is He who
through grace has brought many of us to a saving knowledge of Himself. He is our Lord Jesus
Christ. You will never find in the Bible that un-
due familiarity in the use of divine names which
is so common in the irreverent days in which we

live. No one, for instance, in the Scriptures ever addresses our blessed Saviour merely as Jesus. He is sometimes spoken of as Jesus, and by divine inspiration, when His atoning work is particularly in view, for the angel said, "Thou shalt call His name Jesus: for He shall save His people from their sins" (Matt. 1: 21). But when He is addressed directly, and ordinarily even when spoken of by His followers, He is called, "The Lord Jesus," "The Lord Jesus Christ," or "Jesus Christ our Lord." I am sure there is something in that for each one of us. He has said, "Ye call Me Master and Lord: and ye say well; for so I am" (John 13: 13). Let us ever remember when we approach Him in prayer that He is our Lord; when we speak of Him to others, that "God hath made that same Jesus who was crucified to be both Lord and Christ." These epistles to the Corinthians emphasize His Lordship throughout. Let us beware of calling Jesus, Lord, and then slighting His commands.

> "If He is not Lord of all,
> Then He is not Lord at all."

Thank God, we delight to know Him as our supreme sovereign Master.

In this introductory portion, the apostle who points out in other parts of the epistle a great

many irregularities in the church at Corinth,
who reproves these believers for many things
bringing dishonor upon the name of the Lord, yet
first of all gives God thanks for what His grace
has already wrought. As he remembers the year
and a half that he labored in Corinth, during
which time the greater part of those primarily
addressed in this letter were brought into a saving knowledge of Christ, he says, "I thank my
God always on your behalf." As a soul-winner it
brought great joy to his heart to think of those
he had the privilege of pointing to Christ. "I
thank my God always on your behalf for the
grace of God which is given you by Jesus Christ."
And when he speaks thus, he is not thinking for
the moment merely of the grace that saves. They
were saved by grace; no one is saved in any other
way, and grace is God's free unmerited favor toward those deserving the very opposite. But having been saved we are dowered by grace; God
provides through His grace all we need for our
journey through this world. Among other things,
when He gathers people together in church fellowship, and it is according to the mind of God
that believers should be gathered together in
various localities as churches of God, the Lord
makes Himself responsible through the same
grace that saves to minister that which will profit
and edify and build them up as companies of be-

lievers. It is this particularly on which the apostle is here dwelling.

He thanks God for the grace of God given him by Jesus Christ, "that in everything," he says, "ye are enriched by Him, in all utterance, and in all knowledge." In other words, this Corinthian church was one greatly blessed, from the standpoint of gifts of the Spirit. There were those among them who could minister the Word of God most acceptably, there were others who had the gift of the evangelist who could go out and carry the message to the world, there were some who were gifted as teachers, who could impart spiritual instruction to their brethren; there were many who had miraculous gifts (chap. 12). It is a question if there ever was a Christian church more richly blessed from this standpoint than the Corinthian church, and yet it is a solemn fact that they were very carnal, although so wonderfully endowed. That leads us to realize that gifts in themselves are not preservative. One may be very gifted, one may have great ability individually, and yet not necessarily be walking with God, not necessarily guided by the Holy Spirit in the use of His gift. A church may be blessed with many in its fellowship upon whom God has bestowed special gifts of the Spirit, but these do not themselves prove that that church is spiritual above others. We live in a day when there is a

very unhealthy craving for what we may call
"the miraculous gifts," and people have an idea
that if these were more in evidence in the church
there would be more spirituality and more accomplished for God. I think the history of the Corinthian church proves the unsoundness of such
reasoning. No church that I know of has ever
exceeded them in the grace of God in regard to
gifts, and yet they were anything but a truly
spiritual church. In the epistle to the Ephesians
(ch. 4: 7) a very similar expression is used to
what we have in Corinthians: "Unto every one of
us is given grace according to the measure of the
gift of Christ." And then he mentions the different gifts that the ascended Christ has given to
the Church.

It is grace on God's part that leads the Holy
Spirit to bestow these gifts upon His people. How
much we need to respond to the grace of God by
holding the gift in subjection to Himself and not
becoming occupied with the gift rather than with
the Giver. The Corinthians became so occupied
with the gifts that they all wanted to do miraculous things, and so their eyes were taken off
Christ and fixed upon manifestations, and they
lost the sweetness of communion with Him.

We should be careful never to confound natural
talent with spiritual gifts. For instance, God
gives the gift of wisdom, the gift of knowledge,

He gives the gift of teaching, the gift of preaching, the gift of exhortation, but that is altogether different from any mere natural ability along what we might call oratorical lines. A man may be a natural born orator; it may be just as natural to him to declaim in an interesting way, a compelling way, as it is for another to sing beautifully; but whether speaking or singing one needs something more than mere natural talent, and that is the power of the Holy Spirit. If a man is naturally talented, if a woman has certain natural talents, these are not to be discarded when yielding themselves to Christ, but they are not to be put in the place of spiritual gifts. It is the Holy Spirit of God taking possession of the human instrument, working through it, and anointing it that displaces mere natural talent by spiritual gifts. Very often God takes people who are not at all remarkable for natural talent, and after they are converted and yielded to Him, the Holy Spirit, who divides to every one severally as He will, gives to such amazing power in the presentation of spiritual things. This is a divine gift. The apostle says, "Covet earnestly the best gifts" (1 Cor. 12:31). And so, if you are already saved, if you are trusting Christ as your Saviour, look up to God that He may bestow upon you some special gift of His grace that thus you may be better able to win others to Christ and help

His beloved people. But never confound mere human eloquence with divine ministry, never confound mere oratory with preaching of the Word. Preaching the Word may be oratorical or it may lack that characteristic entirely.

The apostle Paul was naturally a wonderful orator, but when he stood before people to preach the gospel he said he held all that back lest their faith should stand in the wisdom of man rather than in the power of God. Divine gifts enable servants of Christ to minister to edification, to the salvation of sinners, and the building up of saints. But one may have these and be out of fellowship with God; therefore the importance of living day by day in the spirit of self-judgment that He may have the controlling power in the exercise of the gifts.

Through their gifts the testimony of Christ was confirmed in them. Paul had come to Corinth to minister the Word. These Corinthians had believed, and now in turn they ministered to others, and God graciously confirmed that testimony in blessing, so that Paul says, "Ye come behind in no gift." Whereas in other churches there may have been a few with some special gift, in Corinth there were a great many. There was no gift that was not found in that one assembly, and yet as we read the epistle we are amazed to find how far many of them had dropped from faithfulness to Christ and true communion with the Lord. Surely this is a warning to us.

In the last part of the seventh verse he says that they were waiting for the coming of our Lord Jesus Christ. The word translated "coming" is not *"parousia,"* the word generally used for the coming of the Lord to the air when saints rise to meet Him, but it is *"apokalupsis,"* His unveiling, when He is manifested before the whole world. We are waiting for the unveiling of Jesus Christ. This, of course, is the goal. The Lord descending and calling His people to meet Him in the air is a preparation, but the goal is the unveiling. When He shall be manifested in glory, then we shall be manifested with Him. Therefore, we should be content to live quiet, godly, unworldly lives now because in that day we shall have our reward as we shine forth with Him. The apostle put the coming of the Lord, the revelation of Jesus Christ, before these saints as the goal of all their hopes, and then tells them in the eighth verse that the Lord Jesus Christ for whom they wait shall confirm them unto the end.

I wonder whether you have noticed that this is the method of the Spirit of God throughout the Scriptures, particularly when He has to reprove Christians because of failure in the life. He begins by commending them for all that He can and by assuring them that everything is going to

come out all right in the end.   In the first chapter
of Philippians the apostle writes of his assurance
regarding them.   In verse 6 he says, "Being confident of this very thing, that He which hath
begun a good work in you will perform—complete—it until the day of Jesus Christ."   Here he
says He "shall confirm you unto the end, that ye
may be blameless in the day of our Lord Jesus
Christ."   The day of our Lord Jesus Christ is that
day when He returns to call His own to be with
Himself, the day when we shall stand before His
judgment-seat, when we shall all be "turned inside out," when all hidden motives will be brought
to light, when we shall be rewarded according to
the deeds done in the body since His grace saved
us.   And the apostle says "He is going to confirm
you unto the end."   This is our confirmation.
Some people make confirmation a special church
ritual service.   A child is under the care of the
church until a certain year, and then he is confirmed and brought into the full membership of
the church.   The Bible has much to say about confirmation, but it is never presented as a rite.   The
confirmation of the Bible is always the work of
the Spirit of God in the life making His truth
real to the soul.

Now he says, as it were, "I am absolutely sure
that your confirmation will go on until the day of
Jesus Christ."   In other words, the apostle had

not the slightest thought that any one who had
ever been born again would fail to reach heaven.
He knew that many of them might fail grievously
on the way, but he knew also that they were not
responsible to keep themselves but that they were
being kept by the power of God.   People say to
me, "Oh, you are one of those old-fashioned folk
who believe in the perseverance of the saints."
I generally answer, "To be perfectly frank, I am
not at all conceited about the perseverance of the
saints.   My experience with myself and with a
great many other saints is that most of us are not
very much given to perseverance.   We need to be
prodded along all the time."   I heard Sam Jones
say he thought sometimes that the Lord allowed
the Presbyterians to believe once saved always
saved, and the Methodists, that you would only
be saved at last if you hold on, because some of
the Presbyterians are "such an ornery crowd"
that they never would go on if they did not feel
sure they were eternally saved, and some of the
Methodists are such a poor type that if the Lord
did not keep the whip over them, they would
never go through.   That could be said of a great
many, but when we turn to the Word of God we
find that everything for a Christian depends upon
the perseverance of the Saviour.   He who took us
up in grace has undertaken to carry us through to
the end.   He knows how to deal with each indi-

vidual saint in order that he may be confirmed
unto the end. And the final consummation is this,
that every believer will appear "blameless in the
day of our Lord Jesus Christ."

That word, "blameless," may be translated "un-
impeachable" or "unaccusable." In other words,
when we stand at last at the judgment-seat of
Christ, God Himself is going to see to it that no
charge can stand against any believer, because
the Lord Jesus Christ has atoned for all our sins
with His own precious blood. Every failure in
the life will be dealt with there, and all the wood,
hay, and stubble will be burned in the fire of that
day and we shall stand before our Lord unim-
peachable, unaccusable.

In the ninth verse he brings before us a subject that is most precious to every Christian's
heart: "God is faithful." I should like to take
time to dwell on those three words, but I do not
really need to say much about them. You who
have known the Lord for years, do I need to try to
reason with you to show that God is faithful?
As you look back over the years, do not all His
dealings with you tell the story that you have
had to do with a faithful God? And be assured
that when we come to the end of the way, when
at last we meet with loved ones round the throne,
we shall realize then as never before the faithfulness of God.

"When I shall meet with those that I have loved,
Clasp in my eager arms the long-removed,
And know how faithful Thou to me hast proved,
I shall be satisfied."

"God is faithful." I never have been faithful.
I am afraid I never will be faithful in the absolute
sense, but I have to do with a faithful God who
has undertaken to see me through. "God is faithful, by whom ye were called unto the fellowship
of His Son Jesus Christ our Lord." God has not
undertaken to save us merely as individuals, but
having saved us individually He now introduces
us into a wonderful fellowship of which our Lord
Jesus is the risen glorified Head in heaven. That
is why it is called, "The fellowship of His Son
Jesus Christ our Lord," and this is the only fellowship that Christians really need. Every local
church should be an expression of this fellowship;
it is the fellowship of the Body of Christ. You
remember how the apostle in speaking of the
communion says, "The cup of blessing which we
bless, is it not the communion of the blood of
Christ? The bread which we break, is it not the
communion of the Body of Christ?" (1 Cor. 10:
16). So, if you have been redeemed by His blood,
if by the Holy Spirit you have been baptized into
the Body of Christ, you are called into the fellowship of God's Son, and you are one with every
other believer on the face of the earth. We all

belong to one great fellowship. It makes little difference what names people may use, they may be denominational, interdenominational or undenominational, but the great thing is, Are they members of the fellowship of God's Son? That word, "fellowship" really means "partnership." We have been taken into partnership in a wonderful firm of which the Lord Jesus is the Head and in which every other believer has a place. What a fellowship that is! Do you wonder that some of us never crave any other fellowship? We have found all we need in the fellowship of God's Son.

As we trace this word "fellowship" through the New Testament, we shall find many beautiful and suggestive thoughts. In the first epistle of John we find that we have been brought into fellowship with the Father and the Son. Is not that a wonderful thing—in partnership with the Father and the Son! We share their common thoughts. That is one meaning of "fellowship." You are interested in something that I am interested in, and we get together and have fellowship. Just think of it, God the Father and God the Son have taken us into partnership with Them in Their thoughts in regard to redemption, the glorious plan of salvation, and we enter into fellowship with the Father and the Son!

Then this fellowship is called "the fellowship

of the Spirit" because it is not a natural thing.
It is produced by the indwelling Holy Spirit of
God. There is no real Christian fellowship apart
from Him, and that shows the incongruity of unsaved people uniting with the visible church of
God. They cannot have fellowship with God's
redeemed ones because that fellowship is produced by the Holy Spirit and He does not dwell in
unsaved people. It is only as recipients of the
Spirit that we enter into fellowship. The apostle
Paul commends the Philippians because of their
participation in the fellowship of the gospel. Fellowship is not only a sweet and lovely sentiment,
it is a practical thing, that we may labor for the
blessing and for the salvation of a lost world.
Each one is to do his part. The preacher is not
to do all the work. No, we have been called into
a fellowship where each one has his service to
do for the blessing of all, the fellowship of the
gospel. Paul speaks of "the fellowship of ministering," which is not just certain individuals
ministering, but every believer ministering according to his or her ability. This is the Christian ideal, and in the measure in which you and
I seek to walk in accordance with it shall we have
real blessing in church relationship.

I wonder whether I am addressing any who
perhaps are members of some church but have
been saying, "If in order to have fellowship like

this I must possess the Holy Spirit, I am afraid
I got into the visible church too soon, for I am not
conscious of possessing the Spirit of God, I am
not conscious of the indwelling Christ."   What
you need is to come to God as a poor sinner, put
your trust in the Lord Jesus Christ, come right
out into the light where God is, for it is written,
"If we walk in the light, as He is in the light, we
have fellowship one with another, and the blood
of Jesus Christ His Son cleanseth us from all sin"
(1 John 1: 7).

LECTURE III.

BAPTIZED UNTO WHOSE NAME?

✓ ✓ ✓

"Now I beseech you, brethren, by the name of our Lord Jesus Christ, that ye all speak the same thing, and that there be no divisions among you; but that ye be perfectly joined together in the same mind and in the same judgment. For it hath been declared unto me of you, my brethren, by them which are of the house of Chloe, that there are contentions among you. Now this I say, that every one of you saith, I am of Paul; and I of Apollos; and I of Cephas; and I of Christ. Is Christ divived? was Paul crucified for you? or were ye baptized in the name of Paul? I thank God that I baptized none of you, but Crispus and Gaius; lest any should say that I had baptized in mine own name. And I baptized also the household of Stephanas: besides, I know not whether I baptized any other. For Christ sent me not to baptize, but to preach the gospel: not with wisdom of words, lest the cross of Christ should be made of none effect" (1 Cor. 1: 10-17).

✓ ✓ ✓

WE have seen that God has established a wonderfully blessed fellowship here on earth into which He has called His saints: "God is faithful, by whom ye were called unto (or into) the fellowship of His Son Jesus Christ our Lord." The fellowship of God's Son is that communion of saints embracing all believ-

40

ers everywhere, all who have been washed from their sins in the precious blood of Christ and indwelt by the Holy Spirit.

Men have formed denominations, and so the visible Church of God is, in our day, divided into a great many different factions, and unhappily, some of these factions are very markedly un-Christian in their attitude toward others. Yet in all real Christian groups there are those who belong to the fellowship of God's Son and who, I am sure, are often troubled and distressed as they think of the way Christians are divided among themselves. I have heard people justify these denominational divisions by saying that each one represents a different regiment in the army of the Lord. As you have in the army the cavalry, the infantry, the artillery, the air corps, and the engineers, so we have all these different denominations, and each one can choose for himself just which one he prefers, for taking them all together they represent the one army of the Lord. This is a very comfortable way of looking at it if one does not want to have his conscience exercised by present-day conditions, but the fact of the matter is that Scripture tells us that divisions are the work of the flesh. It is not the Spirit of God who divides His people into these different groups. It is the work of the flesh in believers that leads them thus to separate one from another into different companies. You say, "What shall we do under such circumstances? Shall we leave them all and start another company?" In what sense would you then be better than they? This would simply add one more to the many divisions of Christendom. What shall we do? Shall we not recognize the fact that in spite of man's divisions there remains "one Body, and one Spirit, even as ye are called in one hope of your calling" (Eph. 4:4), and so welcome all real believers who hold the truth of God as fellow-members with us in the Body of Christ and thus endeavor to rise above the spirit of sectarianism and denominationalism which prevails in so many places.

It is not denominationalism directly, however, that the apostle is rebuking in this passage. It was rather incipient divisions in the local church; for these Corinthian believers were not as yet separated from one another into various sects. But in the one local church in Corinth there were different cliques and factions, and so there was dissension and trouble. They were losing sight of the blessedness of true Christian fellowship.

Notice how the apostle addresses them, "Now I beseech you, brethren." How in keeping that is with grace. Where grace rules, "I command," becomes, "I beseech." "I beseech you, brethren, by the name of the Lord Jesus Christ, that ye all speak the same thing, and that there be no divi-

sions among you; but that ye be perfectly joined
together in the same mind and in the same judgment." The admonition is to refrain from mur-
muring and complaining and from factiousness
in the local assembly of Christ in order that all
may be bound up in the same mind and in the
same judgment. Of course, the Spirit of God
speaking through the apostle does not attempt to
force all believers to look at everything from exactly the same standpoint. That will never be.
No two people ever see the same rainbow. If you
stood near me looking at a rainbow, you would see
it differently from what I would, because you would
be a little away from me and get a slightly different view, and then, too, my eyes are very astigmatic and yours may be perfect. How foolish it
would be for us to stand there and quarrel about
the rainbow, about its tints, and so on. Rather
let me say, "I am so glad you are able to see it so
much more clearly than I, that with your perfect
eyes you can get so much better a view of it than
I with my astigmatic vision." And you can think
kindly of me and say, "Well, I hope the day may
come when you will be able to see as clearly as I
do." That is the way the apostle puts it in his
letter to the Philippians, "Whereto we have already attained, let us walk by the same rule, let
us mind the same thing....If in anything ye be
otherwise minded, God shall reveal even this unto

you." We do not see eye to eye even as we read the Scripture. So much depends on our education, on our cultural standards, on our environment. We often misunderstand statements of Scripture because of not being more familiar with the languages in which the Bible was originally written.

You say, "But it says we are to be 'perfectly joined together in the same mind and in the same judgment.' How can that be if we do not all see eye to eye about everything?" If we were to insist that we could have no real fellowship unless we did this, I am afraid our church fellowship would become a very small circle indeed. I do not know where you could find a dozen people who see eye to eye on everything. We have all laughed at the old Quaker who left one meeting-place after another, and finally some one said to him, "Well, what church are you in now?"

He said, "I am in the true church at last."

"How many belong to it?"

"Just my wife and myself, and I am not sure about Mary sometimes."

It would simmer down to that if we could not have fellowship with any except those who see things exactly as we do. But what about "the same mind"? "We have the mind of Christ." "The same mind"—that is the lowly mind, the subject mind, the mind that was displayed in

Jesus. You may look at things one way and I look at them differently, but if we have the mind of Christ we are not going to quarrel, but will get along in real happy fellowship considering one another and praying for one another. And then, "the same judgment"—what does that mean? We read that we are to increase in knowledge and in all judgment. That does not mean judging one another, but it means discernment.

Every believer has the Spirit of God dwelling within him to give him discernment, and when things come up about which we differ, if we depend upon the guidance of the Spirit of God, He will give the discernment we need. I am afraid some of us never get very far in real discernment, and the reason is that we neglect the study of our Bibles. We are called "a royal priesthood." In the Old Testament times no man was allowed to be a priest who had a flat nose. What does the nose speak of? It speaks of discernment. Some dish is brought to you and you smell it. You have discerned that there is something wrong with it and do not want to eat it.

Out among the Navajo Indians they had a peculiar idea about the nose. One old Navajo said to me, "Long Coat, where is the mind located?"

I said, "It functions through the brain."

"No," he said, "it is the nose."

"Why do you say that?"

"Well, when you want to go anywhere, doesn't your nose settle it first and then you follow it? When you come to a corner, your nose turns first and then the rest of you goes after it; and when you want to know whether to eat a thing, don't you use your nose first to find whether it is suitable?"

He was a wise Navajo. The nose does speak of discernment, and a flat-nosed priest was one who could not discern, and God said that he could not serve. I am afraid many of us as believers are flat-nosed. We are taken up with almost anything that seems to have some scriptural backing, and we listen to all kinds of teaching, and pay little attention to the careful study of the Word of God. People say, "I go anywhere; I listen to everything, for I can get a little good out of everything." If you do this, you will soon lose all ability to discern the truth as it is in Jesus. It is barely possible that one could so train his digestive powers as to get nourishment out of sawdust, but why eat that when you can eat good substantial oatmeal? And what is the use of going after all kinds of fads and follies when you can have the pure unadulterated Word of God? "Ye shall know the truth, and the truth shall make you free" (John 8:32).

Now the apostle gives one of his reasons for writing this letter. "It hath been declared unto

me of you, my brethren, by them which are of
the house of Chloe, that there are contentions
among you." Observe first, the apostle has heard
a bad report about these Corinthians. He writes
them about it and tells them exactly who brought
the bad report. He would have no sympathy with
these anonymous letter-writers who write, "Dear
Pastor: Perhaps you do not know it, but there is
a woman in the church doing very prominent
work who is a thorough hypocrite. I hope you
will see that she is disciplined. Sincerely yours,
A lover of Christ." The apostle would never pay
any attention to a thing like that, nor would he
have any sympathy with the person who came to
him and said, "Brother Paul, I am sorry to speak
to you about this, but there is one of our brethren—don't for anything say that I told you—but
Mr. So and So, oh, Brother Paul, it is perfectly
dreadful—I do hope you will do what you can—
but don't give him the least idea that I told you."
I think Paul would say sternly, "What business
do you have coming to me slandering a brother
when you are not willing to face him openly about
it?" And so when they sent a bad report to Paul
regarding these Corinthians, he wrote them about
it and said, "I received this report from the house
of Chloe." If it is not true, the house of Chloe
would have to face the fact that they had been
guilty of libeling the Corinthians. In this case it

was true, but Paul is straightforward about it and said, "It hath been declared unto me of you, my brethren, by them which are of the house of Chloe, that there are contentions among you"—there was division right in the local assembly of Corinth. Then he uses an illustration to show what he means. "Every one of you saith, I am of Paul; and I of Apollos; and I of Cephas; and I of Christ."

"I am of Paul"—Paul, the teacher. "I like real Bible teaching, I do not have much use for this other kind of thing, I am not interested in evangelism and exhortation. I like Brother Paul, for he feeds my soul—I am of Paul." And another said, "I am of Apollos." Apollos was an eloquent man and mighty in the Scriptures. "I like a man who can stand up and give a wonderful oration, a man who can give a great address winding up with a marvelous peroration that almost brings you out of your seat. That is the man for me. I am not concerned about these dry Bible teachers, I want something to thrill my blood and stir my soul." And then others said, "I am of Cephas. I like these practical men, these exhorters. Cephas, the man who over and over again used the words, 'I stir you up'." And then others said, "Well, you may have Paul and Apollos and Cephas, but I am of Christ. I am not interested in any one else. I do not need any man to teach me, I am of Christ, and I do not recognize any of the rest of you. Stand by, for I am holier than thou." Have you ever seen that crowd? They are the most conceited of all.

Those were not the actual names that were used. In chapter 4: 6 we read, "These things, brethren, I have in a figure transferred to myself and to Apollos for your sakes; that ye might learn in us not to think of men above that which is written, that no one of you be puffed up for one against another." Paul is saying, "You see, I have simply used this figuratively." It was not actually Paul and Apollos, it was men in their local group, and they were saying, "Well, I am for this brother and I am for this other one," and another, "I am of Christ and am not interested in any of the rest of them." And so Paul put in his own name and that of Apollos and Cephas to illustrate how wrong this was. And then he asks the question, "Is Christ divided?" Is it only a little group who are of Christ? Even those who sometimes say, "I am of Paul, I am of Apollos, I am of Cephas," if they are truly converted, are all of Christ. And so no one group should arrogate that distinction to themselves.

"Was Paul crucified for you?" What does he mean by that? I am not to take any man and make his name the head of a party, I am to remember that the fellowship to which I belong is

that of the One who was crucified for me. We
owe a great deal to Paul. I think after I have
seen the Lord Jesus Christ and my father and
mother, the next one I want to see is the apostle
Paul. I want to have a good talk with him and
tell him how much the messages he left on record
have meant to me. But Paul was not crucified
for me. He helped to give me a better understanding of the One who was crucified for me and
so I value his ministry.

"Were ye baptized in the name of Paul?" Why
does he put this question? The only One that I
am to recognize as the Head of the Church of
God is the One in whose name I was baptized.
Do not get the idea as some have that the apostle
Paul was putting a slur on baptism, that he meant
to imply that baptism was an unimportant thing,
eventually to have no further place in the Church
of God. He is recognizing it as a tremendously
important thing when he bases his argument upon it. When you became a Christian, in whose
name were you baptized? In the name of the
Lord Jesus Christ. Very well then, you belong to
Him. Recognize the entire fellowship of which
He is the Head, but do not try to make His name
the head of a party and do not make the names of
His servants the heads of parties, but recognize
that the only real Head is Christ.

Because of the fact that these Corinthians were

making so much of individuals, Paul says, "I am
very thankful as I look back that I personally did
not do the baptizing in many cases." He is not
saying, "I am thankful that you were not baptized." They were baptized. We read, "Many of
the Corinthians hearing believed and were baptized." Their baptism followed their believing.
But he says, "I am very thankful, since you are
so given to party spirit, that so few of you can
say, 'I have been baptized by Paul.' I thank God
that I baptized none of you, but Crispus (he was
the ruler of the synagogue), and Gaius; lest any
should say that I had baptized in mine own
name." And he adds, "And I baptized also the
household of Stephanas." Evidently Stephanas
was not with them at this time because he was
one who ministered elsewhere. We read in the
last chapter of this epistle, verse 17, "I am glad
of the coming of Stephanas and Fortunatus and
Achaicus: for that which was lacking on your
part they have supplied." Stephanas, apparently,
was a traveling preacher. Elsewhere Paul tells
us that the household of Stephanas had "addicted
themselves to the ministry of the saints" (1 Cor.
16: 15). Finally he said, "Besides, I know not
whether I baptized any other."

Now he gives his closing argument: "For
Christ sent me not to baptize, but to preach the
gospel: not with wisdom of words, lest the cross

of Christ should be made of none effect." Observe, he is not saying that he was not commissioned to baptize, but he is saying that he was not *sent* to make baptism the important thing. He was sent to preach the gospel. As an apostle he went out preaching, and when any believed the gospel they were baptized. This is the opposite to the great church systems of today and also of Roman missions. Where Romanism goes it is its first business to get as many infants together as possible and baptize them, but the apostle says that he was not sent to do that, he was sent to preach the gospel, and when they believed that gospel, they were baptized.

There are many things that are right and proper in their own sphere which must, of necessity, occupy much of a preacher's time, but it was not to do these things he was set apart as a servant of God and sent into the world. He was ordained of God to preach the gospel. And so with Paul. His great ministry was making Christ known, "not with wisdom of words, lest the cross of Christ should be made of none effect." He did not depend upon mere human oratory or rhetoric, but on the power of the Holy Spirit enabling him in all simplicity to present to the people a crucified, risen, ascended, and returning Christ, that all hearts might be taken up with Him and men be brought to put their trust in Him. That is the thing that unifies. As Christ is presented to the hearts of God's people they are drawn together, they are drawn to Him, they are occupied with Him, their glorious Head.

LECTURE IV.

THE SIMPLICITY OF PREACHING

✓ ✓ ✓

"For the preaching of the cross is to them that perish
foolishness; but unto us which are saved it is the power of
God. For it is written, I will destroy the wisdom of the
wise, and will bring to nothing the understanding of the
prudent. Where is the wise? where is the scribe? where is
the disputer of this world? hath not God made foolish the
wisdom of this world? For after that in the wisdom of God
the world by wisdom knew not God, it pleased God by the
foolishness of preaching to save them that believe. For the
Jews require a sign, and the Greeks seek after wisdom; but
we preach Christ crucified, unto the Jews a stumblingblock, and unto the Greeks foolishness; but unto them which
are called, both Jews and Greeks, Christ the power of God,
and the wisdom of God" (1 Cor. 1: 18-24).

✓ ✓ ✓

THE apostle Paul's great business was proclaiming the cross. "The preaching of the
cross is to them that perish foolishness; but
unto us which are saved it is the power of God."
There is a challenge in almost every word in this
verse.

"The preaching of the cross." The word translated "preaching" is not the ordinary word for

"announcing" or "proclaiming," which is so frequently used in the New Testament; it is the "Logos," that which is used for Christ Himself in the Gospel of John. "In the beginning was the Word—the *Logos*—and the Word was with God, and the Word was God" (John 1:1). It is the ordinary term for a spoken message, and the apostle here puts the word of the cross in contrast to the word of wisdom of verse seventeen. There he says that it is his aim to preach the cross not with wisdom of words, or it might be just reversed, to give the exact meaning of the original, not with the words of wisdom. When he presented the cross, the doctrine of the cross, he did not want to hide it by beautiful verbiage, he would not obscure the message by human eloquence, nor weaken or dilute it in any way by charming rhetoric. He did not desire people to listen to him with admiration and go away exclaiming, "What a brilliant preacher, what a splendid orator!" instead of saying, "What guilty sinners we are and how amazing is the love of God that sent His Son to die and bear the shame of the cross for our redemption!"

Some years ago a gentleman living in a country town in England went to London, and while there listened to some of the great preachers of that day. Writing home to his wife he said, "Last Sunday I went in the morning to hear Dr. So-and-

So (he named one of the most eloquent men occupying a London pulpit at that time), and in the evening I went to the Metropolitan Tabernacle to listen to Charles Spurgeon. I was greatly impressed by both of them. Dr. Blank is certainly a great preacher, but Mr. Spurgeon has a great Saviour." Do you see the difference?

It is so sadly possible to spoil the message by dependence on that which simply appeals to the human mind, and so the apostle says, "I try to preach Christ, not by words of wisdom, that is, this world's wisdom, lest the cross of Christ should be made of none effect." Even the most utterly godless man can appreciate eloquence, oratory or rhetoric, whether he believes the message being proclaimed or not, but it is not the will of God that His servants should tickle the ears of their hearers but that they should grapple with the consciences of those to whom they are speaking. If I am addressing any unsaved ones who are still in your sins, let me earnestly remind you that you are in a most precarious position. One moment may seal your doom forever. If the brittle thread of your life were snapped and you should be ushered out into a Christless eternity, how hopeless would be your condition! How foolish then, how wicked would it be of us, if we should simply entertain you when we know, as Archibald Brown once said, "There is only the thickness of your ribs between your souls and hell." How guilty before God we should be if we sought the admiration and praise of our hearers instead of endeavoring to bring them face to face with their sins before God and seeking to get them to flee to the cross for refuge.

It was this that had gripped the apostle Paul. He knew that men were lost without Christ, that there was no hope for them save through the cross, and so he said, "I do not want anything that will hide the cross. I do not want to decorate the cross with flowers and ribbons and tinsel, and make people lose sight of what it really is, the declaration of man's utter depravity and the manifestation of God's infinite love. It is the preaching of the cross, the word of the cross, in opposition to the word of wisdom. 'The word of the cross is to them that perish foolishness'."

What do we mean when we speak of the cross? I wonder sometimes if we have any conception in our day of what the cross meant when Paul wrote these words. Cicero says, "The cross, it speaks of that which is so shameful, so horrible, it should never be mentioned in polite society," and yet you find Paul exclaiming, "God forbid that I should glory, save in the cross of our Lord Jesus Christ. by whom the world is crucified unto me, and I unto the world" (Gal. 6: 14). The cross meant far worse than the gallows or the electric chair

means today, because it declared that the one who
was hanging there was guilty of the vilest, the
most awful crimes, and was utterly unfit to live,
that he was rejected of man and accursed of God.
And this cross bore our Lord Jesus Christ! What
does it mean? It means that man's heart was so
wicked, so sinful, that there was no other way by
which he could be saved than through the Eternal
Son of God becoming Man and suffering the most
ignominious death for his redemption. But it
means too that in the most complete way man's
heart has been fully exposed, for when God thus
sent His Son, man cried, "Away with Him! Crucify Him, crucify Him!" There at the cross man
told out the very worst of his nature, but God told
out the infinite love of His heart. Peter said to the
men of his day, "Him being delivered up by the
determinate counsel and foreknowledge of God,
ye have taken, and with wicked hands have crucified and slain" (Acts 2: 23). If you want to know
how wicked you are by nature, if you want to get
an understanding of the awfulness of the sins of
which your heart is capable, stand in faith before
that cross and contemplate again God's holy,
spotless Son hanging on that tree suffering un-
speakable anguish, the very expression of man's
attitude to God, the word of the cross.

It is not merely the physical suffering that men
heaped upon Jesus that made atonement for sin,

for we read, "When Thou shalt make His soul
an offering for sin, He shall see His seed, He
shall prolong His days, and the pleasure of the
Lord shall prosper in His hand" (Isa. 53: 10).
God made Him to be the great sin-offering. And
so the word of the cross is the story of God's infinite love to guilty men. Righteousness demanded
that sin be punished, and there upon the cross it
was punished to the full in the Person of our
blessed Substitute. And now the word of the
cross goes out to all the world, and as man at
last is going to be judged by his attitude toward
that cross, "the word of the cross is to them that
perish foolishness."

I am sorry they translated that word, "perish,"
for that may throw us off the track. Some may
think that some day if you reject the cross and
the One who died there, you are in danger of
perishing, but that is not what he is saying. It
is something far more solemn, something that
ought to affect you very much more, if you are
unsaved. What he really says is, "The word of
the cross is to them that *are lost* foolishness."
"Them that are lost!" "If our gospel be hid, it is
hid to them that are lost" (2 Cor. 4: 3). Do you
get the solemnity of that? Not in danger of being
lost by-and-by, not that you will be lost if you
finally persist in rejecting Christ and die in your
sins. That is terribly true, but this is more sol-

emn than that. They *are* lost. If the Christ of that cross is not yet your Saviour, you *are* lost. If you get up and walk out unsaved, you go out lost and go down the street lost; if you get into your car and drive off, you drive off a lost man or a lost woman, and if a crash comes and you are suddenly ushered into eternity, you go into eternity lost, to be lost forever. Men do not think of these things, they do not face these things as they are. If the cross as yet means nothing to you, you are lost. "The preaching of the cross is to them that are lost foolishness." "Oh," they say, "I do not understand it at all. The very idea that a man, no matter how good he is, could be nailed to the cross and there make atonement for my sins, is foolish, is repugnant to me." Very well, "If our gospel be hid, it is hid to them that are lost." That is why you do not understand; it is because you are *lost*. What a terrible condition to be in!

Then look at the other side. "But unto us which are saved it is the power of God." "Us who are saved." Of whom is he speaking? He is speaking of a people who once were lost but are now saved. But someone says, "I do not get that. You mean they are in process of salvation for, of course, nobody can be sure of his final salvation until the day of judgment, when at last he stands before God and the question is there definitely de-

cided." That is not what the Book teaches, dear
friend. It contemplates people already lost and
people already saved. "By grace are ye saved
through faith; and that not of yourselves: it is
the gift of God: not of works lest any man should
boast" (Eph. 2: 8, 9).

An old Scotch woman had been very religious,
she had gone to church all her life and she always hoped that at last she would get dying grace
and be fit for heaven. She went one time to a
meeting where two earnest servants of God were
preaching and when she came home, they said to
her, "Well, Grandma, how did you like the preachers?" "Well," she said, "I could not make them
out. The first man got up and talked to folk he
said were saved already, to folk so good I did not
know there were any in our town like them. And
then another man got up and preached to folk
so wicked that he said they were lost and going
to hell. But there was not one word for me."
She was not lost and she was not saved, according
to her own estimation. But there are just the
two classes, "Them that are lost" and "us which
are saved," those who have put their trust in the
Lord Jesus Christ, those who have faced their
sins in the presence of God and have seen in the
cross, in the work of the cross, that which has
satisfied God and that in which their hearts can
rest. They are saved right here and now.

Am I addressing anybody who has been in doubt about that? Perhaps you are a church-member, perhaps you profess to be a Christian, and yet have often had doubts as to whether you are really saved. Suppose that you have never been saved (you had better give yourself the benefit of the doubt), will you, right now, take your place before God as a poor, lost sinner and look up in faith to Him who died on yonder cross and tell Him you are the sinner for whom He suffered and that you are going to rest in Him?

Years ago my father had an old friend who was a familiar figure in our home when I was a boy. One day after he had been saved for many years someone said to him, "Mr. Ross, do you ever doubt that you are saved? Has it ever come to your mind that you have made a mistake and that you are not really saved?" He said, "It is strange that you should ask me that question for, do you know, last night when I was on my way to the meeting where I was to preach the gospel, it just came to me as though a voice spoke, 'Donald Ross, what on old hypocrite you are! You have never been saved at all,' and I could hardly tell whether it was the voice of the devil or whether it might be the voice of the Lord. I said, 'Man, could that be true? After years of preaching Christ to others, could it be true that I have never been saved?' And then I said, 'Well, Lord, if it is all

true that I have just been thinking I am saved,
I am so thankful that Jesus died for hypocrites,
and I come to Him now just as I am.' "

> "Just as I am! without one plea
> But that Thy blood was shed for me,
> And that Thou bidd'st me come to Thee,
> O Lamb of God! I come!"

This dear old saint said that in a moment the
cloud was lifted and he knew that he had been
listening to the voice of the devil and not that of
God.

If you are not clear, let me beg of you, shut
your eyes and ears to everything else just now
and lift your heart to God and trust the One who
died on the cross for you, trust Him as your
Saviour, "Be it known unto you therefore, men
and brethren, that through this Man is preached
unto you the forgiveness of sins" (Acts 13: 38).

Well, then, unto us which are saved the word
of the cross is the power of God. That is, there
is no human energy that converts people, we cannot convert them by any ability of our own.
Somebody said to me a short time ago, "You
know Dr. So-and-So, well, he is a grand man of
God. He converted me ten years ago." I know
that he meant that this dear servant of God had
presented the gospel which he had believed. But
it is not servants of Christ who do the converting.

We cannot save people, we cannot give men peace with God; it is the word of the cross that is the power of God. Here is a poor, troubled, anxious soul not knowing what to do or where to go; suddenly the Spirit of God presents the cross, the fact that Christ on the cross died for our sins according to the Scriptures, and faith leaps up in the heart, and the soul says, "Thank God, He died for me!" In a moment that soul passes from death to life. The word of the cross is the power of God. Sometimes we have to preach about a great many other things, but in a sense I begrudge the time that has to be given to other subjects when I think of men who might be sitting before me who have not seen the truth as it is in Christ Jesus. How all this writes "folly" over everything of the natural mind, for the apostle referring to Isaiah says, "It is written, 'I will destroy the wisdom of the wise, and will bring to nothing the understanding of the prudent.' "

Men pride themselves in their philosophies, in their reasoning powers, but no philosophy in the world would ever have reasoned out the need of the cross nor have suggested that only through the death of Christ sinners could be saved. "Where is the wise? where is the scribe?" that is, the reasoners, for reasoning goes for naught in the light of the cross. "Where is the disputer of this world?" When he mentions the scribe, he is naturally referring to the Jews, the wise men in Israel, who tried to work out a way of salvation through systems and ritual, but the apostle brushes them to one side. What does he know of the word of the cross? And then the disputer, the Greek philosopher, proud of his learning, investigating all the various sciences and systems of thought of his day. But not one of them would ever have dreamed of Christ dying on a cross as the means of salvation for sinners. So he said, "Where is the disputer of this world? Hath not God made foolish the wisdom of this world?" Mere wisdom would never have delved into the mystery of the cross. It is a striking fact that our English word, "world," is made to do duty for two Greek words here. It might be rendered, "Where is the disputer of this *age?* Hath not God made foolish the wisdom of this *world?*" In the first instance it is *aion,* "the age," and in the second instance it is *kosmos,* this "ordered universe" in which we live. The whole trend of the age is against the word of the cross. The wisdom of this age would never have thought that only by the death of the Son of God on the cross salvation could be wrought out, and so far as this ordered universe is concerned, the things that men pride themselves in are only foolishness in the sight of God. "He that sitteth in the heavens shall laugh: the Lord shall have them in derision" (Ps. 2: 4).

Well might the omnipotent God laugh (I do not say this irreverently) as He hears the ravings of these godless professors in our universities, trying to explain the mystery of the universe, as they measure everything by their own little foot-rules, delving into things utterly beyond human comprehension, deliberately turning away from the revelation that would make everything plain.

"For after that in the wisdom of God"—God has permitted man to grope and grope and do his best to find out these hidden mysteries, to come to an end of himself at last—"the world by wisdom knew not God, it pleased God by the foolishness of preaching to save them that believe." What is preaching? It is a simple proclamation, and it has pleased God by what looks to man like foolishness, the simplicity of making an announcement, to save them that believe. I stand up in the name of the God of heaven and declare that "Christ died for our sins according to the Scriptures, and that He was buried and that He rose again the third day according to the Scriptures" (1 Cor. 15: 3, 4). The world says, "Foolishness! You could not prove that if you had to." No, I could not; but I repeat the announcement: "Christ died for our sins according to the Scriptures, and He was buried, and He rose again the third day according to the Scriptures." And whenever a man is humble enough and lowly

enough to believe the announcement, he is saved.
"It pleased God by the simplicity of an announcement to save them that believe. For the Jews
require a sign." They say, "Give us some evidence that this is true; work some miracle." Some
say, "If you could work miracles today, would it
not be wonderful?" I do not know that it would.
If I had apostolic power and could go through an
audience and lay my hands upon some poor crip-
ple and he would leap to his feet well and whole,
I fancy I could fill a building and we would have
all kinds of cripples coming, but I have never
heard of anything like that causing poor sinners
to awake and turn to Christ. Even when the
apostles could do these things, men turned on
them and tried to kill them, as in the case of Paul
at Lystra.

It is the preaching of the cross that saves. That
is what guilty sinners need. "The Jews require
a sign, the Greeks seek after wisdom: but we
preach Christ crucified, unto the Jews a stumblingblock, and unto the Greeks foolishness."
Some one says, "But Paul, if you know it is a
stumblingblock and foolishness, why don't you
serve it up to your audience in such a way as to
get rid of those elements?" And Paul would
answer, "Because if I make it attractive to the
natural man, it will not be the means of salvation
to sinners." "We preach Christ crucified, unto

the Jews a stumblingblock, and unto the Greeks foolishness." This involves the work of the Spirit of God. He must prepare the heart. This is the effectual call.

There is a general call that goes to all men, there is an effectual call when the Spirit of God drives the truth home, and a man realizes that God is tugging at his heart to draw him to Christ. "But unto them which are called, both Jews and Greeks, Christ the power of God, and the wisdom of God." This was the apostolic message. "In whom are hid all the treasures of wisdom and knowledge" (Col. 2: 3). That message still has the same power as of old. God give us to preach it in dependence on the Holy Spirit.

CHRIST, THE WISDOM OF GOD

✓ ✓ ✓

"Because the foolishness of God is wiser than men; and the weakness of God is stronger than men. For ye see your calling, brethren, how that not many wise men after the flesh, not many mighty, not many noble, are called: but God hath chosen the foolish things of the world to confound the wise; and God hath chosen the weak things of the world to confound the things which are mighty; and base things of the world, and things which are despised, hath God chosen, yea, and things which are not, to bring to nought things that are: that no flesh should glory in His presence. But of Him are ye in Christ Jesus, who of God is made unto us wisdom, and righteousness, and sanctification, and redemption: that, according as it is written, He that glorieth, let him glory in the Lord" (1 Cor. 1: 25-31).

✓ ✓ ✓

THE foolishness of God! What a striking expression! I remember on one occasion a friend of mine, a very faithful preacher, advertised on a large signboard in a Canadian city that he would preach on these words. He was almost immediately summoned before the magistrate and asked if he did not know that there was a law in Ontario against blasphemy. He had to explain that the topic advertised was simply a quotation from Holy Scripture. The expression, of course, is akin to that of verse 21, "the foolishness of preaching," and in commenting on the former passage we suggested that it might be rendered "the simplicity of preaching," and so here we learn that the simplicity of God is wiser than men. That is, the program of the gospel that seems so simple to the worldly-wise is after all the source of all wisdom, wiser far than all of man's philosophies.

Then we are told that the weakness of God is stronger than man. The weakness of God refers to the cross. Christ was crucified through weakness. He, the omnipotent One, chose in infinite grace to take the place of a helpless prisoner in the hands of His enemies. At any moment He might have destroyed them by His power, or, if He was still to keep in the place of weakness, He could have prayed for help from above and twelve legions of angels would have been sent to rescue Him. But He did neither of these. He humbled Himself unto death, and that death for the destruction of him who, up to that time, had the power of death, that is, the devil.

The believer's calling is brought out very effectively in verses 26 to 29. In making up the members of the Body of Christ, it has not pleased God to choose many from among the wise, the mighty, the noble, or the great men of this world. Lady

Huntington, the friend of Whitfield and the Wesleys, who took such an active part in the great revival movement of those wonderful days, used to say that she was only going to heaven by an "m." When some one asked her what she meant, she stated that she was so thankful that Scripture did not say, "not *any* noble are called," but "not *many* noble." Therefore she got in by an "m." Had God selected those whom the world admires as the pillars of His Church, to a very large extent it would have destroyed the very thing He had in view. It was His desire to manifest the results of His grace. He works, not with what He finds, but with what He brings. He delights to take up those whom the world looks down upon and to make them devoted saints and faithful servants who will be to the praise of His glory throughout all the ages to come. So we read that "God hath chosen the foolish things of the world to confound the wise." He has, in His sovereign grace, taken up "the weak things of the world to confound the things which are mighty," base things, things that are despised has God chosen, and things that are not, to bring to nought the things that are.

Look back over the history of the Christian Church. What wondrous stories it tells of grace reaching down to the lowest, the poorest, the most insignificant, bringing such to repentance, creat-

ing faith in their souls by the word of truth of
the gospel, regenerating them, justifying them
from all things, sanctifying them by the Holy
Spirit and the Word, and then sending them out
as ambassadors for Christ to turn the world up-
side down by the simplicity of preaching the message of the cross. The earlier followers of the
Lord Jesus Christ were, with very few exceptions,
men from the lower walks of life: fishermen, tax-
collectors, Galilean peasants! Judas was the only
"gentleman" in the entire apostolic band. He
was from Judea, the bursar of the little company,
and he turned traitor. But God filled those men
from the common walks of life with the power of
His Holy Spirit and through them won thousands
more to a saving knowledge of His Son. Saul of
Tarsus stands out himself in vivid contrast, and
one who, whether saved or not, would have had
some great place among the people of that day,
but he is the one who writes the words that we
have been considering, and he counted himself
among the base things, and the things that are
not, and thanked God that to him it was given to
be used of God to bring to nought the things that
are.

The reason for all this comes out clearly in the
29th verse in a succinct statement, "that no flesh
should glory in His presence." Had God taken up
the wealthy and the powerful, it would have given

the flesh a large place in the eyes of men at least, but by choosing the weak things He had the greater opportunity to manifest His own power. In themselves they could accomplish nothing; through Him they did valiantly. Therefore all the glory belongs not to them but to Him. He has said, "My glory will I not give to another."

How we need to remind ourselves again and again of these things today. It has always seemed to me that there is so much mawkish sentiment linked with so-called religious leaders, even in the professing Church of Christ. As teachers and preachers are presented to audiences, it is considered the right thing, the proper thing to laud them to the skies, to expatiate on their brilliancy and learning and wonderful personality, until I myself have often felt grieved and shocked and thoroughly ashamed as I listened to such laudations. One cannot imagine the apostle Peter so introducing his beloved brother, Paul, nor can we think of Paul presenting his fellow-laborers, Epaphroditus, Titus, or Timothy in such a manner to those to whom they were to preach. He does indeed say the kindest things of them all, for he loved them truly and was grateful to God for all the good things seen in them; but as he speaks of them, he does not dwell upon their ability or personality or charm or wonderful gifts, but rather on their devotedness to Christ in suffering for

His name's sake. Surely there is a lesson in all this for us. If we give to man the glory which belongs alone to God, we may be certain that we shall incur the divine displeasure.

Let us now consider the wonderful 30th verse, and as we quote it, let me make a slight change from the text of our splendid Authorized Version, a change which I believe any scholar will recognize as warranted by the original text, and which brings out more vividly the actual truth that the apostle means to set forth: "But of Him are ye in Christ Jesus, who of God is made unto us wisdom: even righteousness, and sanctification, and redemption." That is, Paul is not telling us exactly that Christ is made four things to the believer, but rather one, and out of this one three others spring. Christ is made unto us wisdom. He is Himself the wisdom of God. "In whom," we are told in Col. 2: 3, "are hid all the treasures of wisdom and knowledge." People often speak of the "problem of Jesus," the "problem of Christ." There is no problem of Christ. Christ is not a problem: He it is who explains every problem. Listen to that poor, sinful Samaritan woman at the well. She had many questions over which she had puzzled for years. As she conversed with the Lord Jesus, the conviction evidently grew upon her that here was One whose wisdom was super-human. Timidly, and yet hopefully, I am sure, she exclaimed, "I know that Messias cometh which is called Christ." No doubt the thought in her mind was this: "Oh, if I could only see Him. If He could come in my day, I would go to Him with all my cares, with all my problems and perplexities, and He would explain everything." Jesus, looking at her with those wonderful eyes of His (they had already seen into the very depths of her soul), answered, "I that speak unto thee am He." Startled, she looked again upon Him, feasted her own eyes on that wonderful face until she was absolutely convinced that the words He spoke were true. One might have expected a torrent of questions, but no—she had found the Messiah. Every problem was settled when she knew Him, and away she went to the city to call others to meet Him too. And so I say again, there is no problem of Christ, but Christ is the key to every problem. To know Him is to have all the knowledge that is really worth while. And we who are saved are in Him. That is a remarkable expression which Paul uses over and over again, "In Christ Jesus." It speaks of our new standing before God. It tells of the intimate union that subsists between the risen Lord and all His own. In Him there is no condemnation. In Him we are accepted in all His own blessed perfection. And God has made Him unto us wisdom. Everything we need for our souls' deliverance is found in the knowledge of Christ. Our righteousness, our sanctification, our redemption, all are found in Him.

It is well that we should dwell on each of these words separately, and be clear as to their exact significance. Righteousness. We had none of our own. "There is none righteous, no, not one." All that we thought to be such we have learned is but as polluted rags in the sight of an infinitely holy God. But He has set forth Christ, the risen Christ, who once bore our sins in His own body on the tree, as the expression of the righteousness of God. We are made the righteousness of God in Him. "This is His name whereby He shall be called, Jehovah Tsidkenu," and so we stand before God in a perfect, unchallenged righteousness, complete in Christ.

Sanctification. Whether we think of sanctification as practical or positional, nevertheless all are found in Him. To be sanctified is to be set apart. For us it means, of course, to be set apart to God in Christ in all the perfection of His finished work. This is our positional sanctification. But it also means to be set apart from the sin, pollution, uncleanness, corruption that prevails in this world, even as our Lord prayed, "Sanctify them through Thy truth, Thy Word is truth." It is as our hearts are taken up with Christ that we will know the reality of this.

Redemption. We who had sold ourselves for nought have been redeemed without money. "Redeemed, not with corruptible things, as silver and gold, but with the precious blood of Christ." He gave Himself for us. His life is the price of our redemption, life given up to death in order that we might be delivered from the fear of death and enter into life eternal. We have "everything in Jesus, and Jesus everything."

And so we have nothing for which we can give ourselves credit, but, "As it is written, He that glorieth, let him glory in the Lord." Like David, we can each one exclaim, "My soul shall make her boast in the Lord." John Allen, the converted navvy (or section-hand, as we would say in America), one of the first officers of the Salvation Army, exclaimed as he was dying, "I deserve to be damned; I deserve to be in hell; but God interfered!" Yes, and so may each redeemed one say. The sinning was ours, the disobedience was ours, the curse, the wrath, the judgment—all were our desert. The holiness is His, the perfect obedience unto death is His. He became a curse for us, He drained the cup of wrath, He bore the judgment. Thus He has become in very truth our righteousness, sanctification, and redemption, and to Him belongs all the glory now and through eternal ages.

JESUS CHRIST AND HIM CRUCIFIED

✓ ✓ ✓

"And I, brethren, when I came to you, came not with excellency of speech or of wisdom, declaring unto you the testimony of God. For I determined not to know anything among you, save Jesus Christ, and Him crucified. And I was with you in weakness, and in fear, and in much trembling. And my speech and my preaching was not with enticing words of man's wisdom, but in demonstration of the Spirit and of power: that your faith should not stand in the wisdom of men, but in the power of God. Howbeit we speak wisdom among them that are perfect: yet not the wisdom of this world, nor of the princes of this world, that come to naught: but we speak the wisdom of God in a mystery, even the hidden wisdom, which God ordained before the world unto our glory: which none of the princes of this world knew: for had they known it, they would not have crucified the Lord of glory" (1 Cor. 2: 1-8).

✓ ✓ ✓

IN the book of Acts we have the account of Paul's entry into Corinth where after a year and a half of earnest work he left a church that came behind, we are told, in no gift. Going into that brilliant but godless city where they gloried in human ability and in human attainment, where they made much of the various arts

and where they deified human lust and knew
nothing of the true God, the apostle's soul was
deeply stirred. He had been but a few days before in Athens and there, we read, had gone by
invitation to the place where the philosophers,
the intelligentsia, gathered to hear and to tell
some new thing, and where at their own request
he undertook to explain the message of the gospel.
However, they did not permit him to come to the
crucial point, for they interrupted him as soon as
he spoke of a Saviour who died and was raised
again, and refused to listen further. Probably
never was a more eloquent sermon preached than
that which the apostle delivered that day on Mars
Hill, and yet the results were somewhat meager.
There were a few who clave to him, but the great
majority turned away, rejecting him and his
proclamation.

From Athens he went to Corinth. I do not believe there is any reason to think that he felt he
had made a mistake in preaching as he did at
Athens. His rule was this: "I am made all things
to all men if by any means I might save some."
There he realized that he was addressing men of
the highest culture and had to present the message in a way that he hoped would appeal to
them; but upon going to Corinth he put aside
everything, as far as he possibly could, that was
merely human and went in absolute dependence

upon the Spirit of God with one great message,
"Jesus Christ and Him crucified."

He says, "And I, brethren, when I came to you,
came not with excellency of speech or of wisdom,
declaring unto you the testimony of God." He
realized it was quite possible by the flowers of
rhetoric to cover up, to obscure the shame of the
cross, and so he did not permit himself any
flights of fancy or of the imagination in presenting the glad tidings; but seriously, earnestly, solemnly, as became a man who stood between the
living and the dead, he preached the message of
the cross in all simplicity, for he determined, he
said, "not to know any thing among you, save
Jesus Christ, and Him crucified." And that
should still be the method of the servant of God;
for after all, there is no other message that will
avail for the salvation of sinners or the edification of God's beloved people. Everything centers
in the cross of our Lord Jesus Christ. "Jesus
Christ and Him crucified." That is the Person
and the Work. Always Christ personal was presented in apostolic preaching. Men were not
asked to believe a creed, they were not asked to
subscribe to a system of doctrine, but they were
asked to receive a Person, and that Person, the
Lord Jesus Christ.

I think we make a mistake in supposing that
just pinning our faith to a verse of Scripture is

salvation. I wonder whether many have not been
deceived in that way. I hear people speak of
knowing they are saved, and when asked why,
they reply, "Because I believe John 3: 16 or John
5: 24," and you look for some evidence of a new
life in them and do not find it. They never appear at a prayer-meeting, but if there is a social
affair, or something like that, they are present.
Apparently they have no real interest in the study
of the Word of God; you never see them at a Bible
lecture. They have time for anything that ministers to the flesh, but very little time for spiritual
food, and it makes one tremble for them. I cannot think of anything more dreadful than to have
gone through life thinking that one was really
saved, and then at last to be suddenly ushered
into eternity and wake up forever lost. You see,
believing a text does not save anybody. Believing
in CHRIST saves all who trust Him. I believed
every text in the Bible before I was converted.
I never thought of doubting one of them until
after I was converted. That may seem like a
strange thing to say, but as a lad I believed all
that I was told, that the Bible was the Word of
the living God. I accepted it all. Some years
after I was converted I became perplexed over
certain things and began to doubt, and it led me
to a deeper investigation, and then my faith was
confirmed. But in all those years that I believed

everything in the Bible I was not saved. I had never been regenerated, I had never received a new nature. I was lost. And if I had died in my sins, I could have quoted hundreds of Bible texts, I could have repeated chapter after chapter of Holy Scripture in the flames of hell while bewailing the fact that I had never been acquainted with the Person that these passages of Scripture glorified. Do not make any mistake here, for it is one that can never be remedied if you go into eternity resting on a false hope. Examine your foundation, ask yourselves, Is Christ Himself precious to me? If He is, why do I not enjoy His Word more? Why do I not love to spend more time with Him in prayer? Why is there so much frivolity and levity and carelessness in my life? Why do I do so many things that I know the Lord Jesus would never do and cannot approve in me if I really love Him? He has said, "If a man love Me, he will keep My words" (John 14:23). "If ye love Me, keep My commandments" (John 14:15).

What is the use of professing to be a Christian if there is no evidence of it in the life? What is the use of speaking of the new birth, of talking about having eternal life if I live the same kind of a life that tens of thousands of respectable Christless men and women live all around me? What is the difference between my life and theirs? If this change has ever taken place in me, when did it take place? When did I open my heart's door to Christ and receive Him? If I have received Him, then He has come to dwell in me and that changes everything for me. "As many as received Him, to them gave He power to become the children of God, even to them that believe on His name: which were born, not of blood, nor of the will of the flesh, nor of the will of man, but of God" (John 1: 12, 13).

Now observe, it is "Jesus Christ, and Him crucified." Some say, "We preach Christ," but the Christ who lived on earth for those thirty-three wonderful years could never save one poor sinner apart from His death. Jesus Christ was crucified? Why? The crucifixion of our Lord Jesus Christ throws into relief several tremendous facts. First of all, it emphasizes the wickedness, the corruption, the vileness of the human heart. Who was Jesus Christ? He was God manifest in the flesh. He was here in the world His hands had made, and His own creatures cried, "Away with Him, away with Him; crucify Him!" Could we have any worse commentary on the iniquity of the human heart than that? Man, as far as he was capable, was guilty of the awful crime of deicide, he would murder God, drive Him out of His own universe. "The fool hath said in his heart, no God" (Ps. 14: 1). It is not exactly as in our Authorized Version, "The fool hath said in his heart, There is no God." Many a man admits there is a God who says, "No God," and that is what that verse really tells us, in the Hebrew. "The fool hath said in his heart, no God." "No God for me." He has said, "I do not want God to come into my life, I do not want to be troubled about God, I want to take my own way, to do my own will." And because men were set on that, they nailed the Christ of God to a cross. If there is anything that tells out what man is, this does.

Stand in faith by that cross, see the blessed Saviour suffering, dying there; see the nails upon which He hangs and the blood dripping from those awful wounds; see the thorns crushed upon His sacred brow and the blood enwrapping His naked body as with a crimson shroud. That is what sin has done, the sin that is in your heart and in mine. That tells out the story of the wickedness, the deceitfulness of our hearts. The men who thronged about that cross and cried out in derision, "Thou that destroyest the temple, and buildest it in three days, save Thyself. If Thou be the Son of God, come down from the cross" (Matt. 27: 40), were no different from ourselves; their hearts were like our hearts. They were representative men. We may see ourselves there. The cross brought out, declared all the malignity that was in the heart of man, but it also told out the infinite love that was in the heart of God. One might well have understood it if God looking down upon that scene had let loose the thunders of His wrath and the lightnings of His judgment and had destroyed that throng in a moment; if He had said, as He did so long ago, "My Spirit shall not always strive with man . . . I will destroy man whom I have created from the face of the earth" (Gen. 6: 3, 7). But no; "God so loved the world, that He gave His only begotten Son, that whosoever believeth in Him should not perish, but have everlasting life." When man cast Him out and nailed Him to a tree, God in infinite love for sinners made His soul an offering for sin. It was as though He said, "That cross, the symbol of shame and agony, shall become the great altar upon which will be offered the one supreme Sacrifice which atones for the sin of the world—Jesus Christ and Him crucified." What wonderful evidence of God's love for sinners is seen in that cross!

In the light of that cross how can men still go on doing the things, living in the sins, that led to it? The cross of Christ is that which casts light on everything that men glory in in this world and stains all its glory, so that the apostle could say elsewhere, "God forbid that I should glory, save in the cross of our Lord Jesus Christ, by whom the world is crucified unto me, and I unto the

world" (Gal. 6: 14). Did you ever think of it in
this way? You profess to be a Christian, you say
that you owe everything for eternity to the One
whom the world rejected. What effect does that
have upon your life? Do you still have fellowship
with that world that cast Him out? Do you still
participate in the things that characterize that
world?

A Christian walked down the street one day
intending to go to the theater. Something was
on that he thought he would be interested in. He
came to the very entrance, even stepped up and
bought his ticket, and the next moment there
came flashing into his mind, "If I go in there, I
crucify the Son of God afresh and put Him to an
open shame." He tore the ticket up, and ran from
the place, thankful to be delivered. If you as a
Christian go back into the things of the world
from which the death of Christ has separated
you, you are denying the cross of Christ. That
is what it means. If we understood this, what a
separated people we would be, how it would do
away with all this dilly-dallying with the world
and its folly. How we would realize that we owe
too much to the One whom the world rejected to
go on with that system which has thus treated
the Eternal Lover of our souls—"Jesus Christ and
Him crucified."

"I was with you in weakness, and in fear, and

in much trembling." I think every servant of Christ knows a little of that. How often as one thinks of facing an audience, the heart fails and the spirit cries out, "O Lord, what can I do, what can I say? Suppose I should make a mistake, suppose I should give the wrong message, how dire the effect might be on some! I can never undo it for eternity!" I can see Paul bowing before God every time he contemplated going out to preach the Word, and crying out, "O Lord, keep me from mistakes, let me have just the right word, give me to be Thy messenger, save me from trying to attract attention to myself, save me from glorifying man."

"My speech and my preaching was not with enticing words of man's wisdom, but in demonstration of the Spirit and of power." Paul recognized the fact that there is such a thing as meeting man on the soul-plane instead of the spiritual. A man may preach the gospel and yet do it "soulishly," on the soul-plane, depending upon that which simply appeals to the human mind, and finding perhaps, that at the psychological moment he had gotten a grip on the audience by a tender story, ask for decisions. And when the people respond, he says, "There now, what a lot of people have come to Christ," and perhaps not one in the crowd has had the conscience reached or has had to do with God about his sins. Paul was afraid

of that. He said, "I do not want to preach things
in such a way that my human effort will persuade
them. I am depending upon the Holy Spirit of
God and divine power to do the work."

"That your faith should not stand in the wisdom of men, but in the power of God." Because,
you see, if I make a profession of salvation on
the strength of a discourse that has stirred simply my emotions and made me feel that I ought
to do something about it, and also because of my
admiration for the preacher; then, when the
preacher is gone and my emotions are no longer
stirred, I will find myself wondering whether I
am converted or not, whether there is any reality
in this thing or not. I felt so differently under
the spell of that emotion; now I do not feel that
way at all. If the Holy Spirit of God has presented Christ to me and I have received Him,
never mind about my feelings, I am saved and
saved for eternity. My faith stands, "not in the
wisdom of men, but in the power of God." I rest
upon His sure testimony.

We do not mean by this, the apostle says, that
we have nothing but the simplicity of the gospel
message to give to men, we seek also to lead believers into the deep things of God. "We speak
wisdom among them that are perfect." What
does that mean? Did you ever see a perfect
Christian? Surely not in the absolute sense, but

it means perfect in the sense of well-developed. When he talked to the unsaved or to young believers, he had one message, and when he talked to mature saints he sought to lead them on into the deeper things of God. He does that in this epistle and elsewhere.

"We speak wisdom among them that are perfect: yet not the wisdom of this world." Christianity is a divine revelation, not a human theory. "Not the wisdom of this world, nor of the princes of this world, that come to naught: but we speak the wisdom of God in a mystery"—something that is hidden from the Christless, that which the Spirit of God reveals to believers—"even the hidden wisdom, which God ordained before the world unto our glory." There are rich treasures of wisdom, wonderful truths to make known; for in Christ are "hid all the treasures of wisdom and knowledge." And as we go on with Him we enter into a depth of understanding that the world knows nothing about.

"Which none of the princes of this world knew: for had they known it, they would not have crucified the Lord of glory." If they had only known that the Man who stood in Pilate's judgment-hall that day, so meek, so lowly, answering never a word as He was vehemently accused, was God manifest in the flesh, they would not have crucified the Lord of glory. And so God takes mankind up on the ground of ignorance and says, "I am going to excuse your ignorance, but there is one thing I will never excuse. After I enlighten you and present My Son to you, if you do not receive Him, I will never excuse that." Men are excused because the light has not come, but not excused when the light has come. "This is the condemnation, that light is come into the world, and men loved darkness rather than light, because their deeds were evil" (John 3:19).

This is not to say that God will not judge sin wherever it is found. But simply that He holds men responsible for what knowledge of His truth they have, and not for what has never come to them. "All have sinned" and all "are guilty before God," but judgment will be according to works and in perfect righteousness.

But when one trusts the Lord Jesus he is delivered forever from judgment. What a wonderful thing it is to know Him—"Jesus Christ, and Him crucified!"

LECTURE VII.

DIVINE REVELATION

✓ ✓ ✓

"But as it is written, Eye hath not seen, nor ear heard, neither have entered into the heart of man, the things which God has prepared for them that love Him. But God hath revealed them unto us by His Spirit: for the Spirit searcheth all things, yea, the deep things of God. For what man knoweth the things of a man, save the spirit of man which is in him? Even so the things of God knoweth no man, but the Spirit of God. Now we have received, not the spirit of the world, but the spirit which is of God; that we might know the things that are freely given to us of God. Which things also we speak, not in the words which man's wisdom teacheth, but which the Holy Ghost teacheth; comparing spiritual things with spiritual" (1 Cor. 2: 9-13).

✓ ✓ ✓

THE apostle declared that in making known the gospel he sought to use all simplicity of speech, but when it came to opening up the truth of God to believers, there are deep things, wonderfully precious things, that cannot be given to the world at large, which form the hidden wisdom of God. The world has its various schools of philosophy, its deep things to which the average man on the street does not pay much attention; and so God has His deep things which are not for the world outside, but for those who have already received the gospel message. The Lord Jesus Himself warned His disciples against casting pearls before swine. What did He mean by that? Simply this, the unsaved man, the man who has never been regenerated, has no more ability to appreciate, to enter into and enjoy spiritual unfoldings than the swine has ability to set a value on beautiful pearls, and therefore, the message for the unsaved is the gospel; but to the Lord's own people He would impart this hidden wisdom, that which none of the princes of this world knew, for, he says, "Had they known it, they would not have crucified the Lord of glory. But as it is written, Eye hath not seen, nor ear heard, neither have entered into the heart of man, the things which God hath prepared for them that love Him."

The apostle is quoting from the sixty-fourth chapter of the book of the prophet Isaiah. The singular thing is that a great many people stop here with the Old Testament quotation and say, "You know we cannot understand, we cannot be expected to understand or enter into the things which God hath prepared for us, because the Word tells us that, 'Eye hath not seen, nor ear heard, neither have entered into the heart of man, the things which God hath prepared for them that love Him.' " And so they settle back and conclude that we must be content to be ignorant of

these things, for God has said that they are not
for us to know. Let us look at the passage in the
Old Testament and see the connection in which
it is found. In verse 4 we read, in our English
Bibles, "For since the beginning of the world men
have not heard, nor perceived by the ear, neither
hath the eye seen, O God, beside Thee, what He
hath prepared for him that waiteth for Him."
This is the translation from the Hebrew. That
which we find in the New Testament is the translation of the Greek Version of the Old Testament,
hence the difference in words, though the meaning
is exactly the same. What is it that Isaiah tells us?
It is that no man apart from divine revelation
can understand what God has in store for His
people in times to come. That was true in Old
Testament days, but when we come to the New
Testament since God has revealed Himself in the
Person of His Son and given this new revelation
of the new covenant in the Gospels and in the
Epistles, we must not stop with the verse in
Isaiah. We must not be content to take for
granted that we are still where they were in the
Old Testament days, for that is the very thing
the apostle tells us is not the case.

"*But* God hath revealed them unto us by His
Spirit: for the Spirit searcheth all things, yea,
the deep things of God." In other words, the Old
Testament speaks of times when there were great

and wonderful mysteries which were kept hidden
from all men; even the prophets themselves, as
enlightened as they were, knew nothing of the
special truths of this dispensation, but God has
made them known now. Read the books of the
Old Testament, read the Psalms, for instance,
which give you the highest inspiration of the
saints before the veil was rent, and you get no
inkling of the heavenly calling or of believers en-
tering through the rent veil into the very presence of God without an officiating priest between.
You get nothing of Christ exalted at God's right
hand and of believers linked with Him so that
we can say, "He hath raised us up together, and
made us sit together in heavenly places in Christ
Jesus" (Eph. 2:6). The Old Testament gives us
the preparation time. There we have God's people as children going to school, learning through
symbols and types and shadows, but with no realization of the wonderful truths now made known,
and therefore, Isaiah could say, "Eye hath not
seen, nor ear heard, neither have entered into
the heart of man, the things which God hath
prepared for them that love Him." But all that
has changed today. Now our eyes do see, our
ears do hear, and our hearts should be able to
comprehend the wonderful things which God
hath prepared for those linked up to Himself
through the Lord Jesus Christ. "God hath re-

vealed them unto us by His Spirit," and so we still need the Old Testament, for the things written there were for our learning.

We go back in the Old Testament and see the exercises of the people of God in years gone by, but we do not stay there; we learn wondrous lessons, but we move on to the full and glorious revelation that God has given in the new dispensation. It is here our souls revel in the precious truths now made known. Christians sometimes imagine that if they come to God in worship, for instance in singing, in the very words of Holy Scripture, like some of our friends who sing the Psalms, their worship takes a higher character than that of Christians using what they call "man-made hymns," and yet what is the fact? We might gather together and sing the Psalms week after week and year after year, and always be conscious of the fact that we are singing the very words of Scripture, but there would not be a syllable that would give us our place within the holiest, accepted in the Beloved; and you will find that where Christians are content thus to approach God in worship, they have no realization of the fulness of the Christian's position. It could not be, because the Psalms as all other Old Testament Scripture lead us up to the door, but they do not carry us inside into the fullest blessing. Therefore, you will generally find people who are wedded to the Psalms, precious as they are, a legal people, knowing very little of the fulness of grace, and most of them are content to go through life thinking it is altogether too much to believe that a man can be saved and know it in this life, just let them go on trusting and hoping, and perhaps God will give them dying grace at last.

You have heard of the good old Scotch woman who said, "We will not sing any of these man-made hymns, we will sing just the Psalms of David to the tunes that David wrote!" The fact is that a Spirit-taught Christian today can enjoy in a hymn precious and wonderful truths which would have been amazing to David, truths of which he knew absolutely nothing. What a wonderful thing it is to think that we live in the dispensation of the grace of God. By the Holy Spirit God has now revealed these things formerly hidden unto us, "for the Spirit searcheth all things, yea, the deep things of God." That may seem like a peculiar expression. The Holy Spirit is One with the Father and with the Son; our Lord Jesus puts the Trinity all on an equality when He tells His disciples to teach and to baptize in the name of the Father and of the Son and of the Holy Spirit. You could not think of putting a creature in there and saying, "In the name of the Father and of the Son and of the blessed Virgin

Mary," or, "In the name of the Father and of the
Son and of the holy apostles." You could not do
that, for you would be bringing His creatures on
a level with God. But when you say, "In the
name of the Father and of the Son and of the
Holy Spirit," everything is in keeping because all
are co-equal and co-eternal.

In what sense does the Holy Spirit have to
search to find out the mind of the Lord? "For
the Spirit searcheth all things, yea, the deep
things of God." In Himself He does not need to
search, He does not have to study to learn the
mind of God. But the wonderful thought is that
in our dispensation the Holy Spirit has come to
dwell in us, and it is through Him that we do the
searching and the studying, and the Spirit of God
opens the truth of God to us. People say, "I do
not know how it is that some folks get such wonderful things out of their Bibles. I do not get
them out of mine. I know I ought to read my
Bible, and I do read it, perhaps a chapter a day,
but I do not have much appetite for it, I do not
get much out of it." I will tell you why. It is
because you do not sit down over your Bible in a
self-judged, broken spirit, putting out of your
life everything carnal, everything worldly, everything unholy, and then depending absolutely on
the Holy Spirit who dwells within you to search
into the Scriptures for you, to open the truth of

God to you. God has given you the Holy Spirit for that very purpose. The Lord Jesus Christ said, "Howbeit when He, the Spirit of truth, is come, He will guide you into all truth: for He shall not speak of Himself; but whatsoever He shall hear, that shall He speak: and He will show you things to come. He shall glorify Me: for He shall receive of Mine, and shall show it unto you." Take a poor, simple, ignorant Christian who can barely read or write and put him down over his Bible in dependence on the Holy Spirit of God, and he will get more out of a given passage of Scripture in half-an-hour than a Doctor of Divinity or a Doctor of Psychology, who studies it with a lot of learned tomes about him depending upon his intellect instead of upon the Holy Spirit. The Spirit of God opens the truth to those who depend on Him. I am afraid that many of us are absolutely careless of the Holy Spirit who dwells within us. We are trying to make our own way through the world, trying to find out what is right and wrong in spiritual things, instead of handing over everything to the Spirit of God and depending on Him to guide and lead and unfold the Scriptures. He came to do this very thing and He delights to fulfil this mission.

How strikingly the apostle illustrates this in verse 11: "For what man knoweth the things of a man, save the spirit of man which is in him?

even so the things of God knoweth no man, but
the Spirit of God." What does he mean by "the
spirit of man which is in him?" Materialists tell
us that the spirit of a man is the breath of a
man. It is a striking thing that in Greek and
Hebrew the same word may be translated "spirit,"
"air," "breath," "wind." They say the spirit is the
air that you breathe, there is no personality about
it, the body is all there is of man as far as personality is concerned. If that were true, would it not
be absurd for the apostle to speak as he does
here? Translate the word "spirit" by "breath"
and you would read, "What man knoweth the
things of a man, save the breath of man which
is in him?" Is that not remarkable?—an intelligent breath! Is it your breath that knows things?
Is it your breath that reasons and weighs evidence? Surely not. It is the spirit of a man.
And what is the spirit of a man? It is the real
man.

When God created man He created him a spirit
living in a human body, and therefore God is
called "The Father of spirits." Translate that,
"God, the Father of breaths," how would that
sound? No; God is a Spirit and man is a spirit,
and therefore, in that sense, even unregenerated
men are God's sons. The spirit is the personality.
It is that which differentiates him from the lower
creation, enables him to think, to weigh evidence,

to reason, to investigate. "What man knoweth the things of a man, save the spirit of man which is in him?" I cannot read your thoughts, you cannot read my thoughts. We find people who profess to be able to do so, but they always make a botch of it. We try to read people's minds by their faces, but we often accuse them of things that are not so, as Eli falsely accused Hannah.

"What man knoweth the things of a man, save the spirit of man which is in him?" I might talk as humbly as possible and you might be foolish enough to go away and think, "What a lowly man that is!" and all the time I might be a kind of Uriah Heep with a false humility. Another might seem to you to be proud while in reality he might be very humble. So Jesus said, "Judge not that ye be not judged." We are not to try to read other persons' minds for we will often be mistaken if we do. "What man knoweth the things of a man, save the spirit of man which is in him?" If my human spirit understands my thoughts, if my human spirit knows what is going on in my mind, do you not see the apostle's argument? The Holy Spirit knows everything that goes on in the mind of God. Is not that a wonderful thought?

"Even so the things of God knoweth no man, but the Spirit of God." And He has chosen to make them known to us. I can make known my thoughts to you, and you can make yours known

to me. Very well, the Holy Spirit of God makes
known the thoughts of God to us. "Now we have
received, not the spirit of the world, but the spirit
which is of God; that we might know the things
that are freely given to us of God." This blessed
Holy Spirit has been received by believers. He
has come to indwell us, to control us, for the glory
of the Lord Jesus Christ in order that we might
know the things that are freely given to us of
God. That is the secret of learning the Bible,
and understanding the truth. You come to the
Book and study it in dependence on the Holy
Spirit who dwells within and He will open it up.
But let me give you another secret. He won't do
that if you are grieving Him. As long as the
Spirit is happy within you because you are living
in a godly, unworldly, consistent manner, it is
His delight to take the things of Christ and open
them up; but the moment you grieve Him, the
moment you give yourself to unholy thoughts or
worldly behavior, yield to carnality, to things
contrary to the Lord Jesus Christ whom you are
called upon to represent here, then you grieve the
Spirit of God and instead of the Holy Spirit being free to do what He delights to do, take of the
things of Christ and show them unto you, He has
to occupy you with your own failure and sins and
shortcomings, in order to bring you to repentance
and confession where you will seek to put every-

thing right before God. So the secret of getting the mind of God as you study His Word is to live in the power of an ungrieved Spirit and go to the Book in dependence on Him.

"We have received, not the spirit of the world, but the spirit which is of God; that we might know the things that are freely given to us of God." We have them here, but do we know them? It is one thing to have a vast amount of knowledge shut up between the covers of a book, it is another thing really to know it.

You may have a large library. Everything in all those books is yours. But it is quite another thing to make all that accumulation of knowledge yours practically. It requires diligent study and careful reading. So with God's wonderful Library, the Bible. We need the illumination of the Holy Spirit as we meditate upon its wondrous truths, for it is only in this way we can enter into its treasures. This Book was not written by men, except as they were used as penmen; it was given by God. "Holy men of God spake as they were moved by the Holy Spirit." And think of the folly of expecting to understand it if I just approach it from a carnal or intellectual standpoint. That is not the way to get God's truth. He has given it to me, but if I would appreciate it the Spirit must open it up, and I must walk in the Spirit

"Which things also we speak, not in the words which man's wisdom teacheth, but which the Holy Ghost teacheth; comparing spiritual things with spiritual." Some people wonder what we mean when we speak of the verbal inspiration of the Bible. There are those who talk of the Bible being inspired in the sense that God gave to the writers of the different books certain thoughts and they embodied them in their own language to suit themselves, but that is not the truth of inspiration as taught in the Book. "Which things also we speak, not in the words which man's wisdom teacheth." They did not take divine truths and write them down in their own words. They expressed divine truths in the words that the Holy Spirit gave. He gave the words as well as the thoughts. Verbal inspiration means inspiration of the words. If the Bible is inspired at all, it is in its words, and that is what the apostle insists upon. When you come to the study of this Book and recognize the fact that the words were given of God, you will have such a conception of the wonder of the Book that you will delight in lingering over every syllable. How often we have studied the Book and one little word seemed to jump at us; we have looked it up and found the original meaning in the Hebrew or the Greek, found what the root is, and as we delved into it we have found there was not any other word that would have expressed that truth. It is like God Himself; it is perfect. "Which things also we speak, not in the words which man's wisdom teacheth, but which the Holy Ghost teacheth."

He concludes this section with an expression that is a bit peculiar, one about which theologians have had a great many different views. "Comparing spiritual things with spiritual." That may suggest a comparison of one divinely-imparted line of truth with some other opening up of eternal verities. That is blessedly true, and that was perhaps the thought that the translators had in mind, but there is something deeper than that. Others have translated it, "Expounding spiritual things to spiritual minds," and that is surely important. If men are not spiritual, they cannot take in spiritual truth. One might endeavor to give them the deepest and most wonderful revelation from the Word of God, but they would not be able to take it in. It is the same in spiritual things as in natural things. Take music, for instance, if you do not have music in your soul, if you do not have a real sense of music, you cannot understand it.

I heard a man once tell of going to hear Jenny Lind, the famous "Swedish Nightingale," who eventually gave up the concert stage for love of Christ. Beside him sat a sea-captain who had paid five dollars for his ticket but who drowsed and slumbered all through the concert. He went, out of curiosity, to *see* the noted singer, but he had no ear to enjoy her marvellous tones. He was unable to appreciate that wonderful voice that thrilled myriads who had a sense of musical values. To enjoy music one must have music in his own soul. This is just as true in regard to spiritual things. That is why people need to be born again and then they need to walk in the Spirit, for one cannot understand spiritual things unless he is living a spiritual life.

On the other hand, this last expression is not exactly personal in the Greek, it does not necessarily refer to individuals, and a better translation might be, "Communicating spiritual things by spiritual methods," or "by spiritual words." That seems to be a very satisfactory translation. It is the business of servants of Christ to communicate spiritual things by spiritual methods, not stooping to the cheap claptrap methods of the world as they seek to expound the Word of God, but in a reverent way opening up spiritual truths and using suited words in accordance with the testimony that the Holy Spirit Himself has given men. God give to each one of us a deeper appreciation of this marvelous revelation which we have in His Word.

NATURAL, CARNAL, AND SPIRITUAL MEN

✔ ✔ ✔

"But the natural man receiveth not the things of the Spirit of God: for they are foolishness unto him: neither can he know them, because they are spiritually discerned. But he that is spiritual judgeth all things, yet he himself is judged of no man. For who hath known the mind of the Lord, that he may instruct Him? But we have the mind of Christ. And I, brethren, could not speak unto you as unto spiritual, but as unto carnal, even as unto babes in Christ. I have fed you with milk, and not with meat: for hitherto ye were not able to bear it, neither yet now are ye able. For ye are yet carnal: for whereas there is among you envying, and strife, and divisions, are ye not carnal, and walk as men? For while one saith, I am of Paul; and another, I am of Apollos; are ye not carnal? Who then is Paul, and who is Apollos, but ministers by whom ye believed, even as the Lord gave to every man? I have planted, Apollos watered; but God gave the increase. So then neither is he that planteth any thing, neither he that watereth; but God that giveth the increase. Now he that planteth and he that watereth are one: and every man shall receive his own reward according to his own labor" (1 Cor. 2: 14—3: 8).

✔ ✔ ✔

IN this passage we have three men brought before us; the natural, the carnal, and the spiritual. What are we to understand by these expressions? We often say there are only two classes of people in the world, those who are

regenerated and those who are not; or, to put it
in another way, those who are saved and those
who are lost; and of course that distinction
stands. But here the apostle divides mankind into three classes: the natural, the carnal, and the
spiritual.

Who is the natural man? We read in verse 14
of chapter 2, "The natural man receiveth not the
things of the Spirit of God: for they are foolishness unto him: neither can he know them, because they are spiritually discerned." The natural man is the man who has simply been born
according to nature. Our Lord Jesus says in
John 3, "That which is born of the flesh is flesh."
That is the natural man. "That which is born of
the Spirit is spirit." That is the genesis of the
spiritual man. But the word translated "natural"
does not merely mean of the flesh. The word
really means, psychical. In 1 Thessalonians 5: 23
the apostle Paul says, "And I pray God your
whole spirit and soul and body be preserved
blameless unto the coming of our Lord Jesus
Christ." He shows that man is tripartite. The
spirit, the highest part of the man, is that which
differentiates him from the lower creation, is that
to which God speaks. We read, "What man knoweth the things of a man, save the spirit of man
which is in him?" It is the spirit that gives
man intelligence above the brute. By the spirit

man reasons, is able to weigh evidence, by the spirit he is able to listen to the voice of God.

On the other hand, the second part of man is called the soul, the *psyche*, and this word "natural" is an adjective formed from that word, psychical. "The psychical man, or the soulual man, receiveth not the things of the Spirit of God." When God created man, somebody has well said, he was like a three-story house; the lower story, the body; the second-story, the soul, the seat of his natural instincts and emotions; and the third-story, the spirit, the highest part of man by which he could look up to God. But when man sinned, there was a moral earthquake, and the top-story fell down into the basement, and that leaves him a psychical man, it leaves the soul in the preeminent place instead of the spirit. When you remember that the soul is the seat of man's emotional nature, you will realize that the natural man is a creature led not by conscience, not by an enlightened spirit, but following the desires of his own heart as a soulish man because he follows his own affections and desires. He is a creature of emotions, and that is why it is so easy to say that every sin appeals in some way to the emotions of the natural heart. At base all sin is selfish; we sin because we think we shall find a measure of satisfaction in that sin. Sin is always selfish, and the psychical man is a selfish being, he is a

self-centered person, for after all, the soul is the
self. The natural man, therefore, is the man who
lives the self-life, the man whose spirit has never
been quickened into newness of life; it is still
down there a captive in the basement, if you will.
You can see at once where that applies to you.
What is your motive in life? Are you living to
glorify God or are you living to enjoy yourself?
Are you seeking your own desires or are you seeking to please the Lord Jesus Christ? As every
saved person looks back to the old life, he can
say:

> "I lived for myself, for myself alone,
> For myself and none beside;
> Just as if Jesus had never lived,
> And as if He had never died."

That is the psychical man. He may be outwardly
a very good man, a very gracious man, a very
courteous man, a very kind man, as long as he
can have his own way. He lives for himself and
finds a certain satisfaction even in doing good.
He learns as he goes through life that honesty is
the best policy, that he is happier if he is honest,
and therefore many an unregenerate man is a
model of integrity. He gets a degree of happiness out of meeting the needs of other people; he
may be a very kind man, and there is a glow of
warmth in his heart when he hands something to
a needy person and that person responds, "God

bless you, sir, you don't know how much good you are doing." There may be all that and yet no thought of living for God, no thought of glorifying the Lord Jesus Christ. Some natural men descend into things groveling and debasing, their appetites lead them into licentiousness and inebriety, but other natural men take what has been called the clean side of the broad way, the higher way of the natural man, but it still is the way that leads to destruction. As you walk down that broad way you find all classes and conditions of people, some openly immoral, some vicious, some abominably unclean, others eminently respectable, looked upon with admiration by their fellows; some of them very religious and finding a certain amount of satisfaction as they wend their way to the great cathedral or little chapel, as the case may be; as they sit in a Christian, Jewish or some other service, and as the meeting goes on they find satisfaction in feeling that they are doing the right thing. They are affected by the service, they love the music; if the preacher happens to be eloquent and appealing, they enjoy listening to him, and sometimes even though he is not eloquent, if he is earnest they like to listen to him.

When Charles Spurgeon was at the height of his fame as one of the greatest preachers of the gospel, many an unbeliever thronged to hear him, many a man who rejected Christianity delighted to listen to his sermons. On one occasion as a man, well-known as an infidel, was returning from Spurgeon's meeting, he met a friend who said, "Where have you been today?"

"I have been to hear the great preacher, Charles Spurgeon," he said.

"You surprise me," said his friend; "you do not believe a word he says."

"No, I do not, but he does, you know; and I get a certain amount of satisfaction in listening to a man preach as though he really believed what he was preaching."

Even a natural man can appreciate that, for he may set a certain value upon earnestness and intensity. It is very possible that one may be outwardly good, his life may be a very righteous one, he may be a man of integrity in business, be very kind and benevolent, and have a certain amount of religious feeling, and yet be a natural man.

What is needed to bring a man out of that state into that of a Christian? There must be a new nature, a renewing of the mind, he must be born of God. "Except a man be born again, he cannot see the kingdom of God" (John 3: 3). This natural man at his best with all his amiability and respectability cannot enter into nor understand divine things. Talk to him of the wondrous truths of the Word of God and he will look at you in amazement and will say, "I do not see the im-

portance of these things." Tell him that God became Man for our redemption, that He was born
of a virgin, and he smiles tolerantly and says, "If
you get any comfort in believing that, all right,
but as far as I am concerned it involves a biologi-
cal miracle which I cannot accept." Tell him that
Christ died for our sins upon Calvary's cross and
that it was there He shed His blood for our redemption, and he will smile again and say,
"Rather an old-fashioned idea, that idea of blood
atonement. I notice in my studies it has rather
a large place in all the ancient religions, but of
course I do not see it at all." "If our gospel be
hid, it is hid to them that are lost" (2 Cor. 4:3).
Talk to him of the physical resurrection of our
Lord Jesus Christ, and again he says: "Of course
it does not make very much difference whether
His body rose; that is a small thing. His principles have been resurrected after being rejected
by the men of His day, and they abide, and if we
follow the rules He laid down everything will be
all right."

It is only as the Spirit of God lays hold of him
and gives him to see his lost condition that the
gospel appeals to this man. Believing it he ceases
to be a natural man, he is no longer to be placed
in that category. He may be a babe in Christ
but he is a Christian. However, when you turn
to consider Christians, you find two classes sug-

gested in these words of the apostle Paul. He uses these words in verse 15, "He that is spiritual," and then in the first verse of chapter 3 he says, "I could not speak unto you as unto spiritual, but as unto carnal." Let us look at the word "carnal." Literally it means "fleshly," it is an adjective formed from the Greek word for "flesh." The term "flesh" as used doctrinally in Scripture does not refer to human flesh, but rather to the nature which we have received from Adam, "That which is born of the flesh is flesh." Now a carnal man, strange as it may seem, is a fleshly believer. There are many such persons. The carnal man has been regenerated, he has received a new nature, his spirit has been quickened into newness of life, and that spirit that fell into the basement is being elevated into its proper place by divine power, but the man finds he is still under the power of that old carnal fleshly nature in a large measure. Many a Christian's life is made up of mingled victories and defeats. As he walks with God, as he takes the place of lowliness and humiliation before God, as he feeds upon the Word, as he breathes the atmosphere of prayer, his spiritual life is developed and he grows in grace and in the knowledge of God. But if this believer is slothful in availing himself of the means of grace, he may find that even after being saved for some years he is still far from being the kind of a Christian that it is the desire of the Lord that he should be.

What is a carnal believer, a fleshly believer? It is best to find out from Scripture. In verse 3 we read: "For ye are yet carnal: for whereas there is among you envying, and strife, and divisions (or factions), are ye not carnal, and walk as men?" Here is a Christian, one who has really trusted the Lord Jesus Christ, but as you get intimately acquainted with him, you find he is a very selfish person. He is delightful to get along with as long as he can have his own way. As long as he can run everything to suit himself he is perfectly happy and agreeable, but cross him in the least degree, bring something before him that is contrary to his own desires, and at once there is a stirring of the flesh within him and he is manifested as a carnal man because there is strife. Think of the Lord Jesus Christ. They could treat Him as they would, but He was always the meek and lowly One; they could not rouse His temper by ill-treatment and yet He had a temper. A spiritual Christian is not one who has no temper. Just as that knife of yours would amount to very little if not properly tempered so the Christian amounts to nothing if he is not properly tempered. We read of our Lord Jesus Christ being angry. He was in a synagogue on a Sabbath Day and there was a poor woman there bowed with disease, and His enemies were watch-

ing Him to see whether He would heal her on the
Sabbath. He asked the question, "Is it lawful to
do good on the sabbath days?" (Mark 3: 4) but
they would not answer Him, and we read, "He
looked round about on them with anger, being
grieved for the hardness of their hearts" (Mark
3: 5). What made Him angry? It was their
hypocrisy. Hypocrisy always stirred the indignation of the Lord Jesus Christ. They could heap
every indignity upon Him they desired, that
never stirred Him to anger; but let them heap
indignities upon one of the least of His children
and that stirred Him to the very depth of His being. When Saul of Tarsus was persecuting the
Christians, Christ Jesus spoke to him and said,
"Saul, Saul, why persecutest thou Me?" (Acts 9:
4). He never talked in that way to people when
they ill-treated Him on earth, but when they ill-
treat His own while He is in glory, He feels it
keenly. When you find a Christian quick to resent what you do to him but not at all quick to
resent what is done to others, you may be sure
he is still carnal.

Then there is envying. A person who envies
another manifests the marks of carnality. We are
members of one Body. If that is really so, if I
am a member of one Body with every other
Christian, I ought to be just as delighted when
my brethren are honored as though it were I,

and I ought to be as deeply concerned when my brethren are distressed and in trouble as if I were in their place. Scripture says, "If one member be honored, all the members rejoice with it" (1 Cor. 12: 26). And we are exhorted to "rejoice with them that do rejoice, and weep with them that weep" (Rom. 12: 15). How different it often is! I can do something reasonably well, somebody else is preferred before me and I cannot appreciate what they do. I think I can preach a little bit, but somebody else is enjoyed more than I am, and instead of saying, "Thank God for the way He is using His servant," I sit in a corner and think, "What is it that makes the people so interested? I don't see anything in that kind of preaching." When I do this, I am carnal. You can apply that to everything else. If you cannot enjoy to have somebody else preferred before you, you are carnal.

Then there are the faction-makers, the division-makers, those who try to bring in strife among the people of God. Here at Corinth they were divided into little cliques and were saying, "I am of Paul; and another, I am of Apollos," and every one had his favorite. Paul says, "That is just carnality. When you go on like that, you are acting like little babes." "I, brethren, could not speak unto you as unto spiritual, but as unto carnal, even as unto babes in Christ." If Christians could realize that when they compare one with another, say unkind things about some and laud others to the skies, it is just baby-talk, they would be ashamed of it. Paul is telling us that it only shows carnality. It is not anything to be proud of; it is something that may well cause one to bow the head in shame. Paul says, "Here you are in Corinth, you have such wonderful attainments and are so proud because you come behind in no gift, and yet you are just babies, so that I cannot unfold to you the things that I would like to. I have had to feed you with milk, and even now you are not able to be fed with meat. You are still big babies." Paul was very faithful. The Corinthians gloried in men and they gloried in great swelling words; and some, I suppose, listened to Paul and said, "We don't see anything in his preaching; we learned that years ago. Why doesn't he go into the deeper things?"

A colored brother was a candidate for the pastorate of a church and he preached for the congregation on the text, "Thou shalt not steal." The congregation thought it was great, and the Pulpit Committee met after the service to decide whether to give him a call. Finally one of the brethren spoke up and said, "I don't believe in calling any man on one sermon. That was a fine sermon he preached, but I think we should ask this brother to come back again before we call him." So they decided to ask him to come back the next Sunday. He did and he used the same text, "Thou shalt not steal," and preached the same identical sermon. At the close the Committee met again and said, "He must have forgotten that he preached that sermon last Sunday, we had better ask him back again." So the next Sunday he got up in the pulpit and said, "You will find my sermon in the twentieth chapter of Exodus, 'Thou shalt not steal.'" Before he could go on a member of the Pulpit Committee got up and said, "You are forgetting that you preached that sermon here twice already; we want to hear you in something else." The preacher replied, "I am going to preach on that text every time I come to this church until you learn to keep away from Widow Jones' hen-coop of a night."

So Paul says, "I cannot unfold the great things to you, you are still little babes, you are not developed yet, you are just carnal." But now he says, "The spiritual are a different class." Who are the spiritual? Those who walk in a spiritual way, those who are guided by the Spirit of God. The highest part of the man is now in ascendency. Self does not predominate in this man, he lives to glorify Christ and walks on a higher plane than the carnal man.

"He that is spiritual judgeth all things, yet he himself is judged of no man." What does he

mean by this? The word translated "judgeth" is
the same as in the fourteenth verse, "But the natural man receiveth not the things of the Spirit
of God: for they are foolishness unto him:
neither can he know them because they are spiritually *discerned.*" "He that is spiritual *discerneth* all things, yet he himself is discerned of no
man." He is able to see the difference between
what is of God and what is of man, what is of the
flesh and what is of the Spirit, what is of the
new and what is of the old nature. The spiritual
man discerneth all things but he himself is discerned of no man. Other men cannot understand
him, if they are not spiritual. They say, "He is
a queer kind of a man; he does not seem to be
actuated by the motives of other men, he is not
dominated by the principles that dominate other
men." Sometimes they even say as in Isaiah's day,
"The spiritual man is mad, he is not normal." Of
course not, according to the present order, because he is controlled by a higher power. One of
those old New England philosophers wrote, "If I
do not seem to keep step with others, it is because
I am listening to a different drum-beat." And if
a man of God does not seem to keep step with the
carnal and the worldly and the Christless, it is
because his ear is attuned to heaven and he is
getting his instructions from above. I remember
reading, about forty years ago, a little poem that

seems to me to bring out very preciously what
should characterize the spiritual man:

> "There is no glory halo around his devoted head,
>   No luster marks the sacred path in which his footsteps
>   tread;
>   But holiness is graven upon his thoughtful brow,
>   And all his steps are ordered in the light of heaven e'en
>   now.
>   He often is peculiar and oft misunderstood,
>   And yet his power is felt by both the evil and the good,
>   And he doth live in touch with heaven a life of faith
>   and prayer,
>   His hope, his confidence, his joy, his all are centered
>   there."

Would you like to be a spiritual man, a spiritual
woman? If you would, there is a price to pay.
You must surrender your own will, you must
yield yourself unreservedly to the control of the
indwelling Holy Spirit of God. And that means
the end of all human ambitions, that means that it
makes no difference henceforth what men may
think or say, you have only One to please, and
that is the Lord Jesus Christ. There is a great
deal of talk about surrender, about spirituality,
on the part of Christians who manifest by their
very demeanor the carnality that controls them.
God give us to be controlled by Him!

Let us then as believers not be occupied with
man but with Christ. "Who then is Paul, and
who is Apollos, but ministers by whom ye be-

lieved, even as the Lord gave to every man." And what are ministers? They are servants, and so God's ministers are servants of the people of God. Just imagine a family with a number of servants. Here is Chloe and Nellie and Tom and Bill, and the whole family is upset because some are saying, "I am of Chloe, I am of Nellie, I am of Tom, and I am of Bill." What, the whole family divided over the servants? What absurdity! God's ministers are the servants of the people of God; let them accept the service thankfully, but never let them put the servant in the place of the Master. "I have planted, Apollos watered; but God gave the increase." The servant has no power to cause the Word to produce fruit.

"So then neither is he that planteth any thing, neither he that watereth, but God that giveth the increase." The servant is nothing, but God is everything. "Now he that planteth and he that watereth are one." And what is that? They are both just nothing; they are two ciphers. But put Christ in front of the ciphers and then you have something worth while. "And every man shall receive his own reward according to his own labor."

THE TESTING OF THE BELIEVER'S WORKS

✓ ✓ ✓

"For we are laborers together with God: ye are God's husbandry, ye are God's building. According to the grace of God which is given unto me, as a wise masterbuilder, I have laid the foundation, and another buildeth thereon. But let every man take heed how he buildeth thereupon. For other foundation can no man lay than that is laid, which is Jesus Christ. Now if any man build upon this foundation gold, silver, precious stones, wood, hay, stubble; every man's work shall be made manifest: for the day shall declare it, because it shall be revealed by fire; and the fire shall try every man's work of what sort it is. If any man's work abide which he hath built thereupon, he shall receive a reward. If any man's work shall be burned, he shall suffer loss: but he himself shall be saved; yet so as by fire. Know ye not that ye are the temple of God, and that the Spirit of God dwelleth in you? If any man defile the temple of God, him shall God destroy; for the temple of God is holy, which temple ye are. Let no man deceive himself. If any man among you seemeth to be wise in this world, let him become a fool, that he may be wise. For the wisdom of this world is foolishness with God. For it is written, He taketh the wise in their own craftiness. And again, The Lord knoweth the thoughts of the wise, that they are vain. Therefore let no man glory in men. For all things are yours; whether Paul, or Apollos, or Cephas, or the world, or life, or death,

or things present, or things to come; all are yours; and ye
are Christ's; and Christ is God's" (1 Cor. 3: 9-23).

✓ ✓ ✓

W E have noticed how the apostle warns
the people of God against putting His
servants in a place that should belong
only to the blessed Lord. Every minister is simply what that name implies, a servant, and the
danger is that the servant will be exalted and the
Master lost sight of, or the servant be so censored
and blamed that the message will be refused and
the Master dishonored. The servants in themselves are nothing but channels through whom
God speaks to His people. The important thing
is the message they bring. And so Paul speaks
of himself and his fellow-servants in this way:
"We are laborers together with God."

The wonderful thing is that God could do all
His work without us. It is not necessary that He
should take up any of us and use us to spread
His gospel. He could write it in letters of fire
upon the heavens, He could send angels of glory
to preach the "unsearchable riches of Christ,"
even as of old they came to proclaim the birth of
Christ and to direct the shepherds to Bethlehem's
manger. But He has chosen to give to us the
privilege of making known the riches of His
grace, a holy privilege, and yet a very responsible

one. It should lead every servant of Christ to ask himself, "Am I really in touch with God, am I seeking my own interests, can it be that I am actuated by selfish motives, by vain-glory, simply trying to attract attention to myself and my ministry instead of taking a place like that of John the Baptist of old who pointed the people away from himself to Christ saying, 'He must increase, but I must decrease'" (John 3: 30)? This was the attitude of Paul and this will be the attitude of every true minister of God. "We are laborers together with God." They are not left to work in their own strength, but are to give out their message in dependence upon the indwelling Holy Spirit. That is the difference between preaching and worldly oratory. An orator may take a passage from the Bible and read it in a most thrilling way, but that would not be preaching, because he would not be doing it in the power of the Holy Ghost. A poor unlettered man may stand up and preach the gospel in halting English, and yet in such divine power that men would break before it and be led to confess their sins and trust the Saviour. That is what He means when he says, "The preaching of the cross is to them that perish foolishness; but unto us which are saved it is the power of God" (1 Cor. 1: 18). God's servants would preach better if you prayed for them more; there would be more response to

the preaching if they were more upheld in the
secret closet by the people of God. How the
apostle felt his dependence on the prayers of
God's people! You find him pleading with the
saints to remember him in prayer that he might
preach as he ought to preach. That is the peti-
tion that we bring to you, and we plead with you
for Christ's sake and for the sake of dying men,
bear up the ministry before God, take it daily to
God in prayer that those who preach the Word
may give it out in the demonstration of the Spirit
and in power. "We are laborers together with
God," and it is only as God works in and through
us that anything is accomplished.

Then he turns to the servants as a whole and
likens them to a field and a building. First we
read, "Ye are God's husbandry"—or God's tilled
field. You remember how the Lord Jesus Christ
used that figure. The sower sows the Word and
when the Word is sown and people believe it, He
likens them to wheat in a field. That is a beautiful picture of His people, God's tilled field. One
lovely thing about a field of wheat is that the
heads are rising up toward the sun and they are
very much on a level. We are all members one
of another; one is not to tower above the other,
but together we are to bring forth fruit to the
glory of the Lord Jesus Christ.

Second, "Ye are God's building." The building

is really the temple referred to in verse 16,
"Know ye not that ye are the temple of God, and
that the Spirit of God dwelleth in you?" Of old
when Solomon built the temple, he built it upon
the solid rock of Mount Moriah. That was an
oval-shaped hill and so it was necessary to make
a level foundation. Vast stones were brought
from the quarries below and thus made a great
platform upon which the building stood, and so
the apostle says, "Ye are God's building," God's
temple. That is, the Church of God collectively is
the temple of God. He is not speaking of the individual now. In the sixth chapter and the
nineteenth verse he says, "What? Know ye not
that your body is the temple of the Holy Ghost
which is in you?" That is another thing. In
that sense you are a temple of God apart from
every other believer, but here he is speaking of
the assembly of God who as a whole constitute
the temple of God, "The Church of the living God,
the pillar and ground of the truth" (1 Tim. 3:15).

"According to the grace of God which is given
unto me, as a wise masterbuilder (or as a wise
architect), I have laid the foundation." Just as
that foundation had to be laid before the temple
was erected, so Paul came to Corinth and there
laid the foundation by preaching the Word, and
was used to bring the first members into the
Church of God in that locality. Very few of us

can do foundation work like that in these days.
Our missionaries have that privilege, they do not
have to build upon another man's foundation; but
with most of us the foundation has been laid, and
so in the same way the foundation of the Church
in Corinth was laid when Paul first went there to
labor. Now he says, "That foundation does not
need to be laid again. Others build upon it—but
let every man take heed how he buildeth thereupon." In other words, they must preach the
truth of God in the power of the Holy Ghost and
not allow unscriptural and worldly and carnal
things to come in to mar the work that the Spirit
of God is doing.

"Now if any man build upon this foundation
gold, silver, precious stones, wood, hay, stubble."
That word "precious" should be "costly," like
the great and costly stones built into the temple
of old. It is not the thought of diamonds and
rubies, but great costly stones, built into the
spiritual temple of the Lord. If unconverted,
worldly, careless people are brought in, all these
hurt and hinder the work of Christ; and so if you
apply this to every individual believer, though
primarily it has to do with building up the
Church through the servants of God, the same
principle abides. You rest on the one foundation,
Christ, and you are building a life, a character,
that must stand the test of that coming day. How

are you building and what are you building? You
may build with gold which speaks of divine righteousness, silver which speaks of redemption,
costly stones speaking of that which will abide
the day of testing. Or, on the other hand, you
may build with wood, hay or stubble—wood,
which may be fashioned to be very beautiful and
has a certain value attached to it, but which will
not stand the fire; hay, which is of less value than
the wood and yet also has a certain measure of
worth because containing nourishment; stubble,
that which is utterly worthless, that which should
have no place whatever in the thoughts of the
people of God. How are you building?

God has undertaken for us so marvelously. We
have often wondered what we were going to do,
how we were ever going to get through; and yet
God has brought us through, and we have found
that a great deal we worried about we had better
left with Him. Someone has said, "I have had a
great many troubles in my life, but most of them
never happened." God has been so gracious. Is
this not a good time to look back and take stock?
How have we been building? Everything that
has been to the glory of God will be looked upon
in that day as the gold that has His approval.
Everything in our life that has been the result of
our recognition of redemption, if we have acted
as men and women redeemed by the precious

blood of Christ, will shine out as silver in that day. Everything that has been in accordance with the Word and has sprung from that renewed nature which we have through grace, will be as costly stones built into this edifice of our life. How have you been building? Do you see a great many things that give you pause? Do you say, "There has been so much selfishness, so much carnality, so much downright bad temper, so much just of the flesh and so much that was un-Christlike"? Then, dear believer, go to God and judge all these things in His presence, and they will be burned up now and you won't have to face them later. If you do not judge them now, you will have to face them at the judgment-seat of Christ. "If we would judge ourselves, we should not be judged" (1 Cor. 11: 31). We are called to confess all these things that the Spirit shows us are just of the flesh.

A great deal that is called Christian work may be only the energy of the flesh. It is not done for the glory of God at all. What motives actuate us? How do we feel if others are preferred before us? This is a good way to test ourselves as to whether what we are doing is for the Lord. Only that which is done for Christ will be rewarded in that day. Notice, it is He Himself who will point out the differences.

'Every man's work shall be made manifest."

This is at the judgment-seat of Christ, not at the judgment of the Great White Throne. Believers will stand before the judgment-seat of Christ at the Lord's coming. "For the day (that is, the day of Christ) shall declare it, because it shall be revealed by fire"—the purging, testing fire of divine approval, discernment, righteousness; for He is going to judge everything by His standards, not by ours. "And the fire shall try every man's work of what sort it is." I beg of you, consider that little word, "s-o-r-t." "Of what *sort* it is." Not, how much it is. There may be much that amounts to very little in that day, but "of what *sort* it is." It is the character of our work that counts, the motives that lie behind our service. The secrets of the heart are to be made manifest. God will test everything in the light of His own truth. It is a great comfort sometimes when you cannot do all you would like to do to know that if it is of the right character, you will be rewarded just the same.

That is so lovely in connection with that dear woman who anointed the feet of the Lord. When others objected, Jesus said, "She hath done what she could." Is that what the Lord will be able to say of you in that day?—"He hath done what he could"—"she hath done what she could." And then, I do like that word that the Lord spake to David. Solomon tells how David wanted to build a temple to the Lord, but God did not allow him to do so, but the Lord said, "Thou didst well that it was in thine heart" (1 Kings 8:18). Possibly there is a sister who wanted to be a foreign missionary, but she lost her health and was not able to do so. She has been perhaps a semi-invalid at home for years, but has been able to write kind and helpful letters to those in distress. She gave of her slender means to others to take the gospel to the ends of the world, yet she says, "I feel as though my life has amounted to so little; I wanted to be a missionary, and instead of that I have lived this humdrum existence." Do not be discouraged; if done for Christ, He will say, "She hath done what she could." "Thou didst well that it was in thine heart." Perhaps there is a brother who as a young man thought, "How I would like to go into the ministry, how I would love to devote my life to proclaiming the gospel." But that necessitated study, years of preparation, and during those years when he would like to have gone to school perhaps he had a dear aged mother depending upon him, or a sick father, and he had to be the wage-earner of the family. And so he has toiled on, labored on, helping to keep these dear ones, and many a time he has said, "Well, I have missed it; my life has not been the kind I wanted it to be; I wanted to be a minister of the gospel and here I have had to live in this matter-of-fact kind of way, handling butter and eggs, working in an office, or something like that." My dear brother, the Lord has taken note of all that self-denying care you have given that dear father or mother. He is not going to lose sight of any of it, and in that coming day He will say, "Thou didst well that it was in thine heart," and will give you the same kind of a reward as you would have earned if you could have gone out and preached the gospel. It is the heart God looks at—"of what *sort* it is." God grant that our work may be of the right sort.

"If any man's work abide which he hath built thereupon, he shall receive a reward." This is in addition to salvation. We are saved by grace, but this is for faithful service. After we have been saved, there is superabounding grace for, of course, the reward too is of grace, for we could not have earned anything but by divine power. He enables us and then rewards us. But, on the other hand, "If any man's work shall be burned, he shall suffer loss." What does that mean? Will I not feel unhappy even in heaven if I suffer loss in that day? You see, I will come before the Lord and He will go over my life from the day His grace saved me. It will pass like a panorama before me, and for everything that was the out-working of His Holy Spirit, for everything that was in accordance with His Word, He will give a reward.   He will gather that which was for His glory together, and will say, "I am going to reward you for that." But He will bring everything to light which was of self, contrary to the Spirit of Christ, and say, "All that is just so much lost time. If you had devoted all that time to My glory, I could have rewarded you, but I cannot reward you for that which did not please Me. But I tell you what I am going to do with it, I am going to burn it up, and you will never hear of it again for all eternity."   There will be nothing left but that which was to the glory of the Lord Jesus Christ.

Suppose that in that day I have really nothing to glorify Him, I have trusted Him as my Saviour but my life seemingly amounted to nothing. "If any man's work shall be burned, he shall suffer loss: but he himself shall be saved; yet so as by fire."   You may have a beautiful home, you may have spent a long time in building it, but one day it takes fire, and you are wakened in the middle of the night to find the flames roaring through the halls. You leap out of the window and are saved, but the house is burned up. That is the way it will be for many a believer; the life will go for nothing, the life and testimony will be wasted, there will be no reward, but the individual believer will be saved yet so as by fire. Look at Lot. He spent years in Sodom building up a great reputation, he became a judge, but he had no business being there. We read: "That righteous man . . . in seeing and hearing, vexed his righteous soul from day to day with their unlawful deeds" (2 Pet. 2: 8), but Abraham's soul was not daily thus distressed. Why? Because he was not there at all, he was separated from it all. Finally God destroyed Sodom with fire and saved Lot. "Saved yet so as by fire." Everything he had lived for was burned up. Believer, what a solemn thing if that should be true of you or of me, when the blessed Lord takes account of our service.

The apostle goes to the farthest extreme here, but in the next chapter he shows that there will be no believer of whom that is actually true. Chapter 4 verse 5 reads: "Therefore judge nothing before the time, until the Lord come, who both will bring to light the hidden things of darkness, and will make manifest the counsels of the hearts: and then shall every man have praise of God." He will find something in every believer's life that He can reward, some little act of unselfishness, some trembling testimony for Himself, everything that was of the Spirit will be rewarded in that day. But he puts it in the third chapter in the strongest way that we may distinguish between salvation, which is of grace alone, and reward which is for service.

In the last part of the chapter he refers to another class. He has been speaking of members of the Church of God, in the temple of God, some who build gold, silver, precious stones, and some who build wood, hay, and stubble. Now he speaks of a third class in verse 16, "Know ye not that ye are the temple of God, and that the Spirit of God dwelleth in you?" And then in verse 17, "If any man defile the temple of God, him shall God destroy; for the temple of God is holy, which temple ye are." Of whom is he speaking now? "If any man defile the temple of God"—those who are the enemies of God's truth, those who try to destroy His Church, seek to ruin the work of the Lord, men from the outside who creep in. I tremble when I think of what it will mean for men who today profess to be servants of Christ and ministers of God but despise this Book and deny every fundamental truth of Holy Scripture, and yet for filthy lucre's sake get into pulpits of orthodox churches, and instead of building gold, silver or precious stones are only building wood, hay, and stubble, and they are destroying, as much as in them is, the temple of God. God says, "I will destroy them; they will have to account to Me by-and-by." I dwell upon this because some have misunderstood this passage and think of the temple as the temple of the human body; they have thought it might mean if somebody fell into some kind of habit that defiled the body it would mean that God would destroy him. If you allow yourself to indulge in any habit that injures this body, you will have to have answer for that; but here He is talking about the temple that is being built upon the one foundation, the Church of the living God.

"Let no man deceive himself. If any man among you seemeth to be wise in this world, let him become a fool, that he may be wise. For the wisdom of this world is foolishness with God." "The wisdom of this world," not the knowledge of this world. Knowledge is perfectly right and proper; gain all you can; but the wisdom, that is, the philosophy, the reasoning of this world is foolishness with God. "For it is written, He taketh the wise in their own craftiness." Men may think they are very wise but God is ahead of them, and therefore because He has made foolish all the wisdom of this world, how absurd it is for Christians to glory in that which is just of man. "Therefore let no man glory in men. For all things are your's." Let me give you a title to a fortune. You are rich beyond your wildest dreams. Note carefully this closing passage.

"Whether Paul, or Apollos, or Cephas," the ministers of Christ, "or the world." Is the world mine? Yes, because, "The earth is the Lord's, and the fulness thereof" (Ps. 24: 1). This is my

Father's world. I can say, "Thank God, it all belongs to me, and I am going to reign over it some day." "Or life"—yes, life is mine in which to glorify God. "Or death"—death is the servant to usher me into the presence of the Lord. "Or things present"—they are all mine, the trials, the difficulties, the perplexities as well as the happy things. "Or things to come." What riches are soon to be revealed! "All are your's; and ye are Christ's; and Christ is God's." What a wonderful culmination to this chapter that emphasizes our responsibility!

LECTURE X.

STEWARDS OF THE DIVINE MYSTERIES

✓ ✓ ✓

"Let a man so account of us, as of the ministers of Christ, and stewards of the mysteries of God. Moreover it is required in stewards, that a man be found faithful. But with me it is a very small thing that I should be judged of you, or of man's judgment: yea, I judge not mine own self. For I know nothing by myself; yet am I not hereby justified: but he that judgeth me is the Lord. Therefore judge nothing before the time, until the Lord come, who both will bring to light the hidden things of darkness, and will make manifest the counsels of the hearts: and then shall every man have praise of God" (1 Cor. 4: 1-5).

✓ ✓ ✓

THESE words follow very naturally on what we have been looking at in the third chapter. The apostle has been seeking to put the servants of Christ in their right place before the minds of the saints in Corinth. There had been a tendency to factionalism and sectionalism, they were exalting certain leaders, and rallying round them, instead of recognizing that these leaders, evangelists, pastors, teachers, were simply God-given servants for the blessing of the whole Church. These servants of Christ are God's gift to the Church for the blessing of the whole, whether Paul, the teacher, or Apollos, the eloquent preacher, or Cephas, the stirring exhorter. God has given all to His people for their blessing.

Now he turns to consider the responsibility of the servants of Christ and says, "Let a man so account of us, as of the ministers of Christ, and stewards of the mysteries of God." We are inclined to go to one extreme or the other, either to laud and praise and over-estimate the ability and character of God's servants, or else on the other hand to set them at naught and disdain the instruction and help God intended them to give. He would have us take the middle course, not to foolishly flatter His servants but to recognize that we have a great responsibility toward them as they seek to fulfil their responsibility toward us. They watch for our souls as those who must give account, and we are not to be angry or indignant if they have serious things to say to us at times concerning worldliness, carelessness, and carnality. We are rather to judge ourselves in the light of the Word of God, that they bring to us, for they are ministers of Christ. He does not use the ordinary word for "servant" which we find so frequently in his epistles, that is, "bond-servant," but here it is a word that has the thought of an official minister. They have been specially appointed to this particular service as ministers of Christ.

Notice, Paul links up with himself not only Cephas who was an apostle, but Apollos who was not. Apollos, that eloquent man and mighty in the Scriptures, who first went forth preaching the baptism of John, who was not above being instructed by a godly woman and her husband, Priscilla and Aquila, and went forth to preach the gospel with greater liberty and power when he learned it more fully. He says, Do not put us on pedestals, do not form parties around us, but, "Let a man so account of us as official ministers of Christ." We are sent with a commission from the Most High, sent to sound forth His Word, and we are responsible to do it faithfully. We are "stewards of the mysteries of God." A steward is one to whom certain things are committed which he is to use for the benefit of others. God has committed His truth to us. Writing to Timothy Paul says, "That good deposit which was committed unto thee keep by the Holy Ghost which dwelleth in us" (2 Tim. 1: 14). And he was responsible to proclaim it faithfully.

We then are stewards of the divine mysteries. We have seen that the New Testament mysteries are not abstruse truths difficult to apprehend, but sacred secrets that had not been known in pre-

vious ages. In Deuteronomy 29:29 we hear
Moses speaking to the people of Israel on the
plains of Moab, just before they went over the
Jordan to take possession of the promised land.
He says: "The secret things belong unto the Lord
our God." But when our Lord Jesus Christ came
into the world, He uttered "things that had been
kept secret from the foundation of the world,"
and before He left His apostles He said: "I have
yet many things to say unto you, but ye cannot
bear them now. Howbeit when He, the Spirit
of truth, is come, He will guide you into all truth:
for He shall not speak of Himself; but whatsoever He shall hear, that shall He speak: and He
will show you things to come" (John 16:12,
13). And so the present truth revealed by the
Holy Ghost in our dispensation constitutes the
mysteries, the sacred secrets, that the servants
of God are now to make known. What are some
of them?

We have the mystery of the gospel. And what
is that? It is that grand, wondrous truth that
the mind of man would never have ferreted out
if God had not revealed it, that "God was in
Christ, reconciling the world unto Himself, not
imputing their trespasses unto them" (2 Cor. 5:
19). It is that Christ upon the cross died to put
away sin by the sacrifice of Himself; that having
been delivered for our offences, He has been

raised again for our justification; and now in resurrection life He sends the message out into all the world that he that "believeth in Him shall not perish, but have everlasting life." This is God's great secret. Man never would have thought of it. I know that the gospel is from God for I am somewhat familiar with almost all the different religious systems that are prevalent in the world, and apart from that which is revealed in this Book not one of them ever intimates that God Himself should provide a righteousness for sinful man. They all demand a righteousness from man, but they simply point out different ways by which men are supposed to work out for themselves a righteousness that will make them fit for God. In the gospel alone we have the mystery explained how righteousness is provided for men who never could obtain it themselves. Our Lord Jesus Christ is made unto us wisdom, even righteousness, sanctification, and redemption, and we are stewards of this great mystery.

Then we notice the mystery of godliness or piety, the great mystery of the incarnation of our Lord Jesus, God and Man here on earth in one Person. That is beyond human intelligence. We read, "No man knoweth the Son but the Father." It is utterly impossible for men to understand the union of deity and humanity, and yet this mystery is plain to him that believeth. We simply

accept the revelation that God has given and all
questioning is at an end. People talk about "the
problem of Christ." Christ is not a problem, He
is the key to every problem. Everything else is
made plain when we know Christ in whom dwelleth "all the treasures of wisdom and knowledge."

Paul opens up the great mystery of Christ and
the Church, set forth in two characters under the
figure of a body and its head and that of a bride
and a bridegroom. The Lord Jesus Christ glorified is the Head of the Body, and every believer
indwelt by the Holy Spirit is a member of that
Body and becomes thus the fulness of Him that
filleth all in all. In the other beautiful picture we
are told that He who made them in the beginning
made them male and female, and we read, "Therefore shall a man leave his father and his mother,
and shall cleave unto his wife: and they shall be
one flesh" (Gen. 2:24). Paul says in speaking
about the marriage relationship, "This is a great
mystery: but I speak concerning Christ and the
Church."

Linked with this we have the mystery of the
rapture; and that of the olive tree, Israel's present rejection and future regeneration. These
various mysteries are the revelation to us of
things kept secret from the foundation of the
world. How few who take the place of being ministers of Christ ever unfold these mysteries, and

yet this is the responsibility put upon Christ's servants.

"It is required in stewards, that a man be found faithful." The business of a steward is not to electrify people by his eloquent sermons, not to dazzle them by his wonderful ability, not to please them by flowers of rhetoric, not to so speak that he will simply be to them as a "lovely song of one that hath a pleasant voice, and can play well on an instrument" (Ezek. 33:32), as was said of Ezekiel, but the business of a servant of Christ is to open up the truth of God, to unfold, to expound, to make known these mysteries in order that the people of God may appreciate the heritage that He has given them in the Word. In fulfilling this ministry, the servant of Christ may be open to criticism, but that is a small thing. The apostle says, "With me it is a very small thing that I should be judged of you, or of man's judgment: yea, I judge not mine own self." In other words, as long as I am faithful in opening up the Word of God I am not concerned whether my sermons particularly appeal to you or not; as long as I know that I am pleasing Him that sent me I am not greatly concerned if I displease you. These Corinthians appreciated eloquence, oratory, and other special gifts, and they said of the apostle Paul, "Why, his bodily presence is weak, and his speech contemptible." But he could say,

"Well, that doesn't trouble me at all. Did I give you God's truth? That is what I am concerned about. Your appraisal does not concern me in the least." "It is a very small thing that I should be judged of you, or of man's judgment," or, as the margin puts it, "man's day." That is the entire period of time lasting from the rejection of Christ until He comes back again, while God is letting men try out one scheme after another to see what they can make of a world out of which they have cast the Lord Jesus Christ.

"Yea, I judge not mine own self." I do not attempt to appraise my own service, I have no right to say, "Well, I think I did pretty well today; that was an excellent address." That may be simply the pride of the natural heart. On the other hand I am not to go into a funk and throw myself down under a juniper tree, and say, "It was all a failure; I certainly did make a mess of things." No servant of God is capable of appraising his own service. That which he might think to be excellent may be so much wasted time. That which he thinks wasted time may have just the message for the moment.

Then we read, "I know nothing by myself." It is really, "I know nothing *against* myself." I am not conscious of anything in my ministry of a harmful character. "Yet am I not hereby justified," for I may be blundering even when I do not realize it. "But he that appraiseth me is the Lord." He appraiseth everything rightly in accordance with His own holy Word.

He then warns the saints against attempting to get upon the judgment-seat. It is not our place. "Therefore judge nothing before the time." What time? The time when the Lord shall come. We have seen that when He returns He is going to carefully examine all the service of His people. He will separate the precious from the vile, He will distinguish between the gold, silver and precious stones, and the wood, hay, and stubble. He will pronounce correct judgment upon the labors of His ministers. You and I cannot do that now, and it is better for us just to wait.

"Therefore judge nothing before the time, until the Lord come, who both will bring to light the hidden things of darkness, and will make manifest the counsels of the hearts." You see, that is what you and I cannot do; we can hear what comes from the lips or note the actions, but we do not know the hidden springs behind all this, but when the Lord Jesus examines all our labor, He will bring everything to light, all the hidden things of darkness. Yes, if there was envy and jealousy and pride and carnality, He will drag it all out into the light, and many a sermon that sounded very beautiful, that was almost perfect as a piece of oratory, will be shown to be utterly spoiled in that day by the pride that was behind it.   He will bring out all these "hidden things of darkness, and will make manifest the counsels of the hearts."   He will show where there was earnest preaching to glorify Him, even though the speech was faltering and the expressions used were not all they should have been.   He looks upon the heart, not merely the outward appearance.

Then observe, he says: "Then shall every man," and he is speaking of believers, "have praise of God."   But some people say, "Oh, dear, I can do so little and do not seem to have any gifts.   I am afraid there won't be anything the Lord can reward me for in that day."   If you are in Christ, the Holy Spirit of God is dwelling in you, and in that coming day it will be made manifest that every Christian has accomplished something for God for which he can be rewarded.

At the close of a meeting a brother said to me, "Didn't you go a little strong there?" I said, "No, I do not think I did."   "Well," he said, "think of the dying thief, that man was saved just as he hung by the side of Christ; what opportunity did he have to do anything for which to get a reward?"   "Why, my dear brother," I said, "think of the dying thief again.   There he hung nailed to a cross, he could not move a hand nor a foot, but he recognized in the Man on the central cross the coming King of the ages and said, 'Lord, remember me when Thou comest into Thy kingdom,' and he turned to his fellow and rebuked him and bore witness to the perfection of Christ and said, 'We suffer justly; for we receive the due reward of our deeds: but this Man hath done nothing amiss' (Luke 23:41). At the judgment-seat of Christ I think I see that redeemed man coming before his Lord, and he says to himself as he comes, 'I was saved only a few minutes before my Saviour died, and I have had no opportunity to serve Him, to witness for Him, I cannot expect any reward.' And then I think I hear my Lord say, 'Every one present who was converted through some sermon you heard about the dying thief, come here,' and I imagine I see them coming until there are thousands and thousands of them, and I see my blessed Lord turn to that man and say, 'I want to give you this crown of rejoicing for all these souls that you have helped to win to a knowledge of My salvation.'" Do you not see it? "Then shall every man have praise of God."

TRUE APOSTOLIC SUCCESSION

✓ ✓ ✓

"And these things, brethren, I have in a figure transferred to myself and to Apollos for your sakes; that ye might learn in us not to think of men above that which is written, that no one of you be puffed up for one against another. For who maketh thee to differ from another? And what hast thou that thou didst not receive? Now if thou didst receive it, why dost thou glory, as if thou hadst not received it? Now ye are full, now ye are rich, ye have reigned as kings without us: and I would to God ye did reign, that we also might reign with you. For I think that God hath set forth us the apostles last, as it were appointed to death: for we are made a spectacle unto the world, and to angels, and to men. We are fools for Christ's sake, but ye are wise in Christ; we are weak, but ye are strong: ye are honorable, but we are despised. Even unto this present hour we both hunger and thirst, and are naked, and are buffeted, and have no certain dwellingplace; and labor, working with our own hands: being reviled, we bless; being persecuted, we suffer it: being defamed, we entreat: we are made as the filth of the world, and are the offscouring of all things unto this day. I write not these things to shame you, but as my beloved sons I warn you. For though ye have ten thousand instructers in Christ, yet have ye not many fathers: for in Christ Jesus I have begotten you through the gospel. Wherefore I beseech you, be ye followers of me" (1 Cor. 4: 6-16).

H ERE we have the true apostolic succession. A great deal is said in certain circles about a ministry that can date back to the days of the apostles, the first followers of our Lord Jesus Christ, whereby one clergyman after another, all down through the centuries, has received ordination first from the apostles and then their successors without a break to the present time. As though that in itself would confer any particular grace upon them! Undoubtedly Charles H. Spurgeon was right when he said, "When men count on receiving the Holy Spirit through the laying on of hands and because of any fancied apostolic succession, you can depend upon it, it is just a case of empty hands laid on empty heads." Even if we could show an uninterrupted line from apostolic days to the present time there would be no merit in anything like that. But in these eleven verses we have emphasized for us true apostolic succession.

In the earlier part of the epistle the apostle warned against making overmuch of the servants of God. He told how in Corinth they were already divided into sections in the local church, some saying, "I am of Apollos," some, "I am of Paul," some, "I am of Cephas," and some even making Christ's name the head of a party, and boasting to be of Christ to the exclusion of others. "And these things, brethren, I have in a figure transferred to myself and to Apollos for your sakes." That is, it may not actually have been his name or the name of Apollos or that of Cephas that was used in this sectarian way, but he put himself and Apollos, his fellow-laborer, who was thoroughly of one mind with him, to the front and used their names as illustrations in order that he might reprove this tendency to sectarianism among the people of God. "That ye might learn in us not to think of men above that which is written." You will notice that the words, "of men," are italicized, which, I am sure you already know, means that there is nothing in the original that answers to those particular words. They were put there because the translators thought they were needed to help make clear the sense of the Greek text. It has been translated like this: "That you might learn in us nothing above that which is written." That is, you are not to put men in such a place of authority that you rally to them and to their instruction, and are carried away with admiration for their abilities and forget that they as well as yourselves have to be tested by that which is written. The great question is, "What is written?" and the Bible is open to you just as it is to the learned doctors and great commentators, and you need not, in this respect, that any man teach you, for the Holy Spirit will teach you concerning all things as you ponder over the Word of God. The reason why so many are constantly referring to the thoughts of others, men like themselves, is because there is so little real familiarity with the Book. "That you might learn," says the apostle, "in us nothing above that which is written." God has given His written Word, and outside of that the thoughts of even the best, the greatest teachers will be mere speculation.

God has not given teachers to the Church in order that they may supplant the Bible and save His people the trouble of studying the Word for themselves, but that they may spur the people of God on to more intensive searching of the Scriptures. If men get occupied with teachers, they get puffed up one against another.

In verse 7 we learn that for Christians to attach themselves to certain gifts, to the neglect of others who may also have a special ministry from God, is to become very one-sided and to be only partially developed. Take for instance a Christian who says, "I am not interested in teaching, I like the preaching of the gospel. I like to go to an evangelistic meeting, but I am not interested in teaching." You will find that person is very easily carried away by all kinds of winds of doctrine. As long as there is plenty of emotional appeal, a great deal to enthuse and excite, they are there; but when there is something that neces-

sitates thought and meditation, they are not interested. Such Christians lose a great deal.
On the other hand, you will find other Christians
who speak sneeringly and slightingly of evangelistic efforts, of gospel preaching, and say, "I like
to go to a meeting where some able teacher un-
folds the Word of God, for that builds me up in
Christ, but I am not interested when it is only
the gospel."—*Only* the gospel? The gospel is the
most precious thing that I know anything about.
It is the glad, glorious message of God's love to a
needy world, a very rare jewel in these days.
Somebody said to me recently, "How is it that
one can wander about from church to church, and
go Sunday after Sunday, and month after month,
and never hear the gospel? It was such a re-
freshment to come in today and listen to the gospel." Oh, yes; some people who talk about, "only
the gospel," had better try tramping about a bit
to find out what is being preached. After you
have sampled a lot of the rubbish that is going
out in place of the gospel, perhaps you will have
a higher opinion of gospel preaching. Another
says, "Well, there is So-and-So, I like to hear
him; he is an exhorter, and he always stirs me
up, but I am not interested in dry teaching." Dry
teaching! Teaching, of course, may be very dry
if the power of the Holy Spirit is not manifested.
But mere exhortation, if not backed up by the

Book, will not accomplish very much. Yet exhortation is a gift given by the risen Christ to the Church.

"Who maketh thee to differ from another? And what hast thou that thou didst not receive? Now if thou didst receive it, why dost thou glory, as if thou hadst not received it?" There is no reason for any servant of Christ to exalt himself over another. If one has a gift that God has given, he is to use that for the glory of God and not to attract attention to himself.

Then Paul turns to consider another phase of things. When people are not profiting by the ministry that God has given them, you can be sure that it is because of a low spiritual condition. We read in verse 8: "Now ye are full, now ye are rich, ye have reigned as kings without us: and I would to God ye did reign, that we also might reign with you." What does he mean? Why, these Corinthians were settling down to enjoy the benefits of the gospel without the self-denial that should go with it, and they were making themselves comfortable in the world. They received the good things that God's servants brought to them, they congratulated themselves upon the fact that they were saved and going to heaven, and then settled down to enjoy the world, and Paul exclaimed, "You are reigning like kings now, before the time." "Already," he says, "ye are full, already ye are rich, already ye reign as kings." We shall reign by-and-by, but the reigning time has not yet come. This is the suffering time. This is the time when we are to show our loyalty to Christ by our identification with Him in His rejection.

"I think that God hath set forth us the apostles last, as it were appointed to death." In other words, we are like men who are already under sentence of death and going out to die. On another occasion he said, "We have the sentence of death in ourselves." And so he went on in his devoted service. "For I think that God hath set forth us the apostles last, as it were appointed to death: for we are made a spectacle." The word translated "spectacle" is *"theatron,"* that is where we get our English word, "theater." A theater is a show, something displayed upon the boards, and the apostle says, "We are made a spectacle, we are like performers on a stage, for others to look at and see in us something of the lowliness and gentleness and rejection of our Lord Jesus Christ." "We are made a spectacle unto the world," and the word he uses for "world" is the word, *"kosmos,"* the entire universe. "We are made a spectacle unto the universe, both to angels, and to men." From heaven angels are looking down on the servants of Christ: here on earth men are looking at them. If they are proud and haughty and self-indulgent and self-seeking men, the hearts of angels are grieved and the hearts of men are filled with contempt. When they see lowly, devoted, Christlike, unworldly Christians, then angels rejoice and men recognize their reality.

I remember years ago when I was a young Salvation Army officer, our old Colonel had called us in for what we called an Officers' Council, and I shall never forget his advice to us. He said, "Comrades, remember as you go about your work, men will forgive you if you are not eloquent, they will forgive you if you lack culture, if your educational privileges have been greatly curtailed, if you sometimes murder the king's English as you try to preach the gospel, but they will never forgive you if they find that you are not sincere." Men look for reality, and the Lord looks for reality in His servants, and so the apostle says, "We are like actors on the stage, and two worlds are looking upon us, angels and men, and we must do our part well to the glory of God."

Then he puts the apostles and these Corinthians in vivid contrast, "We are fools for Christ's sake, but ye are wise in Christ." Notice the double contrast. Everywhere we go men brand us as fools. Why? Because we have given up earthly privileges, we have given up the opportunity of settling down comfortably here, in order that we might devote our lives to the gospel of God. And men say, "What fools they are!"

That is the way the world looks at it. The apostle says, "We are fools for Christ's sake." Notice the word, "for," for I want you to see the contrast in the next clause: "We are fools for Christ's sake," we are throwing our lives away as the world looks at it; but you who are settling down making money, getting on in the world, having a comfortable time and saying, "We would not be so foolish as those others are," "Ye are wise in Christ." Do you notice that it does not say, "wise for Christ," but "wise in Christ"? They are real Christians and, as real Christians, were in Christ, and they fancied they were wise because they were holding on to a place and position in this world. He cannot say, "Ye are wise *for* Christ." The apostles who were accounted as fools for Christ were really wise *for* Him. And then he says, "We are weak, but ye are strong." Oh, the irony of all this! You fancy you are the strong ones and we are the weak because we give our lives to propagating the gospel. "Ye are honorable, but we are despised." Men look up to you for, "Men will praise thee, when thou doest well to thyself" (Ps. 49: 18), but we have given up everything for Christ's sake and of course we are despised.

In verses 11 to 13 he gives us an outline of what

true apostolic testimony and experience really are. "Even unto this present hour we both hunger, and thirst, and are naked, and are buffeted, and have no certain dwelling-place: and labor, working with our own hands." The apostle was not one of these men who had such regard for "the cloth" that he could not dirty his fingers to take up some temporal occupation. When there was not sufficient to take care of his needs, he got a job making tents. He was simply a humble servant of Christ, and was not above anything that the Lord would have him put his hand to. "And labor, working with our own hands: being reviled, we bless." It is not, "Being reviled, we give them as good as they give us," but, "Being reviled, we bless; being persecuted, we suffer it: being defamed, we entreat: we are made as the filth of the world, and are the offscouring of all things unto this day." There is apostolic example. He did not look upon the service of Christ as something that introduced one into the first place in cultured society. To be a servant of Christ was to be misunderstood, rejected, it meant a path of self-denial all along the way; but now he says so tenderly, "I write not these things to shame you." Why, then? To exercise them, to stir them up, to get them to realize how selfish their own lives were—"But as my beloved sons I warn you." He is saying, "You are mine, I

brought you to Christ, and I grieve when I see
you are forfeiting future reward for present
ease." How often the servants of Christ are bur-
dened like that and people do not understand.

You can take your choice. If you want to get
a place and a position in the world and be thought
well of down here, go on with the frivolity; but
if you want to be thought well of up there, and
want to be a Christian who will really count for
God, then make a clean break with everything
that would hinder fellowship with Him. You will
get far more pleasure in a prayer-meeting than
in a frivolous social, once you get better acquainted with the Lord Jesus.

So the apostle says, as it were, "Ye are mine,
my sons in the gospel, and I love you, and it is
because I love you that I warn you that you will
lose out by wasting your time in things that just
appeal to the flesh when you might put in that
time in self-denying service for the glory of the
Lord Jesus Christ." "For though ye have ten
thousand instructors in Christ, yet have ye not
many fathers: for in Christ Jesus I have begotten
you through the gospel." He did not use the word
which means "teacher." They did not have many
teachers; there are not a great many real teachers
of the Word of God, and he is not slurring teachers as though their gift might be a very small
thing, but he used the term from which we get

our word, "pedagogue," which means, "child-trainer." There are ten thousand child-trainers but only one father. The child-trainer looked after the minor children, and he says, "You Corinthian babes, you have plenty of child-trainers, but only one father. I brought you to Christ, and I am your father in Christ." How can you tell when people are still in spiritual babyhood? One thing is they cannot enjoy the deep things of God. "I have fed you with milk," he says in another place, "and not with meat: for hitherto ye were not able to bear it, neither yet now are ye able" (1 Cor. 3:2). I have known young Christians who, after being converted a number of years, say, "I am not interested in Bible lectures, they are too dry for me, I do not understand them. I like something simple," and you get the impression that they would like to lie down on a couch and have a nursing-bottle and a nipple on it, in order to suck down a little weak truth. Many of you ought to be teachers yourselves by this time and you are still just babies.

Another way you can tell them is by the things with which they play. Paul says, "When I was a child, I spake as a child, I understood as a child, I thought as a child: but when I became a man, I put away childish things" (1 Cor. 13:11). Many have been converted long enough to put away all childish things and get down to real business for God, but they are still spiritual babies. Some have been saved so long they ought to have a whole host of spiritual children, but they have never yet led one soul to Christ!

And then what a wonderful climax when he says, "Wherefore I beseech you, be ye followers of me." A man must live for God in order to speak like that, and the apostle could do it. He stood there before them and said, "I want your life to count well." They may have said, "But we do not know what to do." "Well then, imitate me. As an apostle for the Lord Jesus Christ I have counted everything loss for Him. My one desire is to glorify Him." In another place he says, "Follow me as I follow Christ." That is a safe thing, that is apostolic succession, and if you will follow that line, you will find apostolic blessing in your life and God will use you to win others to Christ.

DISCIPLINE IN THE CHURCH OF GOD

✶ ✶ ✶

"For this cause have I sent unto you Timotheus, who is my beloved son, and faithful in the Lord, who shall bring you into remembrance of my ways which be in Christ, as I teach everywhere in every church. Now some are puffed up, as though I would not come to you. But I will come to you shortly, if the Lord will, and will know, not the speech of them which are puffed up, but the power. For the kingdom of God is not in word, but in power. What will ye? Shall I come unto you with a rod, or in love, and in the spirit of meekness? It is reported commonly that there is fornication among you, and such fornication as is not so much as named among the Gentiles, that one should have his father's wife. And ye are puffed up, and have not rather mourned that he that hath done this deed might be taken away from among you. For I verily, as absent in body, but present in spirit, have judged already, as though I were present, concerning him that hath so done this deed, in the name of our Lord Jesus Christ, when ye are gathered together, and my spirit, with the power of our Lord Jesus Christ, to deliver such an one unto Satan for the destruction of the flesh, that the spirit may be saved in the day of the Lord Jesus. Your glorying is not good. Know ye not that a little leaven leaveneth the whole lump? Purge out therefore the old leaven, that ye may be a new lump, as ye are unleavened. For even Christ our passover is sacrificed for us: therefore let us keep the feast, not with old leaven, neither with the leaven of malice and wickedness; but with the unleavened bread of sincerity and truth. I

wrote unto you in an epistle not to company with fornicators: yet not altogether with the fornicators of this world,
or with the covetous, or extortioners, or with idolaters; for
then must ye needs go out of the world. But now I have
written unto you not to keep company, if any man that is
called a brother be a fornicator, or covetous, or an idolater,
or a railer, or a drunkard, or an extortioner; with such an
one, no, not to eat. For what have I to do to judge them
also that are without? Do not ye judge them that are
within? But them that are without God judgeth. Therefore put away from among yourselves that wicked person"
(1 Cor. 4: 17—5: 13).

✓ ✓ ✓

WE have already noticed that this first
epistle to the Corinthians is the charter
of the Church and that it brings before
us certain divinely-given rules and regulations
for the ordering of the local churches of God here
on earth. This portion deals with the question
of the discipline of an open offender against holiness and righteousness. The Church is the house
of God. When I use that word, I do not mean a
building. God had one house made of stone and
mortar, the temple at Jerusalem. He has never
owned another. His present house is made of living stones, men and women built together for an
habitation of God through the Spirit. This is the
house of God, the assembly of God, which is the
Church of the living God in this present age of
grace; and holiness becomes God's house. He

dwells in His Church, that is, in the assembly of His saints, and therefore it must be a holy assembly. That is why again and again in the New Testament we are exhorted to absolute separation from the world and its ways.

Sometimes when those who watch for your souls seek to be very careful regarding worldliness and carnality and unholy things cropping out in the Church of God, they are looked upon as censorious and harsh and possibly unkind, because they try to deal with matters of this character, and people fall back on a scripture like this, "Judge not, that ye be not judged. For with what judgment ye judge, ye shall be judged: and with what measure ye mete, it shall be measured to you again" (Matt. 7: 1, 2). In these verses our Lord is speaking of the motives of the heart. You have no right to judge my motives; I have no right to judge your motives. If I see one put a ten-dollar bill in the offering basket and I say to myself, "Oh, yes; he is just trying to be ostentatious, he did not give that out of real love for Christ," I am wrong, for I am judging one's motive, and I have no right to do that. This may apply to a thousand things. But the Church of God is called upon to judge concerning the unrighteous behavior of any of its members. Verse 12 of chapter 5 says, "For what have I to do to judge them also that are without? Do not ye judge them that are within?" The world outside goes on its way and the Church of God has no jurisdiction there.

The Church of God is responsible as to the character of its fellowship, and it is responsible as to those who sit down together at the table of the Lord and are linked up in Christian service. Where there is failure, the individual who fails is responsible before God. It is a serious thing to profess to live the life that should characterize members of the Church of God. Ours is a high and holy calling, and if we lower the standard, we are not only dishonoring Christ individually, but we are giving the wrong testimony to the world.

The story is told of a man who wanted to hire a coachman. He lived in a mountainous region and the road to his home ran along a precipice. A number of men applied for the position. He said to one of them, "Tell me, are you an adept at handling fractious horses?"

"Yes, I am," he said.

"Can you drive a six-horse team?"

"Yes."

"How near can you drive to the edge of the cliff without going over?"

"I have a steady hand and my eye is pretty true; I can get within a foot of it and not go over."

"You step outside," said the man, and he called another and asked him the same questions.

He said, "I am an expert in handling horses; I can drive right along the edge and not go over."

"Step outside," and he called another and asked the questions.

"If you want a man to drive on the edge of the precipice," said this man, "you do not want me. When I drive, I keep as far away from the edge as I can."

"You are the man I want. I will take you."

Christian, be careful of the edge of the precipice. Do not get near it, for the first thing you know you will go over, and this will mean not only the ruin of your own testimony, but the sad thing is, you are liable to drag others over with you. Keep away from the edge, and do not resent it if those who watch for your souls as those who must give account try to impress upon you the solemnity of these things.

The apostle Paul had heard serious things concerning certain internal conditions in the church at Corinth, but he had been hindered from getting to them, and certain persons in the church who were carnally minded themselves and who knew that the apostle's coming would probably mean rebuking them for their worldly behavior were saying, "Paul is really afraid to come to Corinth, he knows he hasn't the influence he once

had." But he says, "No, I am not afraid to come.
Some of you are puffed up, as though I would not
come to you. But I will come shortly, if the Lord
will, and will know, not the speech of them which
are puffed up, but the power." In other words,
when he should come (and he was speaking with
apostolic authority), there were some things he
was going to look into very carefully. He would
find out whether the power of God was working
in their lives or whether it was just bravado and
conceit that led them to justify themselves. There
is a tremendous lot of pretence among professing
Christians: pretending to a piety that they do
not possess, pretending to a devotedness that is
not genuine. He would know not only the talk of
their lips but would inquire into the behavior that
characterized them. "For the kingdom of God is
not in word," is not merely lip profession, "but in
power," it is the manifestation of the Holy Spirit
in the life.

The apostle says, "I want to come to you, but
do you want me to come with a rod"—a rod of
discipline? Did they want him to come as the
representative of the Lord to chastise them for
their bad behavior, or to come in the spirit of
meekness so that they and he might sit down together over the Word of God and enjoy the
precious things of Christ? If they desired him
to come in this last way, there were some things

to be settled first, and he told them what they were. "In the first place, it is reported commonly"—this was not merely a matter of some individual's gossip, it was widely known—"that you are tolerating one of the vilest forms of immorality that has ever been heard of even among the heathen Gentiles; it is known that one of your members actually has taken his father's wife (not of course his mother, but his stepmother) as his own wife. This is an abomination in the sight of God, but you have not recognized the wickedness of it. You have rather prided yourselves on the breadth and liberality that would enable you to go on with a thing like that. You are puffed up when you ought to be broken-hearted." "Ye are puffed up, and have not rather mourned, that he that hath done this deed might be taken away from among you." Even if they felt that they did not know how to handle a thing like this, they could have been down before God with breaking hearts crying to Him to undertake for them, and He would have intervened and taken the wicked man from among them. But since he had received the evil report, as the representative of the Lord Jesus Christ he was going to tell them how to handle the situation, and in so doing he gave instruction concerning the handling of similar questions all down through the centuries.

"For I verily, as absent in body, but present in

spirit, have judged already." In other words, because we are all one in the Lord I have looked into this matter already, I have discerned, I have investigated and have the facts concerning him that has done this deed. This is the verdict, "In the name of our Lord Jesus Christ, when ye are gathered together, and my spirit, with the power (or authority) of our Lord Jesus Christ, to deliver such an one unto Satan." What does that mean? John says, "We know that we are of God, and the whole world lieth in wickedness," or, "in the wicked one" (1 John 5: 19). This man was in the circle of those who are "of God." Somebody might say, "The way to help him is to keep him in the circle, let him sit down with you at the Communion table; do not be hard on him, try to win him back, throw your arms of love about him and sympathize with him." The unrepentant man will be more hardened in his iniquity if you do that. Put him outside in the devil's domain, let him know that he has forfeited all title to a place with the people of God—that he has been put back into the world where Satan rules. That is what he means when he says, "Deliver such an one unto Satan for the destruction of the flesh." What has caused all this trouble? The activity of the flesh. Very well, put him out in that sphere where he will find out that "it is an evil and a bitter thing to forsake the Lord his

God." When he finds himself abhorred by men
and women who love Christ, when he finds his sin
is a stench in the nostrils of Christian people, he
may break before God. If, in spite of his sin, he
has really been born again, he will break. If he
has been a false professor, he will plunger deeper
and deeper into evil things.

"Deliver such an one unto Satan for the destruction of the flesh, that the spirit may be saved
in the day of the Lord Jesus." We do not like
to carry out extreme commands like these, but
this is the Word of God, and the greatest kindness
that the people of God can do to a man who is deliberately going on in wilful sin is to refuse Christian fellowship to him. As long as you treat him
as a brother he will only be puffed up in his ungodly ways and it will be harder to reach him.
But if you obey the Word God will work toward
his recovery and restoration.

"Your glorying is not good. Know ye not that
a little leaven leaveneth the whole lump?" House-
wives know that. What is the nature of leaven?
You have a great pan of dough and insert a little
leaven, and if you leave it all night, the whole
thing runs over on the table by morning. Very
well, you allow one wicked man to go unrebuked
and undealt with after the wickedness has been
fully manifested, and the thing will go on like an
infection working, working, working to the ruin

of others and to the harm of the entire testimony.

The Church of God is largely afraid to exercise discipline today, but where this is carried out in obedience to the Word of God the Church is kept in a condition where God can work. The apostle was not acting upon mere hearsay, there was definite evidence as to the guilt of this man. The Church of God is not to jump at conclusions. We are not to believe every scandal that people try to circulate. We have a rule, "If thy brother shall trespass against thee, go and tell him his fault between thee and him alone: if he shall hear thee, thou hast gained thy brother. But if he will not hear thee, then take with thee one or two more, that in the mouth of two or three witnesses every word may be established. And if he shall neglect to hear them, tell it unto the Church: but if he neglect to hear the Church, let him be unto thee as an heathen man and a publican" (Matt. 18: 15-17). If he will not hear the Church, he has to be put under discipline. If one knows of definite wickedness, he should go first to the guilty person and try to set it right. If he does not succeed, he is then to take another witness, but if he will not hear them, they are to take it to the Church of God and be prepared to back up everything.

"Purge out therefore the old leaven, that ye may be a new lump, as ye are unleavened." Before

God the whole Body is looked upon as unleavened, for "Christ our Passover is sacrificed for us." We are men and women who began with the blood of the cross. Like Israel in Egypt, when sheltered by the passover, they were to put all leaven away. Leaven is the type of wickedness.

Leaven is mentioned in Galatians 5:9: "A little leaven leaveneth the whole lump." There he is speaking of evil and unsound teaching which permeates and leavens the assembly of God. "Christ our Passover is sacrificed for us," and if we have been redeemed by the precious blood it is incumbent upon us to recognize our responsibility to keep the feast, the feast of communion and fellowship with Him, not with old leaven, that is, the corruption of the old nature, nor with malice. Is there a child of God who is still tolerating unjudged malice in the heart? "Neither with the leaven of malice and wickedness; but with the unleavened bread of sincerity and truth." Our God looks for reality. It is not enough to say, "Lord, Lord, have we not prophesied in Thy name?...and in Thy name done many wonderful works?" (Matt. 7:22). The great thing is for all who have been redeemed by His precious blood to manifest subjection to the Lord in the life.

In the concluding verses the apostle stresses the treatment that should be meted out to evil-

doers who have gotten into the church. You cannot discipline the world. He says, "I wrote unto
you in an epistle not to company with fornicators;
yet not altogether with the fornicators of this
world, or with the covetous, or extortioners, or
with idolaters." If you should try to regulate all
immorality in the world, you would have a tremendous job upon your hands, but here is the
point: if a man who calls himself a brother is an
immoral man or a covetous man—what is that?
Does he couple covetousness with fornication?
"The love of money is a root of all evil," and covetousness, reaching out and grasping for wealth,
is just as vile a thing in God's sight as indulgence
in unholy lust in other lines. "If any man that is
called a brother be a fornicator, or covetous, or
an idolater, or a railer." What is a railer? It is
a person who has a tongue loose at both ends and
on a pivot in the middle, a vicious talker, an evil
speaker, one who can destroy the reputation of
another just as the murderer drives a dagger into
the heart and destroys a life. A railer is a wicked
person in the sight of God. "Oh," somebody says,
"I don't mean any harm, but I am so careless
with my tongue." What would you think of one
who goes around with a machine-gun and keeps
firing away on this side and that, and some one
says, "What are you doing?" "Oh," he replies,
"I don't mean any harm, but I am so careless with

this machine-gun." A character assassin is as
wicked in the sight of God as one who would take
another's life. "Or a drunkard." No drunkard
shall inherit the kingdom of God. You young
people in these vicious days in which we live, if
you never want to be a drunkard, do not fall in
with the current idea of thinking it is fashionable
for everybody to drink a little bit. No man ever
became a drunkard who was not first a moderate
drinker. Somebody may say, "I do not believe in
that; I can take a little and it does me no harm."
But it may do your brother harm, and Paul said,
"If meat make my brother to offend, I will eat no
flesh while the world standeth" (1 Cor. 8: 13).
Here is God's standard. "If any man that is called
a brother be a fornicator, or covetous, or an idolater, or a railer, or a drunkard, or an extortioner;
with such an one no not to eat." An extortioner
is one who squeezes the poor. Maybe he tries to
cover up his sin in this way: he squeezes the poor
and makes an extra thousand dollars, and then
on Sunday comes down to the church and says, "I
want to give you a hundred dollars for missions."
God says, "Keep your dirty money, you got it in
the wrong way." God wants holy money to use
in holy service. An extortioner is a wicked person and God says, "With such an one no not to
eat." You are not to sit down to the table with
such an one. That would cut down our dinner-

parties considerably, and I take it that he also includes the Lord's table. People should be warned
to stay away from the Lord's table if living as
depicted here.

"For what have I to do to judge them also that
are without? Do not ye judge them that are
within?" Outside in the world God judges, He will
deal with them in due time, but He calls upon the
Church of God to maintain careful discipline over
its members for the glory of the Lord Jesus
Christ. His good name is at stake. People say,
"What! Is that one of your Christians? Does
that person belong to Christ and do thus and so?"
That is one reason why the Church of God is responsible to maintain holiness as it goes on
through the world.

And now the concluding word: "Therefore put
away from among yourselves that wicked person." Of course there is a great deal of other
instruction in Scripture for discipline, as in the
case of a brother overtaken in a fault, and the
Word says, "If a man be overtaken in a fault,
ye which are spiritual, restore such an one in the
spirit of meekness; considering thyself, lest thou
also be tempted" (Gal. 6: 1). Every effort should
first be made to restore the wanderer, but if he
will not be restored, if he persists in his sin, if
he goes on defying the discipline of the Church
of God, then the time comes when the Word has

to be acted on: "Put away from among yourselves that wicked person."

Perhaps some of you feel like saying what one of the Hopi Indians said to me one time after I had tried to put before them the responsibility of a Christian. They had a rather peculiar name for me; it was, "The Man with the Iron Voice;" and he said, "Man with the Iron Voice, you have made the way very hard today. I thought I was saved by grace alone, but now it looks as though I have to walk to heaven on the edge of a razor." We are saved by grace alone, but we are called to walk in holiness, and while we have no ability to do it ourselves, the Holy Spirit has come to dwell in every believer and He is the power of the new life. If we live in the Spirit, let us also walk in the Spirit, and we will be enabled thus to honor the Lord Jesus Christ by holy, unworldly, devoted, godly lives.

ON GOING TO LAW

✓ ✓ ✓

"Dare any of you, having a matter against another, go to law before the unjust, and not before the saints? Do ye not know that the saints shall judge the world? and if the world shall be judged by you, are ye unworthy to judge the smallest matters? Know ye not that we shall judge angels? how much more things that pertain to this life? If then ye have judgments of things pertaining to this life, set them to judge who are least esteemed in the Church. I speak to your shame. Is it so, that there is not a wise man among you? no, not one that shall be able to judge between his brethren? But brother goeth to law with brother, and that before the unbelievers. Now therefore there is utterly a fault among you, because ye go to law one with another. Why do ye not rather take wrong? Why do ye not rather suffer yourselves to be defrauded? Nay, ye do wrong, and defraud, and that your brethren. Know ye not that the unrighteous shall not inherit the kingdom of God? Be not deceived: neither fornicators, nor idolaters, nor adulterers, nor effeminate, nor abusers of themselves with mankind, nor thieves, nor covetous, nor drunkards, nor revilers, nor extortioners, shall inherit the kingdom of God. And such were some of you: but ye are washed, but ye are sanctified, but ye are justified in the name of the Lord Jesus, and by the Spirit of our God" (1 Cor. 6: 1-11)

✓ ✓ ✓

WE have noticed in our study of this epistle that the apostle was used of God to correct a great many erroneous thoughts, and to suggest a remedy for many wrong prac-

177

tices in the Church of God in ancient times, also
that this letter with its varied instructions was
intended not only for the Church of God some
1900 years ago but that it is addressed "to all that
in every place call upon the name of Jesus Christ
our Lord." If the churches of God today would
be subject to the teachings of the first letter to the
Corinthians, we would be delivered from a great
many things that hinder the progress of the gospel and impede the working of the Spirit of God
among us.

In this section Paul inveighs against a practice which was growing in Corinth, and which I
am afraid has been in evidence in many other
places since, of Christians quarreling with other
Christians about temporal matters, and dragging
one another into the world's law courts for the ad-
judication of their difficulties. This is utterly
abhorrent to the spirit of Christianity. It puts
the Christian in a false position before the world
and before his brethren. It is saying to the
world, "We Christians are just as covetous and
just as quarrelsome, we are just as much concerned about having our own way and about self-
pleasing as you of the world are. We recognize
your judges as having authority over the Church
of God," and it is degrading to the Christian thus
to act.

The apostle says, "Dare any of you?" He is

stirred with indignation and his language is very strong, "Dare any of you, having a matter against another"—he means, of course, another brother —"go to law before the unjust and not before the saints?" This chapter does not teach that a Christian should never go to law. It is quite impossible at times to avoid it, and even the writer of these words when falsely accused before a Roman governor said, "I appeal to Caesar," and stood upon his natural rights as a Roman citizen and insisted that his case should be heard in the imperial court. I know some brethren are wiser than the apostle Paul and feel that he made a mistake. They are quite sure that if they had been in his place, they would have acted more wisely. It is a pity that the apostle could not have availed himself of their advice! He acted quite within his right as a Christian, for that was a matter not of going to law with his brethren before the unjust but of having things heard in a clear, straightforward way before the supreme tribunal of the Roman empire. When in Philippi, the judges would have dismissed him and would have him go out under cover without a clear, public justification, but he said, "No, we have been wrongfully accused and unjustly treated. You admit you have made a mistake; make the admission publicly." That was perfectly right and proper.

But here is an entirely different case. Now we have brethren dragging each other before the world's courts. He says, "Dare any of you, having a matter against another, go to law before the unjust, and not before the saints?" If Christians have disagreements which they are not able to iron out between themselves, let them consult their brethren, bring in others in whom they have confidence, and let them agree to abide by their brethren's judgment just as truly as they would have to abide by a decision from a worldly court.

"Do ye not know that the saints shall judge the world?" This refers to something that many Christians have lost sight of. Our Lord Jesus Christ is coming again to reign for a thousand wonderful years. Then judgment shall return to righteousness, and when He reigns we shall reign with Him. It is written, "The time came that the saints possessed the kingdom" (Dan. 7:22). If we are going to reign with Christ, going to sit on thrones of judgment with Him in that coming glorious kingdom age, what an absurd thing to think that we are not fit to judge matters having to do with temporalities here on earth when our brethren are in difficulty.

"Do ye not know that the saints shall judge the world? And if the world shall be judged by you, are ye unworthy to judge the smallest mat-

ters?" After all, these things are so trivial;
matters of money, of property, matters concerning personal reputation, are such small things
when viewed in the light of eternity. We may
make a great deal of them, we may magnify them
and give them a place of importance altogether
beyond that which they deserve, but the apostle
declares they are very small matters indeed, and
he strengthens his position as he adds, "Know ye
not that we shall judge angels?" What is that?
Angels who are greater in power and might, are
we going to sit in judgment upon them? Are
angels coming into judgment? Yes, we read
twice in the New Testament of angels coming into judgment. In 2 Peter 2: 4 we read, "For if
God spared not the angels that sinned, but cast
them down to hell, and delivered them into chains
of darkness, to be reserved unto judgment," and
then certain conclusions follow. Then in the Epistle of Jude, verse 6, we read, "And the angels
which kept not their first estate (their own prin-
cipality), but left their own habitation, he hath
reserved in everlasting chains under darkness
unto the judgment of the great day." Now it is
the final judgment that is in view, and at that
last great assize these fallen angels shall be all
brought into judgment. And who will sit upon
that throne of judgment? Our Lord Jesus Christ,
and all the redeemed throughout the ages will be

associated with Him. We will be there with our Lord as assessors, we may say, in that last great assize. If this dignity is to be ours, if we are to judge the world during the kingdom age, if we are to judge angels when eternity begins, are we then unfit to judge affairs of this life? How much more should we be able to judge between our brethren!

In verse 4 he says something that evidently was not very clear, it seems to me, to the minds of those who years ago prepared this wonderful Authorized Version of ours. It says, "If then ye have judgments of things pertaining to this life, set them to judge who are least esteemed in the Church." The thought then would be, these matters are so trivial, they are of so little importance that even those who are least esteemed in the Church ought to be fit to adjudicate in such cases. And yet I question if that is what the apostle is really saying, for in the next verse he tells us, "I speak to your shame. Is it so, that there is not a wise man among you? no, not one that shall be able to judge between his brethren?" There he implies that if the Church is to take up matters of this kind, there should be wise men giving decisions, and that would hardly seem to be in harmony with the rendering that we have in verse 4. But if you put an exclamation point after that verse, it changes the entire meaning

of it. "If then ye have judgments of things
pertaining to this life, set them to judge who are
least esteemed in the church!" The Revised Version makes it a question, "If then ye have judgments of things pertaining to this life, do you set
them to judge who are of no account in the
church?" If you drag your Christian brother before one of the unconverted judges of this world,
you are bringing him before a man who, whatever
his place in the world, is of no account in the
Church of God unless he himself happens also to
be a Christian. So I take it this is what the apostle means to say: "Don't you see what you are
doing? You are dragging your brother before
men who have no place in the Church of God
whatever; their dignity and probity do not give
them place in the Church of God. Whether honorable or not, if they have not been born again, if
not converted men, they are of no account in the
Church of God."

"I speak to your shame—in doing this you are
degrading yourselves and you might well bow
your heads in shame—is it so, that there is not
a wise man among you? no, not one that shall be
able to judge between his brethren? But brother
goeth to law with brother, and that before the
unbelievers." This is altogether wrong. He
says, "There is utterly a fault among you, because ye go to law one with another." Even

though you say, "I do not know of any Christian
to whom I could submit this case," there is another way out.   "Why do ye not rather take
wrong? why do ye not rather suffer yourselves
to be defrauded?" You do not have to stand on
your own rights, it is not necessary that you
should always be cleared, it is not necessary that
you should always prove that you have been
wronged in matters of this kind.   You can, if
you will, bow your head and say, "I leave all with
God. I am not going to say anything about it;
if they wrong me, He understands."

Many years ago as a little fellow I attended a
meeting in Toronto where some difficulty had
come up between brethren and they did as the
apostle suggests. My dear mother took me along.
"Little pitchers have big ears," and I well remember how horrified I was to see men I esteemed and
had been taught to respect apparently so indignant with each other. I can remember one man
springing to his feet and with clenched fists saying, "I will put up with a good deal, but one thing
I will not put up with, I will not allow you to put
anything over on me; I will have my rights!"
An old Scotch brother who was rather hard of
hearing leaned forward holding his ear and said,
"What was that, brother? I did not get that!"
"I say, I will have my rights," said the man. "But
you did not mean that; did you? Your rights?

If ye had your rights, you would be in hell; wouldn't you? And you are forgetting—aren't you?— that Jesus did not come to get His rights, He came to get His wrongs, and He got them." I can still see that man standing there for a moment like one transfixed, and then the tears broke from his eyes and he said, "Brethren, I have been all wrong. Handle the case as you think best," and he sat down and put his face in his hands and sobbed before the Lord, and everything was settled in three minutes. When in this spirit it is so easy to clear things up; when we bow before the Lord, He straightens them out.

And then think of what grace has already done for you. Think how marvelously God has dealt with you in spite of all the sin and iniquity that you have been guilty of in the past. In the next verse he reminds them that the unrighteous shall not inherit the kingdom of God, and then he sets forth a fearful catalogue of sins and transgressions against God, nature, and man, and as he repeats this awful list, he turns to that redeemed company and says, "And such were some of you." These are the things from which you have been saved, these are the trangressions that have been forgiven you, from these unholy, wicked, impure things you have been cleansed. You were sinners of five hundred pence, but God has forgiven all. Shall you hold your brother accountable because he owes you a small debt when God has so graciously dealt with you?

"Such were some of you: but ye are washed, but ye are sanctified, but ye are justified in the name of the Lord Jesus, and by the Spirit of our God." Notice the order here: "washed—sanctified—justified." I went into a mission in San Francisco years ago and sat for perhaps half-an-hour listening to marvelous testimonies of redeeming grace. One after another rose and painted a dreadful picture of his past life and then told how God had saved him. I had come to that meeting with a little sermon all made up, but as I sat listening to these testimonies, I said, "O dear, my stupid little sermon! To think I imagined I could go into my study and develop a little discourse that would suit a congregation like this, when I had no idea of the kind of people I was going to address." So I just "canned" my sermon; I put it out of my mind, and when I rose to speak, I took this text: "And such were some of you: but ye are washed, but ye are sanctified, but ye are justified in the name of the Lord Jesus, and by the Spirit of our God." It was easy to preach to them then without a lot of study. These sermons that you get up are so hard to preach, but those that come down are so much easier. At the close a dignified personage came to me and said, "Do you know, you got your theology terribly mixed tonight?"

"Did I?" I said. "Straighten me out."

"You put sanctification before justification. You have to be justified and then you get the second blessing."

"Pardon me, but you are mistaken," I said. "I did not put sanctification before justification."

"You most certainly did."

"I most certainly did not; it was the apostle Paul who did."

"Why, you cannot blame your wrong theology on him."

"I was simply quoting Scripture."

"You misquoted it. It reads, 'Ye are justified, ye are sanctified.' "

"No, no," I said; "read it."

And he began to read, "But ye are washed, but ye are sanctified, but ye are justified," and then he said, "Why, there is a misprint there. Wait a minute; I will get a Revised Bible."

He got it and looked at it, and read, "Washed, sanctified, justified."

"Why," he said, "I never saw that before; but all I have to say is the apostle Paul was not clear on the holiness question when he wrote that!"

But what does the apostle really say? "Ye are washed." What does that mean? It is the washing of regeneration. When the Word of God is applied to the heart and conscience, when first awakened and turned to the Lord, it results in deliverance from the impurity of the old life. We are cleansed by the washing of water by the Word.

"But ye are sanctified"—What is it to be sanctified? It is to be set apart to God in Christ, and that is true of everyone who turns to the Lord Jesus Christ. There is a work that begins even before a man is conscious of his justification. Were it not for that, not one of us would ever turn to Christ. The Spirit begins that work which exercises and convicts and leads us to feel our need, and through the Word we are washed and cleansed, and thus Christ is revealed to our souls, and putting our trust in Him we are justified from all things.

"Washed"—that has to do with the practical cleansing. "Sanctified"—set apart to God in Christ. "Justified"—that means we are judicially cleared before the throne of God. God has nothing against the man who stands justified before Him. These are our blessings, they are true of every believer. How our hearts ought to thrill with worship and praise as we think how God has dealt with us!

THE BELIEVER'S BODY: THE TEMPLE OF THE HOLY SPIRIT

✦ ✦ ✦

"All things are lawful unto me, but all things are not expedient: all things are lawful for me, but I will not be brought under the power of any. Meats for the belly, and the belly for meats: but God shall destroy both it and them. Now the body is not for fornication, but for the Lord; and the Lord for the body. And God hath both raised up the Lord, and will also raise up us by His own power. Know ye not that your bodies are the members of Christ? Shall I then take the members of Christ, and make them the members of an harlot? God forbid. What? Know ye not that he which is joined to an harlot is one body? for two, saith He, shall be one flesh. But he that is joined unto the Lord is one spirit. Flee fornication. Every sin that a man doeth is without the body; but he that committeth fornication sinneth against his own body. What? Know ye not that your body is the temple of the Holy Ghost which is in you, which ye have of God, and ye are not your own? For ye are bought with a price; therefore glorify God in your body, and in your spirit, which are God's" (1 Cor. 6: 12-20).

✦ ✦ ✦

FOLLOWING what we have seen in the early part of this chapter as to the believer's cleansing, sanctification, and justification in the name of the Lord Jesus and by the Spirit of our God, we are now asked to consider some of

189

the practical results of all this. If we have been redeemed to God by the precious blood of His beloved Son, if we have been regenerated by the Word and the Holy Spirit, then we are no longer to live to please ourselves but the One who has made us His own at such a cost. And so the apostle stresses particularly the importance of recognizing our bodies as belonging to our risen Lord.

The honor of the body was never really revealed until our Lord Jesus Christ came. If you are at all familiar with the different heathen philosophies and pagan religions, you know that men as a rule distinguish between the inner man and his relation to God and the body and its relation to earth. A great many of these philosophers and teachers said, "It does not make any difference to what use you put the body. It is merely physical, and when you die it is gone. Even though your soul may persist after death the body will never rise again, and it is impossible to defile the soul by anything you may do with the body." That was the very essence of the philosophy that was taught in Corinth where the apostle had been used of God for the calling out of this company of redeemed ones whom he addresses as "The Church of God," and therefore, there was very grave danger that they might bring over to the new Christian position some of the old pagan conceptions,

and in that way fail to appreciate the holiness,
the purity, that should be connected with the
physical life of the believer as well as with his
spiritual life.

The apostle shows that the believer has not
come into any legal relationship with God. He is
not under law; he has marvelous liberty, but not
liberty to do wrong. He must distinguish between
license and liberty. An instructed believer will
never say, "I am in Christ, and it does not make
much difference what I do." A man who talks
like that shows that he has never apprehended
the reality of what "in Christ" means. The very
fact that I am in Christ means that God has
claims upon me that He did not assert when I belonged to the world. Then I was allowed to take
my own way, but now that I am in Christ I am
called upon to present my body, not merely my
spirit, as a "living sacrifice, holy, acceptable unto
God, my intelligent service." And so He tells us
here, "All things are lawful unto me, but all
things are not expedient," or befitting. If it is
just a question of law, I am not under law but
under grace. But on the other hand, there are
many things that are utterly unsuited to a Christian; things that would bring my testimony into
disrepute. There are a great many things about
which there is no direct instruction in the Word
of God, and because of this some think of them

as things indifferent. But the question is, "What effect would it have on other people if I as a Christian were to indulge in them?" I belong to Christ, and men will judge of Christ as they look upon me, and my behavior therefore must be such as will commend Christ. And then again, "All things are lawful for me, but I will not be brought under the power of any." It is an answer to those who say, "Well, why should not a Christian feel perfectly free to indulge himself if he wants to?" And so they excuse the use of intoxicants and tobacco. It is a bad thing to create habits that are not easily broken, and the apostle says, "I will not be brought under the power of any." I will not allow myself to be a slave to appetite. There are things with which one cannot tamper without being brought under their power. Your liberty is gone when you say, "I have liberty to form habits like this," for you become a slave.

You can apply this in a great many different ways. "All things are lawful for me, but I will not be brought under the power of any." I am the Lord's free man, and I am going to preserve my liberty in Christ. I am free to please Him, not free to please myself. And then if it is a question of food, we read: "The drunkard and the glutton shall come to poverty" (Prov. 23:21). Notice, it is not only the drunkard but also the glutton. In their heathen festivals the people gorged themselves in the most disgusting way in honor of their heathen gods, and we as Christians need to be careful as to over-eating. "Meats for the belly, and the belly for meats." The two are suited the one to the other. Food is suited to the digestive tract and the digestive tract is suited to food, but you are not to live for these things, you are not to live to feed the belly. "But God shall destroy both it and them." Do not live therefore as though your great business in life was the gratifying of your appetite. Let there be something higher before you. As Christians your business is to glorify the Lord Jesus Christ.

Then he speaks of the sex instinct, for there were those who said, "God has implanted certain appetites in the very bodies of men and women, therefore it does not make any difference how people indulge these appetites in or out of the marriage relationship." "The body is not for fornication, but for the Lord: and the Lord for the body." It is not to be used for vile gratification, that is contrary to the holiness of God, but it is to be kept for the Lord, and as it is kept for the Lord, the Lord is for the body. What a wonderful relationship we have been brought into. It is the resurrection of the body of the Lord Jesus that has put dignity upon all our bodies. If I am going to have my body in resurrection, then I must remember it is not to be used for any degrading purpose here on earth.

"God hath both raised up the Lord, and will also raise up us by His own power. Know ye not that your bodies are the members of Christ?" You know that your spirit is a member of Christ, you know your soul belongs to Christ, but do you think as often as you should of the fact that your body is a member of Christ? We read of the Church as the Body of Christ. It is not merely as an aggregation of redeemed souls that the Church is the Body of Christ, but as men and women having physical constitutions we belong to Christ, and my body is to manifest the holiness of Christ, my body is to be used in devotion to Him. I am to present my body as a "living sacrifice, holy, acceptable unto the Lord," as already intimated.

"Know ye not that your bodies are the members of Christ?" Very well, shall I take the members of Christ, this body of mine, and defile it, put it to an unholy purpose? How can I do that, I who profess to have been bought with the blood of God's dear Son? "Shall I then take the members of Christ, and make them the members of an harlot? God forbid. What? Know ye not that he which is joined to an harlot is one body? for two, saith He, shall be one flesh. But he that is joined unto the Lord is one Spirit." What a mystic union this is into which we have been brought! The same Holy Spirit who dwells without meas-

ure in the Head now dwells in every member of
Christ's Body here on earth. Then, the body is
for the Lord. How this will solve every problem
in regard to sensual pleasure and worldly folly.
You are invited out somewhere where you are not
quite sure you can glorify God, and you stop a
moment and say, "My body is a member of Christ;
is it consistent for me, as a member of Christ, to
go where He will be dishonored?" You must not
go where you cannot glorify Christ. That is the
Christian standard.

"He that is joined unto the Lord is one Spirit."
Then I must flee everything that is of a carnal,
corrupt nature. "Flee fornication. Every sin
that a man doeth is without the body." Other
sins do not affect the body, but this one sin is
ruinous to body and soul alike, and so, Paul says,
"Flee fornication," run from anything that would
tend to stir the body to unholy lust. In his "Con-
fessions" St. Augustine tells how in his unconverted days he had allowed himself to become the
willing victim of vile and fleshly lusts. He lived
his careless life as the pagans of that day, and
associated with the corrupt and wicked members
of society. When he got converted, the great
question upon his mind was this, "Will I ever be
able to live according to the Christian standard of
holiness, will I ever be able to keep myself from
the vile, sensuous life in which I have lived so

long?" When he first yielded himself to Christ, he took as his life-text Romans 13: 13, 14, where the apostle exhorts the believer to put on the Lord Jesus Christ and make no provision for the flesh, to fulfil its lusts. For long after his conversion he did not dare even to go near that part of the city where his godless companions of former days lived. But one day a matter of business called him there, and as he was walking along the street he suddenly saw one of the beautiful yet wicked companions of his folly. The moment her eyes lit upon him her face was illuminated with delight, and she came running with outstretched arms and said, "Austin! where have you been for so long? We have missed you so," and he turned and gathered up his long philosopher's gown and started to run. It was not a very dignified proceeding for a doctor, a professor of rhetoric, to run up the street with a godless girl running after him. She called to him, "Austin, Austin, why do you run? It is only I!" He looked back and exclaimed, "I run because it is not I." And he was off again. "The life which I now live in the flesh I live by the faith of the Son of God, who loved me, and gave Himself for me" (Gal. 2: 20). That is our standard, and so in all our behavior in the use of the body we are thus to glorify Him.

Now he comes to the crux of the whole matter. "What? know ye not that your body is the temple

—the sanctuary—of the Holy Ghost which is in you, which ye have of God, and ye are not your own?" See how the Holy Spirit links us again with Christ. When He was here on earth, He said to the Jews of His day, "Destroy this temple, and in three days I will raise it up" (John 2: 19), and they, misunderstanding, looked at the great temple on Mount Moriah and said, "Forty and six years was this temple in building, and wilt Thou rear it up in three days?" But we are told, "He spake of the temple of His body." He, the Holy One, had a real human body, and that body was the sanctuary of deity. Now He has gone back to heaven, He has saved our souls, and He claims our bodies and has sent His Holy Spirit down to dwell in the body of the believer. He says, "Your body is the temple of the Holy Ghost." Do we think as much of this as we should? Would you allow many things about which you are careless if that were constantly before your mind? You think of a church building as a sanctuary set apart for the work of the Lord. You step in from the outside, and immediately your hat comes off, for you realize that you are in the sanctuary. We teach our boys and girls not to be boisterous or frivolous in the church building for it is the house where we meet with God, and we realize that reverent behavior should characterize us. But think of this, your body is the sanctuary, it is the temple in which the Holy Spirit dwells. How careful you and I ought to be that we grieve not that blessed One who dwells within, that we do not bring dishonor upon the name of the Saviour who has sent His Spirit to live in our body. Say the words over and over again to yourself until they get such a grip on you that you will never forget them: "My body is the temple of the Holy Spirit. God dwells in me." It will give you to realize the dignity of the body and the responsibility that attaches to it.

"Ye are not your own." Does your heart respond to that? "Ye are not your own. For ye are bought with a price." And what price? The precious blood of God's dear Son. Yonder at Calvary He purchased us to be His own. An old Puritan writer said, "Calvary was the marketplace where the Saviour bought us with His blood, but He never got His money's worth." We have been such poor servants, we have responded so poorly to His love. We used to sing years ago:

> "Not my own, but saved by Jesus,
>   Who redeemed me by His blood,
> Gladly I accept the message,
>   I belong to Christ the Lord.
>
> "Not my own, to Christ my Saviour
>   I believing trust my soul,
> Everything to Him committed,
>   While eternal ages roll.

"Not my own, my time, my talents,
   Freely all to Christ I bring,
To be used in joyful service
   For the glory of my King.

"Not my own, the Lord accepts me,
   One among the ransomed throng
Who in heaven shall see His glory,
   And to Jesus Christ belong."

It will be wonderful to be His own up there. I would not want to miss it then, but it is a greater privilege to be His own as we walk the streets of this world than it will be when we walk the streets of gold, for this is the world in which we have the privilege of glorifying Him in our bodies. And so he says, "Ye are bought with a price: therefore glorify God in your body." If you have the Revised Version, you will see that the text really stops here. In our Authorized Version it adds the words: "And in your spirit, which are God's." I think somebody making a copy of this in the old Greek text got down this far and had not got the thought at all, but felt that there was something left out and so added these words in the margin. That is the very thing the apostle is not saying. What he is saying is, "Keep to this thought; your body is the temple of the Holy Spirit; if you glorify Him in your body, you will in your spirit." Glorify God in your body and the spiritual side will take care of itself.

THE NEW TESTAMENT TEACHING ON MARRIAGE AND DIVORCE

✓ ✓ ✓

"Now concerning the things whereof ye wrote unto me: It is good for a man not to touch a woman. Nevertheless, to avoid fornication, let every man have his own wife, and let every woman have her own husband. Let the husband render unto the wife due benevolence: and likewise also the wife unto the husband. The wife hath not power of her own body, but the husband: and likewise also the husband hath not power of his own body, but the wife. Defraud ye not one the other, except it be with consent for a time, that ye may give yourselves to fasting and prayer: and come together again, that Satan tempt you not for your incontinency. But I speak this by permission, and not of commandment. For I would that all men were even as I myself. But every man hath his proper gift of God, one after this manner, and another after that. I say therefore to the unmarried and widows, It is good for them if they abide even as I. But if they cannot contain, let them marry: for it is better to marry than to burn. And unto the married I command, yet not I, but the Lord, Let not the wife depart from her husband: but and if she depart, let her remain unmarried, or be reconciled to her husband; and let not the husband put away his wife. But to the rest speak I, not the Lord: If any brother hath a wife that believeth not, and she be pleased to dwell with him, let him not put her away. And the woman which hath an husband that believeth not, and if he be pleased to dwell with her, let her not leave him. For the unbelieving husband is sanctified by the wife, and

the unbelieving wife is sanctified by the husband: else were
your children unclean; but now are they holy. But if the
unbelieving depart, let him depart. A brother or a sister
is not under bondage in such cases: but God hath called us
to peace. For what knowest thou, O wife, whether thou
shalt save thy husband? or how knowest thou, O man,
whether thou shalt save thy wife? But as God hath distributed to every man, as the Lord hath called every one, so let
him walk. And so ordain I in all churches" (1 Cor. 7: 1-17).

1 1 1

THIS seventh chapter deals with a subject
that has caused a great deal of confusion
down through the centuries. The marriage
relationship occupies a large place in the Word of
God, both in the Old Testament and in the New.
The teaching of our Lord Jesus Christ and the
direct ministry of the Holy Spirit after our Lord's
ascension puts this whole matter on a very high
plane, so that marriage for a Christian becomes
God's own wonderful picture of "the mystic
union," as we often say in the marriage ceremony, "that subsists between Christ and the
Church." We can quite understand that in the
early Church there were a great many irregularities to be corrected in regard to this entire subject. There was a certain laxity permitted in
Israel under the law which our Lord Jesus Christ
forbade in the dispensation of grace. Then again
in the heathen world around conditions were such

that it was probably a difficult thing to find persons whose attitude in regard to marriage was at all like that of the New Testament Church. Therefore, there was of necessity very plain speaking.

In the first part of this chapter the apostle is evidently dealing with questions that have been propounded to him and says, "Now concerning the things whereof ye wrote unto me: It is good for a man not to touch a woman." People have drawn from this that the apostle was an advocate of celibacy, and the Roman church is very fond of pointing to this verse as though it taught that the unmarried monk or priest or the unwedded nun is a holier person just because of their state and condition in regard to this matter than the Christian husband or wife, father or mother. The apostle does not say that; but he speaks of serving the Lord without distraction particularly in a time of persecution, and this passage does refer to such a time. Farther on he says, "It is good for the present distress." He wrote in a day when to become a Christian, to be publicly baptized as confessing Christ, meant to put one's very life in jeopardy. Under such conditions it might really be best that a man should not be married at all. Yet he recognized certain inherited tendencies of human nature which might make such a condition a very dangerous one and might work against purity, against the highest type of morality, instead of working for greater holiness, and so says, "Nevertheless, to avoid fornication, let every man have his own wife, and let every woman have her own husband." He stresses the mutual relationship of each to the other. The husband is to render to the wife due benevolence, as the apostle Peter very beautifully puts it, "to give honor to the wife as to the weaker vessel," and the wife on her part is to see that she reverences her husband. They are to remember that having entered into this relationship neither is any longer his or her own master, but they have agreed to subject themselves one to another, and there can be no happy Christian home unless that is recognized.

"The wife," he tells us, "hath not power of her own body, but the husband: and likewise also the husband hath not power of his own body, but the wife." And so they are to be sure that they pay due regard to one another's conjugal rights. There may be circumstances when they might draw apart from each other, they might separate the one from the other for a limited time, but let them be careful not to do so, "Except it be with consent—by mutual agreement—for a time, that ye may give yourselves to fasting and prayer; and come together again, that Satan tempt you not for your incontinency." All down through the Christian dispensation there have been sects and strange teachers who have advocated the celibate condition even for persons already entered into the marriage relationship, and have sought to inculcate the idea that in order to serve the Lord better husbands and wives should live entirely apart one from the other. The apostle says that to attempt such a life as that is only to place yourself in a position of great temptation, and therefore is not only unwise but is thoroughly opposed to the divine institution of marriage. But if husband or wife say, "We think it would be best that we dwell apart from each other for a little time that we may be more entirely devoted to the Lord, that we might wait upon Him in fasting and prayer to be more fully conformed to His image, and come together again," very good, but let them be careful that they do not run off into some strange inconsistency if they attempt this.

"I speak this by permission, and not of commandment." Some people have pointed to this verse and said, "You see, the apostle himself does not always claim to be inspired. In this portion he declares that he is speaking only by permission and not commandment, and therefore he was not inspired of God." Oh, no; he is just as truly inspired to give this permission as he is a little farther on to give a direct command. But what may be permitted in one family might throw another family into hopeless confusion. Here is a family with a number of little children, and the wife gets a high notion of the demands of personal holiness and comes to her husband and says, "My dear, I want to be altogether for God, and so I am going to request that I separate entirely from you for a time. I am going to some spiritual retreat. You get along with the children as best you can!" It would throw the entire family into confusion. She would glorify the Lord better by looking after the children than by spending the time on her knees in some retreat, just as many a Christian today would glorify God far better looking after the growing children at home than being out to meeting every night.

Let us not forget that God established the home before He created the Church, and when people are married they have a tremendous responsibility resting upon them. No one feels that more keenly than one who like myself is separated to the gospel of God. I do not know how often I have felt like crying out with the bride in the Canticles, "They made me the keeper of the vineyard, but mine own vineyard have I not kept." It is one of the difficult things for a servant of Christ called to travel through the world with the gospel message to give the time he should give in training his children in the fear of God, but where people do not have such a calling they should be especially concerned about their responsibility in the home. I think God must have some special place in heaven for preachers' wives. They have had so much more to contend with than the average woman. If the children go wrong, folks wag their heads and say, "Queer kind of a mother." Probably the trouble was that the father was not able to co-operate with her more, and the children may have stepped to one side. And yet how God honors preachers' wives. Somebody said that preachers' children are always the worst. I cannot boast of my own, though I do thank God for saving them all. But you will find that some of the greatest names on the pages of history are preachers' children. In the Second Book of Chronicles where the kings of Israel and Judah are given, when you read of a man being especially wilful or especially good, you read, "His mother's name was so and so." Sad indeed when a child has an evil mother! Then you can scarcely expect much good from him.

The household, you see, might be thrown into hopeless confusion if husband and wife were to separate one from the other, but in other households such times of retirement may be arranged. And so the apostle does not mean that he is not inspired when he says, "I speak this by permission, and not of commandment," but he does mean that the Spirit of God allowed him to give them this permission but not to command them. It is nowhere commanded that husband and wife should for any time separate from each other.

And then Paul says, "I would that all men were even as I myself." For the gospel's sake he chose *to* remain unmarried, and in circumstances such as many were passing through the single state was to be preferred, other things being equal.

Having once entered into the marriage relationship he says in verse 10: "Unto the married I command" (now we have not merely permission but commandment), "yet not I, but the Lord." What does he mean by that? Simply this, He was just repeating something that the Lord has already said unto the married. He was reminding them of what the Lord has already said in Matthew 5: 31, 32: "It hath been said, Whosoever shall put away his wife, let him give her a writing of divorcement: but I say unto you, That whosoever shall put away his wife, saving for the cause of fornication, causeth her to commit adultery: and whosoever shall marry her that is divorced committeth adultery." Those are the solemn words of the Lord Jesus. In the nineteenth chapter of the same Gospel, he gives just one change which permits the innocent party in a divorce to marry again according to Scripture. There we read: "For this cause shall a man leave father and mother, and shall cleave to his wife:

and they twain shall be one flesh. Wherefore they are no more twain, but one flesh. What therefore God hath joined together, let not man put asunder" (Matt. 19:5, 6). I have heard people try to get around that by subterfuge and say, "I don't believe the Lord joined us together; I think the devil did it; and therefore, I think we are free to get a divorce and marry somebody else."

God pronounced the words in the garden of Eden, "Therefore shall a man leave his father and his mother, and shall cleave unto his wife: and they shall be one flesh" (Gen. 2:24). It is He who joins people together in the marriage relationship, and once joined in that relationship they should never break it.

"They say unto him, Why did Moses then command to give a writing of divorcement, and to put her away?" (Matt. 19:7). In the law of Moses this was permitted. In a hard, rough age when men were often very uncouth and cruel, God commanded that instead of holding a wife who was disliked and hated as a kind of slave or chattel, she should be given a writing of divorce and permitted to go home to her people. But now under the dispensation of grace when men are born again and transformed by the Spirit of God, no such thing is tolerated. "Moses because of the hardness of your hearts suffered you to put away your wives: but from the beginning it was not so. And I say unto you, Whosoever shall put away his wife,"—now observe—"*except* it be for fornication, and shall marry another, committeth adultery: and whoso marrieth her which is put away doth commit adultery." Notice, there is a sin which dissolves the marriage relationship and if one partner is guilty of that sin, he may be put away and the other party is free, and if married again, the new marriage is not called adultery. There are those who are so legal that they refuse to take note of that "except," but the Son of God has put it there in order that the innocent party may not have the onus of immorality on him. There you have the New Testament standard given by the Lord Himself.

"And unto the married I command, yet not I, but the Lord, Let not the wife depart from her husband." But he immediately adds, "But and if she depart." What is implied there? There may be circumstances where no self-respecting woman could continue in the marriage relationship with some man, there may be circumstances where a man is so absolutely brutal or so vile and filthy and perverted in his whole character, that no decent, good woman could live with him, and in that case it is evident from this that she is free to leave him but not to be divorced and remarried unless she has definite New Testament ground for

it. "If she depart, let her remain unmarried."
Circumstances may make it necessary for her to
leave, but if so, let her remain unmarried. "And
let not the husband put away his wife." If she
is obliged thus to leave a brutal man, she can at
least continue to remember him before God in
prayer and it may be that through her prayers
the day will come when he will be broken down
by divine grace and saved. If that day comes,
and he beseeches her now to return to him, she
can go back to find him a new man, and make a
home for him once more, but if she has already
entered into another relationship, think of the
pitiable condition she would be in.

"But to the rest speak I, not the Lord." Is he not
speaking by inspiration? Keep in mind the whole
argument. "Unto the married I command, yet
not I, but the Lord." The Lord has already spoken
in this matter. Then he says, "To the rest speak
I, not the Lord." The Lord has not already spoken,
but Paul speaks now by inspiration of the Holy
Ghost, and he is laying down a divine principle in
regard to a matter on which the Lord had not
already legislated. "If any brother hath a wife
that believeth not, and she be pleased to dwell
with him, let him not put her away." This did
not come up in the Lord's time on earth for He
came to the lost sheep of the house of Israel. Now
Paul is speaking to Gentiles, and it was a com-

mon thing for one member of the family to be converted and the others not. Think of a case where a man in Corinth has been saved but his wife is a devotee of the heathen cults and is indignant that he no longer burns incense to these idols, and yet she is willing to live with him. "Let him not put her away." He is not to assume self-righteous ground and say, "I am a Christian and cannot acknowledge you as my wife any longer."

In Israel if a Jew were married to a pagan, he had to put her away, she was unclean in the sight of God. But under grace if a pagan wife is pleased to dwell with her Christian husband, let him show her all due kindness and consideration and seek to be a blessing to her. And if it is the case of a woman who has been converted, we read, "And the woman which hath an husband that believeth not, and if he be pleased to dwell with her, let her not leave him. For the unbelieving husband is sanctified by the wife, and the unbelieving wife sanctified by the husband: else were your children unclean; but now are they holy." If you turn to the last chapter of Ezra, you will find that in Israel many Jews had entered into alliances with women from among the heathen, and there were many children speaking half in the language of Ashdod and the other half in the language of Israel. When the husband is a Christian and the wife is not, the children will

generally speak half in the language of heaven
and half in the language of earth. It is a difficult thing to bring them up for God in a mixed
home like that. He said, "You will have to put
all these wives and children away as unclean."
But notice the difference in grace. "For the unbelieving husband is sanctified by the wife." He
may be hard, he may be wicked, he may hate the
very name of Jesus, but he has been brought outwardly into a new relationship with God through
the conversion of his wife. There is now somebody in that home to pray, somebody who loves
the Word of God, somebody to live the Christian
life, and let the others see what it means to be regenerated. I may be addressing wives who are
breaking their hearts over unsaved husbands.
Will you not take comfort from this, "The unbelieving husband is sanctified by the wife"? Or
I may be addressing husbands who are grieved
because the wives that they love are still out of
Christ. You too may be comforted, for "the unbelieving wife is sanctified by the husband." Keep
on praying, keep on bearing them up before God,
believing that if He has saved you out of an unconverted family, it is because He wants the
whole household for Himself. That is what is indicated when the pagan jailer cried, "What must
I do to be saved?" and the answer came ringing
and clear, "Believe on the Lord Jesus Christ, and

thou shalt be saved, *and* thy house" (Acts 16:
31). In other words, God is saying, "Jailer, I not
only want you, I not only want to cleanse your
heart, but I want to make your household a Christian one, a testimony to My grace right there in
Philippi," and so it came to pass. So keep on
praying. And your children are sanctified because they have a father or a mother, as the case
may be, to take them to God in prayer and to
teach them the Word of God, and you can count
on Him to bless that ministry to them by bringing
them eventually to Christ.

But, next, we may suppose a case where the
unsaved one will not remain. Very well, "If the
unbelieving depart, let him depart." You cannot
do anything about it. "A brother or a sister is
not under bondage in such cases." But then, you
see, you live your own life in widowhood to the
glory of the Lord Jesus. Do not look around for
another mate. If the unbelieving depart, then
you devote yourself to Christ and His glory and
keep on praying for the wandering one, for "God
hath called us to peace. For what knowest thou,
O wife, whether thou shalt save thy husband?"
Even though he is gone, even though he has left
the home, keep on praying for him, for how do
you know when God may intervene and bring him
back penitent and broken-hearted to try to make
up for the wilfulness of the past by living a kindly

devoted life with you. Farther on we read, "How knowest thou, O man, whether thou shalt save thy wife?" She has gone because you love Jesus and she does not. Do not be too hard in your thoughts, pray and ask yourself, "Was there something in me that should have been different that turned her away. If I had a little more grace and Christlikeness, might she have remained?" Bear her up before God, and if the day comes that she is ready to return, receive her as God receives His erring ones when they come back to Him.

"But as God hath distributed to every man, as the Lord hath called every one, so let him walk. And so ordain I in all churches." These are not just matters with which we may play fast and loose. If you are a Christian and a member of a Christian church, these are divine requirements concerning the marriage relationship ordained for all the churches.

Why is God so insistent about this? Because from the beginning it was His thought that the marriage relationship should set forth the union between Christ and His redeemed, and when people are married they take each other for life. Many of you remember when you stood before the minister and he said, "Do you take this woman to be your lawful wedded wife? Will you love, honor, and cherish her so long as you both shall live?" and you said, "I will." Have you lived up to it?

And you remember when he said to the woman, "Do you take this man to be your lawful wedded husband? Will you love, honor, and obey him so long as you both shall live?" and you answered, "I will." Does your conscience tell you that you have been true to that vow? You entered into a relationship that day that pictures the relationship between the soul and the Saviour. Away back in the Old Testament when Rebecca had become the affianced wife of Isaac, they thought she should not leave her home immediately and so decided to call her and see what she had to say about it. They put the question, "Wilt thou go with this man?" and without a moment's hesitation she answered, "I will go," and she went across the desert to be united to Isaac.

Unsaved one, my blessed Lord has sent me to you with a message of His love and kindness. He wants you to enter into an eternal union with Himself. Wilt thou go with this Man, the Man Christ Jesus?

LECTURE XVI.

THE TIME IS SHORT

1 1 1

"Is any man called being circumcised? let him not become uncircumcised. Is any called in uncircumcision? let
him not be circumcised. Circumcision is nothing, and uncircumcision is nothing, but the keeping of the commandments of God. Let every man abide in the same calling
wherein he was called. Art thou called being a servant?
care not for it: but if thou mayest be made free, use it
rather. For he that is called in the Lord, being a servant,
is the Lord's freeman: likewise also he that is called, being
free, is Christ's servant. Ye are bought with a price; be
not ye the servants of men. Brethren, let every man, wherein he is called, therein abide with God. Now concerning
virgins I have no commandment of the Lord: yet I give my
judgment, as one that hath obtained mercy of the Lord to
be faithful. I suppose therefore that this is good for the
present distress, I say, that it is good for a man so to be.
Art thou bound unto a wife? seek not to be loosed. Art
thou loosed from a wife? seek not a wife. But and if thou
marry, thou hast not sinned; and if a virgin marry, she hath
not sinned. Nevertheless such shall have trouble in the
flesh: but I spare you. But this I say, brethren, the time is
short: it remaineth, that both they that have wives be as
though they had none; and they that weep, as though they
wept not; and they that rejoice, as though they rejoiced
not; and they that buy, as though they possessed not; and
they that use this world, as not abusing it; for the fashion
of this world passeth away. But I would have you without

216

carefulness. He that is unmarried careth for the things that belong to the Lord, how he may please the Lord: but he that is married careth for the things that are of the world, how he may please his wife. There is difference also between a wife and a virgin. The unmarried woman careth for the things of the Lord, that she may be holy both in body and in spirit: but she that is married careth for the things of the world, how she may please her husband. And this I speak for your own profit; not that I may cast a snare upon you, but for that which is comely, and that ye may attend upon the Lord without distraction. But if any man think that he behaveth himself uncomely toward his virgin, if she pass the flower of her age, and need so require, let him do what he will, he sinneth not: let them marry. Nevertheless he that standeth stedfast in his heart, having no necessity, but hath power over his own will, and hath so decreed in his heart that he will keep his virgin, doeth well. So then he that giveth her in marriage doeth well; but he that giveth her not in marriage doeth better. The wife is bound by the law as long as her husband liveth; but if her husband be dead, she is at liberty to be married to whom she will; only in the Lord. But she is happier if she so abide, after my judgment: and I think also that I have the Spirit of God" (1 Cor. 7: 18-40).

✟ ✟ ✟

IN the earlier portion of this chapter the apostle, by the Holy Spirit, laid down for us the Christian standard of marriage, showing that with a single exception, which the Lord Himself has indicated in Matthew 19, marriage is indissoluble, the marriage relationship once entered into cannot be broken with impunity, and if any one attempts to break it and marries another, he is guilty of the sin of adultery, the violation of the seventh commandment. That at once raises a question, for there are many people who have had rather unhappy marital experiences before their conversion, and have been separated from husband or wife. Remarriage has taken place, and while they are in such circumstances the grace of God finds them and they are saved. What of them? The apostle makes that point clear when he says, "Let every man abide in the same calling wherein he was called." He illustrates this in this way: If you were called, if God saved you as a Jew, do not try to Gentilize yourself but just remain a Jew. Though you are now a member of the Body of Christ you cannot undo what you are by nature, and you cannot undo what has taken place before you were converted. On the other hand, if you were a Gentile before you were converted, and now find yourself in a community, as many did in those days, of Jewish believers, do not attempt to Judaize, do not try to make a Hebrew of yourself, for that is impossible. You are saved as a Gentile, God opened the door of faith to you as a Gentile, He took you up as you were; therefore abide with God. To be either Jew or Gentile means nothing now. The great thing for the future is obedience to the Word of God.

Now that you are a Christian you have a new

standard by which to live, for God has given His
Word to you. That applies where people have had
rather mixed experiences along the line of marriage and divorce. When they are converted, all
the past is wiped out by the precious blood of
Christ. God called them and He saved them in
the condition in which He found them. He did
not ask, for instance, that the husband and wife
who had been married contrary to Christian principles separate in order to be saved. He took them
as they were, made them members of Christ, and
He recognizes them as His own who have been
sanctified by the Holy Spirit and cleansed by the
blood of Christ. Now let them abide in the relationship in which His grace has found them, and
by living faithfully as husband and wife adorn
the doctrine of Christ.

The apostle continues by saying, "Art thou
called being a servant?" The word for "servant"
is "bondman," and when this epistle was written
slavery extended over the entire world and many
of the early Christians were slaves. "Art thou
called being a slave? care not for it." Do not get
restless because of that. You are the Lord's freeman, but if you are set at large, then use your
liberty for the glory of the Lord Jesus Christ.
"For he that is called in the Lord, being a servant,
is the Lord's freeman." He is no longer a slave
in God's eyes, he is free to serve Christ; and as

the slave serves the earthly master it is a wonderful thing for him to realize, "I am not simply serving my master, I am serving the Lord Christ. He called me in these circumstances, and here I am to glorify Him." And he that is free is not to say, "Well, I have no master, I am free, I am not a slave; I can do as I will." Oh, no! He says, "He that is called, being free, is Christ's servant," and he uses the same word again, Christ's "bondman." He has been bought, he has been purchased, and so is never to seek to have his own way but is to take the way of the Lord.

"Ye are bought with a price; be not ye the servants of men." And then he reiterates, "Brethren, let every man, wherein he is called, therein abide with God." That brings in a restriction. I may be saved in a certain calling in which, after all, I could not abide with God.

And then he reverts to what he had been speaking of in the early part of the chapter. "Now concerning virgins I have no commandment of the Lord: yet I give my judgment, as one that hath obtained mercy of the Lord to be faithful." Some would say, "Well, the apostle recognized that he was not inspired when he wrote this." Not at all. He is simply telling us that the Lord has given him no commandment to say that a virgin must marry or must not marry, but he gives by inspiration his judgment in the matter. He was a wise pastor who recognized the conditions prevailing at that time, and said, "I suppose, therefore, that this is good for the present distress." The days in which this letter was written were days of great persecution, of fearful suffering, when one might have to flee at a moment's notice and leave home and loved ones for Christ's sake. And so Paul is saying, "For the present distress I should say this is the best thing."

"Art thou bound unto a wife? seek not to be loosed." If you are bound to a wife, do not, of course, seek to break the tie; but, "Art thou loosed from a wife? seek not a wife." But if one says, "Yes, but I have found one who appeals very much to my heart and I would like to make her my wife," if she is willing to share with you the risk and danger, "If thou marry, thou hast not sinned." On the other hand, "If a virgin marry, she hath not sinned." It is not a question of taking vows and saying, "I will or I will not marry." It is a matter of being guided by the Lord under existing circumstances.

"But this I say, brethren, the time is short: it remaineth, that both they that have wives be as though they had none" (ver. 29). The apostle says, "Whatever you do, keep in mind that you are here for only a little while, and you are here to glorify God and that is far more important than to seek your own happiness. You are living

in difficult times, in perplexing days, but your
hope is the Lord's near return." This is always
the blessed hope for the Christian, and they were
to live with that in view. "This I say, brethren,
the time is short: it remaineth, that both they that
have wives be as though they had none; and they
that weep, as though they wept not; and they that
rejoice, as though they rejoiced not; and they
that buy, as though they possessed not; and they
that use this world, as not abusing it: for the
fashion of this world passeth away." In other
words, we are not to allow any temporal relationship or any human occupation to hinder our fellowship with God or our obedience to His will.
When he says, "It remaineth, that both they that
have wives be as though they had none," he does
not mean that they are to disown their wives, to
be cold and indifferent toward them, or hard and
unkind. Nothing like that, for he has already in-
culcated the very opposite principle. He means
that the one thing to live for is not your own happiness as husband and wife, but if you are united
in the Lord, see that your great business is to
live for Him.

A dear friend of mine spent a great deal of his
time traveling around the world giving out the
gospel and his precious wife remained at home
perhaps two-thirds of the year caring for the
little family. I once said to her, "It must get

awfully lonely for you. You hardly have any married life living like this." Her eyes filled with tears, and she said, "The day my husband and I were married we promised each other we would never let our personal comfort interfere with our devotion to the work of the Lord, and I believe He called my husband for this great evangelistic ministry, and therefore I am glad to keep the house while he goes out to his work." I said, "I have a choice tidbit for you. Have you noticed what David said concerning those that abide by the stuff while the others go out to war? He said, 'As his part is that goeth down to the battle, so shall his part be that tarrieth by the stuff' (1 Sam. 30: 24). And so if you carry out your part, when the judgment-seat of Christ is set up and you and your husband stand there before God, if he has thousands of precious souls to his credit for whom he is to be rewarded in that day, you will get half of it, even though you could not go out and do the preaching, for the Lord says that those who abide by the stuff shall share with those that go to battle." That is the principle. Every one is to act in view of the fact that the time indeed is fleeting, the Lord's return is nearing, and no consideration of personal comfort is to be allowed to hinder devotion to the will of God.

And then Paul adds, "They that weep, as

though they wept not." The causes of weeping
will soon be over and God shall wipe away all
tears from our eyes. It does not say that you
must not weep; but if you do, it is to be as though
you wept not. Who are the folk who weep not?
They are the happy people; and though you weep
you can be joyful, even in the midst of sorrow, if
you are looking on to the glad day of the Lord's
return.

And then, "They that buy, as though they possessed not." You cannot get through this world
without buying; it is impossible to live in this
scene without something for physical comfort as
you go along. But do not set your heart upon
such possessions, do not let your affections be entwined about earthly things. As you go through
this world it is perfectly right and proper to enjoy
many privileges: "He giveth us richly all things
to enjoy;" "And they that use this world, as not
abusing it." In other words, do not let the spirit
of the world get hold of you. While enjoying the
good things that God in His grace lavishes upon
you do not set your heart upon them, for they are
all fleeting, they will be gone some day. If your
treasure is all here, if your heart is set upon
things here, when everything here has disappeared, what will you have left? If you have
Christ, you will have that which satisfies the soul
when everything else is gone.

Remember that the "fashion of this world passeth away." The apostle is careful to explain that
in what he has to say in regard to the single life,
as under certain circumstances preferable and
possibly wiser than to enter the marriage relation, he does not mean to put people under legal
restriction. It is evident it was necessary for him
to explain this because within a century-and-a-
half after these words were written monasticism
had come into the Church. People were living in
deserts and caves as hermits; they had dedicated
themselves to the Lord and taken a vow that they
would never marry. Communities of monks and
nuns were supposed to be holier than other people, because thus dedicated to a virgin life. The
apostle says, "I am not urging anything like that
upon you when I speak. It may be wiser for the
present distress that you do not marry," but in
the thirty-second verse he says, "I would have you
without carefulness." That is simply, I would
have you without anxiety.

In the midst of persecution what crushing
anxiety must of necessity rest upon the heart of
a husband and father if away for a time, knowing
that the family is exposed perhaps to a cruel and
awful death. He cannot get them out of his mind
and he will find it difficult if away on a mission,
to serve the Lord without distraction, and so he
says, "He that is unmarried careth for the things

that belong to the Lord, how he may please the
Lord." He may say, "I have only one life any-
way, and if called to lay it down for the Lord,
very well." It may be a great deal harder if he
has to think of wife and children in grave danger
because of affliction and persecution.

"He that is married careth for the things that
are of the world, how he may please his wife."
He that is married is necessarily anxious about
temporal things. When he says, "Careth for the
things of the world," it is not meant as a slur as
though it were wrong, but it means that he cares
for temporal things; he has to think of the provision for and the safety of his loved ones. It is
very right and proper that he should. There is
the same difference between a wife and a virgin.
The unmarried woman, if dedicated to the work
of the Lord, cares for the things of the Lord that
she may be holy in body and in soul. Some of the
most wonderful Christians that have ever lived
have been women who for Christ's sake chose
never to marry, but to devote their lives to the
service of the Lord Jesus Christ. I never quite
understand why married people who have the
comforts of home often speak in a disparaging
and unkind way of unmarried people. I should
think, if marriage is so delightful, that married
people would speak in a very tender and sympa-
thetic way of people who have not married, but

instead of that they speak sometimes in such a
contemptuous way. I never like to hear people
say, "Oh, she is just an old maid!" or, "He is just
an old bachelor!" Wait a moment, he whom you
so designate may be glorifying the Lord in a way
he could not have done if he were the head of a
household, and she of whom you speak may be
one who is rendering wonderful service to God
and humanity. I repeat, some of the most devoted Christians I have ever known have been
unmarried men and women who gave themselves
wholly to the work of the Lord Jesus Christ. All
honor to them!

But now he says, "And this I speak for your
own profit"—I do not want to cast a snare upon
you, you are perfectly free to choose in the Lord
which life you would lead. I am simply exhorting
you concerning that which is seemly—"that ye
may attend upon the Lord without distraction."
But if, after thinking it all over, after living up
to the present time of life unmarried, you think
it might be better for you to marry, very well, do
what you will; you do not sin in being married.
But on the other hand, if you can stand stedfast
in your heart, if you do not feel any particular
yearning for the marriage relationship, and have
decreed in your heart to live singly, do so.
Whether you keep your virginity or whether you
do not, you are doing well, if unto the Lord. "He

that giveth her in marriage doeth well," but under these circumstances, "he that giveth her not in marriage doeth better."

And then he concludes by laying down the definite principle, "The wife is bound by the law as long as her husband liveth." Mark this; do not let any one miss this; it does not say, "as long as the man liveth;" it says, "as long as her husband liveth." If he who was her husband became an adulterer, he has broken the marriage relationship. While he may be forgiven, yet nevertheless, our Lord Jesus shows that there is one sin that dissolves the relationship. "The wife is bound by the law as long as her husband liveth; but if her husband be dead, she is at liberty to be married to whom she will; only in the Lord." What does that mean? It means a great deal more than just following your own fancy. It means a great deal more than, "in Christ." We are distinctly told that the Christian is not to be unequally yoked together with unbelievers. If you are a Christian and unmarried, and you have never thought this through, take it home. If you ever contemplate marriage, put it out of your mind at once that you might possibly marry somebody who is unsaved. That would be positive disobedience to the Word of God. "Be ye not unequally yoked together with unbelievers" (2 Cor. 6:14). Of course if you are saved while married to an unsaved person, we have had instruction not to leave but to pray that they may be brought to Christ. But if you are not married, settle it in your mind that you will never permit your affections to be entwined around an unsaved person.

An old Puritan said, "If you are a child of God, and you marry a child of the devil, you will be sure to have trouble with your father-in-law." Do not forget it. For a child of God to take the devil for his father-in-law will be a fearful mistake; nothing but trouble will follow, for God has said so in His Word. You say, "Well, I am thinking of being married, so I must marry a Christian person." True; but there is something even more than that. Let your marriage be "in the Lord." One is to be led by the Lord in this important matter as truly as in anything else, and so, marriage "in the Lord" is marriage in subjection to Him whom we own as Lord and Christ. "Oh," you say, "then if I marry in the Lord, I will always be happy and never have any troubles!" Not necessarily, but when the troubles come you can say, "The Lord gave me this husband, or wife, and the Lord will give me grace to get along with him, or her." When you know it is of the Lord, the Lord will enable you to get through to His honor and glory.

"But," the apostle says, "she is happier if she so abide, after my judgment;" and he is giving inspired judgment, but not a command. It is good sound judgment. You know it is often proven that the second marriage is a mistake. Of course sometimes it is a blessing.

Then I think there is a little irony in the last part of this verse, for there were some people questioning Paul's apostleship and judgment, and so he says, "She is happier if she so abide, after my judgment. and I think also that I have the mind of Christ." In other words, "They say I haven't, but I think I have." He wrote these words as truly by inspiration as when he penned that matchless eighth chapter of Romans.

Let me bring you back to those words, "This I say, brethren, the time is short." We have but a little while to testify for God. Christian, shall we not seek to use every moment for His glory? Shall we not seek in every calling wherein He has called us to abide and be used in blessing for a lost world? Shall we not put out of our lives anything that hinders fellowship with God and usefulness in testimony?

If you are unsaved, take these words home: "The time is short." The time when mercy is being offered is slipping by.

> "Life at best is very brief,
> Like the falling of a leaf,
> Like the binding of a sheaf:
> Be in time!

"Fairest flowers soon decay,
Youth and beauty pass away,
Oh, you have not long to stay:
Be in time!"

Our Lord's return draws near, death too is ever following on your track and you are still out of Christ. In grace He "came from Godhead's fullest glory down to Calvary's depth of woe" for your redemption. Does He not deserve to have you trust Him and confess Him openly as your Saviour? "If thou shalt confess with thy mouth the Lord Jesus, and shalt believe in thine heart that God hath raised Him from the dead, thou shalt be saved."

CHRISTIAN LIBERTY AND BROTHERLY CARE

1 1 1

"Now as touching things offered unto idols, we know that we all have knowledge. Knowledge puffeth up, but charity edifieth. And if any man think that he knoweth any thing, he knoweth nothing yet as he ought to know. But if any man love God, the same is known of Him. As concerning therefore the eating of those things that are offered in sacrifice unto idols, we know that an idol is nothing in the world, and that there is none other God but one. For though there be that are called gods, whether in heaven or in earth (as there be gods many, and lords many); but to us there is but one God, the Father, of whom are all things, and we in Him; and one Lord Jesus Christ, by whom are all things, and we by Him. Howbeit there is not in every man that knowledge: for some with conscience of the idol unto this hour eat it as a thing offered unto an idol; and their conscience being weak is defiled. But meat commendeth us not to God: for neither, if we eat, are we the better; neither, if we eat not, are we the worse. But take heed lest by any means this liberty of yours become a stumblingblock to them that are weak. For if any man see thee which hast knowledge sit at meat in the idol's temple, shall not the conscience of him which is weak be emboldened to eat those things which are offered to idols; and through thy knowledge shall the weak brother perish, for whom Christ died? But when ye sin so against the brethren, and wound their weak conscience, ye sin against Christ. Wherefore, if meat make my brother to offend, I will eat no flesh while the world standeth, lest I make my brother to offend" (1 Cor. 8).

IN this chapter the Spirit of God deals in a very remarkable way with the great theme of Christian liberty and brotherly care. It is almost impossible for us, in a land like this, to visualize the exact circumstances in which the early Christians were found, but those who have labored for any length of time among a heathen people will understand exactly what the problem was with which the apostle deals in this particular chapter. It was the question of how far a Christian was at liberty to eat meats which at their killing had been dedicated to idols. This was the common practice. In fact, practically all the meats that were sold in the markets had been so dedicated. One can understand that many of the early Christians feared that if they fed upon meats of this character they should be bringing dishonor upon the name of the Lord and possibly appear to countenance idol worship. I have noticed the same thing among the Pueblo Indians of New Mexico and Arizona, and also the Navajo and other Indians when they become Christians; they are concerned as to anything that looks like participation in or recognition of heathen ceremonies, because they want the people to understand that they have made a clean cut with the old life. In Corinth this was quite a problem, and it is evident that they had written to the apostle Paul for information concerning it.

"Concerning the things whereof ye wrote unto me," we read in the opening verses of the seventh chapter, and this expression introduces the rest of the epistle. From that point on the apostle is dealing with matters that had been submitted to him by letter, that he might give his inspired judgment for the guidance of the Church. And so here he says, "As touching things offered unto idols, we know that we all have knowledge." "We all," that is, we Christians, we know the one true and living God and we know the folly of idolatry. However, in these first three verses the apostle stresses the importance of humility, both as to our attainments in grace and our knowledge of the truth. We may know certain things that others do not, and may act upon our knowledge in such a way as to put a stumblingblock in the path of some one else; so he exhorts us to hold that knowledge that God has given us in the spirit of humility. We quite understand that there are no such beings in the world as those represented by the idols, but that does not do away with the fact that back of the idolatry is satanic power. "The things which the Gentiles sacrifice, they sacrifice to demons, and not to God" (1 Cor. 10:20); therefore there must be no compromise whatever between Christianity and pagan religions. We know that those who are in the darkness of heathenism are in the bondage of Satan, and therefore

our missionaries are not to take from their pagan
religions all the good they can and then share
what we have with them. Not at all. To a
people whom we know to be lost in their sins,
worshiping idols that represent nothing that is
real, our missionaries go to turn them from darkness to light and from the power of Satan unto
God. This was what the apostles and their fellow-
workers went forth to do, and their methods
should be our methods. We need nothing new.
The gospel is still "the power of God unto salvation to every one that believeth" (Rom. 1:16),
and where it is preached in dependence upon the
Holy Spirit, miracles will be wrought in the
hearts and lives of heathen men today just as
truly as nineteen hundred years ago and down
through the centuries.

"We know that an idol is nothing in the world,"
but on the other hand everybody does not have
this knowledge, and it may not be wise to say, "It
does not make any difference to me whether these
meats were offered to idols, and so I am at liberty
to eat." Yes; as far as my own conscience is
concerned I am at liberty to eat of it, but let me
stop to consider the effect of that upon others.
"But," you say, "I know." Yes, but "knowledge
(mere knowledge) puffeth up." It is quite possible to be conceited and proud over the fact that
I have a little knowledge that someone else has

not. I may well ask, "What hast thou that thou didst not receive?" (1 Cor. 4:7). There is a tendency to pride in our hearts even in the things of God. We get a smattering of His Word that some others do not have, and instantly we are lifted up in our own conceit. He says, "Knowledge (if it is only that) puffeth up." Do you see the difference? Knowledge puffeth up—love buildeth up. Some of us get to be like a great swollen frog on a log, just puffed out with wind. We imagine that we have advanced wonderfully over other folk. Throw a stone at the frog and he suddenly shrinks to about one-fifth of the size he seemed to be. Yes, knowledge puffeth up but love buildeth up. It makes for real solid growth.

We need to "grow in grace and in the knowledge of our Lord Jesus Christ," and if we put knowledge before grace, it will work harm to ourselves as well as to others. "If any man think that he knoweth any thing, he knoweth nothing yet as he ought to know." Has God given me a little light on His Word? After all, I know very little compared with the many things of which as yet I have no knowledge, and so let me hold in all humility what He has imparted, thanking Him for it, but walking carefully before Him.

"If any man love God, the same is known of Him." We might have expected the apostle to say, "If a man love God, he knows God." That is true,

but the other side is the wonderful part of it.
If any man love God, God knows him, and it is
that in which we can rejoice. I like the way the
apostle John speaks of himself so often, "The disciple whom Jesus loved." If you or I had been
writing that, we might have said, "The disciple
who loved Jesus;" and I do not know whether we
would have stopped there, we might have said,
"That disciple who loved Jesus whose name is So
and So." That is the way most of us do. Naturally we all like to get our own names to the front.
We need to be brought low to the feet of our
blessed Saviour. John gloried in the fact that he
was that disciple whom Jesus loved, and it is for
us to rejoice in the fact that we are known and
loved of God.

Then in verses four to six we have the hol-
lowness and the emptiness of all idolatrous systems. There is a science, a very recent one,
known as "The Science of Comparative Religions." I think it had its origin largely in the
World's Fair held in Chicago in 1893, when there
was a great Congress of Religion and teachers
came from all parts of the world to exchange
thoughts on religious concepts. From that time
on men began comparing one religion with another. There is a "Science of Comparative Religions," but Christianity is not one of them.
Christianity is not a religion, it is a revelation.

It is not something that men have thought out; it is not a system of philosophy, or ethics; it is something revealed from heaven by the power of the Holy Spirit. Idolatrous systems are the works of men energized by the enemy.

"As concerning therefore the eating of those things that are offered in sacrifice unto idols, we know that an idol is nothing in the world, and that there is none other God but one." That God is the God who has been revealed as the Father of our Lord Jesus Christ. "For though—in the world around and in the pagan nations—there be that are called gods, whether in heaven or in earth (as there be gods many, and lords many), yet to us—to those of us who have accepted the revelation that has been given in this holy Word —there is but one God, the Father, of whom are all things, and we in Him; and one Lord Jesus Christ, by whom are all things, and we by Him." Observe, Paul is not speaking here of the doctrine of the Trinity, neither is he intimating that it might be a mistake to put our Lord Jesus Christ as the Divine Eternal Son on the same level with the Father and the Holy Spirit. To us there is one God, and that God is the One who has revealed Himself in the Word as our Father, as the Creator of all men; He is the Father of all that believe. He is the Father of the universe because that through Him it came into existence; it

came out of Him, and therefore there is a sense
in which it is perfectly right to speak of the uni-
versal Fatherhood of God and the brotherhood of
man.   He is the God of the spirits of all flesh;
all men came into existence through Him.   But
man is a fallen creature, he has turned away from
God; he is dead spiritually, and therefore needs
to be quickened into newness of life; and it is only
when regenerated, when born again, that he comes
into the family of God through redemption.   Now
he can look up into the face of God and say, "Our
Father," something that he could not do in his
unconverted state.

The apostle says, "There is but one God," and
this is perfectly true.   Elsewhere in Scripture we
find that He subsists in three Persons: the Father,
and the Son, and the Holy Spirit.   That comes
out very clearly in the baptismal formula.   "Go
ye therefore, and disciple all nations, baptizing
them unto the name of the Father, and of the Son,
and of the Holy Spirit" (Matt. 28: 19).   How in-
congruous it would be to put the name of a mere
creature in there!   Suppose, for instance, much
as we revere the one who was blessed and favored
above all women because chosen to be the mother
of the Son of God, that we should say, "Unto the
name of the Father, and of the Son, and the
blessed Virgin Mary."   How instinctively every
Christian heart would shrink from that.   We

must not put a creature into the place of Deity, but we can say, "In the name of the Father, and of the Son, and of the Holy Spirit," for the Father with the Son and the Holy Spirit is God; the Father without the Son and the Holy Spirit would not be God. The Son with the Father and the Holy Spirit is God: the Son without the Father and Holy Spirit would not be God. The Spirit with the Father and the Son is God; but the Spirit without the Father and the Son would not be God. That is a definition that was coined some years ago by the venerable Dr. Joseph Cook of England, and it sets forth the truth as it is in Scripture.

When we are speaking of Christ in His mediatorial position, we bring Him down to the place He took in grace as a Man without denying His Deity. Someone asked me this question: "Is there any sense in which God the Father is greater than Jesus Christ?" When we think of the Lord Jesus as the Eternal Only-begotten Son, He is co-equal with the Father; and when He speaks of Himself as the Son, He says, "That all men should honor the Son, even as they honor the Father" (John 5: 23). If any man does not honor the Son, he dishonors the Father. "I and My Father are one." But having stooped in grace to become Man, the Man Christ Jesus voluntarily takes a place of subjection to the Father, and therefore,

as the Son born on earth of a virgin mother, He
is the same Person, but the same Person in different circumstances; He voluntarily assumes humiliation and says, "My Father is greater than I."
There is no difficulty about this if we remember
that He is Son of God in two senses: God the Son
from eternity, and the Son of God born of a virgin
mother here on earth, with no human father.

"There is but one God, the Father, of whom are
all things, and we in Him." And then, there is
"one Lord Jesus Christ," one to whom we yield
the allegiance of our hearts and recognize that He
is our Saviour, "By whom are all things, and we
by Him." That is, our blessed Lord is the origi-
nator of both creations—"By whom are all
things." "In the beginning was the Word, and
the Word was with God, and the Word was God.
The same was in the beginning with God. All
things were made by Him; and without Him was
not any thing made that was made" (John 1:
1-3). This entire creation came into existence
through the word of His power. "He spake and it
was done, He commanded and it stood fast." He
who is God is the Son from all eternity. But this
creation fell and a mediator was needed, and so
He came into the world in lowly grace; He
assumed a servant's form and became Man without ceasing for one moment to be God. As Man
He went to Calvary's cross to settle the sin ques-

tion. He was buried, but He rose again in triumph, and as the risen One He is Head of the
new creation. "By Him are all things"—that is
the old creation. "And we by Him"—that is the
new creation. God has "raised us up together,
and made us sit together in heavenly places in
Christ Jesus" (Eph. 2:6). For we who were
dead in sins have been quickened together with
Him, and it is because we know this, because we
know that God has thus revealed Himself, that
we are through forever with idols. Sometimes
when we talk of missions, there are those who
speak slightingly of this work, speak of it as
though it pays very poor returns. We ourselves
have only to go back a few centuries to find that
our ancestors were idolaters, but the gospel came
to them with the knowledge of God, and faith in
the Lord Jesus Christ delivered them from their
idolatry and thus we are what we are today.
Shall we think for one moment of refusing to give
the gospel to those still sitting in the darkness in
which our forefathers once sat?

From verse seven to the end of the chapter the
apostle dwells especially on the importance of concern for the consciences of others. We may not
face exactly the same problems that these Corinthians did, but we need to have the same care
for the consciences of other people. A Christian
may say, "I am quite sure that this thing is right;

I have perfect liberty, and I am not going to let somebody else dictate to me what I should do." But stop a moment; suppose that someone else who does not have light on this thing is quite convinced that you are deliberately and wilfully disobeying the Word of God. If by-and-by that person should come to the conclusion that since you, a stronger Christian, feel free to do that, he is free to do it too, what then? Do you not see that his conscience will be defiled and his testimony eventually be ruined. So the apostle says, "There is not in every man that knowledge: for some with conscience of the idol unto this hour eat it as a thing offered unto an idol," that is, believing that an idol is a reality, and believing that they are committing an idolatrous act. "And their conscience being weak is defiled." Under those circumstances we can deny ourselves of that which might injure and hurt them if they persist in it.

"But meat commendeth us not to God: for neither, if we eat, are we the better; neither, if we eat not, are we the worse." Why do we need to be concerned about non-essentials like these? If this matter will trouble someone else, I will put it out of my life. I will not use my liberty if it causes another to stumble. I will not use my liberty to gratify my own desires. "Take heed lest by any means this liberty of yours become a stumblingblock to them that are weak. For if any man see thee which hast knowledge sit at meat in the idol's temple, shall not the conscience of him which is weak be emboldened to eat those things which are offered to idols?" Perhaps he is just a young convert, or simply an inquirer, maybe one not at all established, perhaps not yet truly regenerated, and if he sees you do something that hurts his conscience and he does the same thing, he defiles his conscience, and it may lead to the shipwreck of his faith. Because you insist upon your liberty, shall that weak brother perish? He is not affirming that any true child of God will ever be lost, but he puts it in the form of a question. Would you be willing so to behave that it would cause another's shipwreck? "Through thy knowledge shall the weak brother perish, for whom Christ died?"

Some years ago I was preaching in a gospel hall in Detroit. A former Mohammedan from India was there who was at the head of a tea business, and he had been brought to know the Lord Jesus Christ. On one occasion when holding a meeting there, the Sunday School had its annual outing and we all went over to a beautiful spot, and spent the day together. I was chatting with this brother, Mr. Mohammed Ali by name, when a young girl came by passing out sandwiches. She said, "Won't you have a sandwich?"

"Thank you," I said, "what kind have you?"

"I have several different kinds."

"I will help myself to several of them."

And then she turned to Mr. Ali and said, "Will you have one?"

"What kind are they?" he asked.

"There is fresh pork and there is ham."

"Have you any beef?"

"No, I do not."

"Have you any lamb?"

"No."

"Fish?"

"No."

"Thank you, my dear young lady, but I won't take any."

Laughingly she said, "Why, Mr. Ali, you surprise me. Are you so under law that you cannot eat pork? Don't you know that a Christian is at liberty to eat any kind of meat?"

"I am at liberty, my dear young lady, to eat it," he said, "but I am also at liberty to let it alone. You know I was brought up a strict Mohammedan. My old father, nearly eighty years of age now, is still a Mohammedan. Every three years I go back to India to render an account of the business of which my father is really the head, and to have a visit with the folks at home. Always when I get home I know how I will be greeted. The friends will be sitting inside, my father will come to the door when the servant announces that I am there, and he will say, 'Mohammed, have those infidels taught you to eat the filthy hog meat yet?' 'No, Father,' I will say; 'pork has never passed my lips.' Then I can go in and have the opportunity to preach Christ to them. If I took one of your sandwiches, I could not preach Christ to my father the next time I go home."

Of course the young lady understood. He was acting exactly as the apostle is suggesting here. We have liberty to refrain from doing these things if they will trouble other people. Love is to be the dominating motive. "When ye sin so against the brethren, and wound their weak conscience, ye sin against Christ."

And so the chapter comes to this striking conclusion, "Wherefore, if meat make my brother to offend, I will eat no flesh while the world standeth, lest I make my brother to offend." This is true Christian liberty coupled with brotherly care.

SERVANT OF ALL

✓ ✓ ✓

"Am I not an apostle? am I not free? have I not seen Jesus Christ our Lord? are not ye my work in the Lord? If I be not an apostle unto others, yet doubtless I am to you: for the seal of mine apostleship are ye in the Lord. Mine answer to them that do examine me is this, Have we not power to eat and to drink? Have we not power to lead about a sister, a wife, as well as other apostles, and as the brethren of the Lord, and Cephas? Or I only and Barnabas, have not we power to forbear working? Who goeth a warfare any time at his own charges? who planteth a vineyard, and eateth not of the fruit thereof? or who feedeth a flock, and eateth not of the milk of the flock? Say I these things as a man? or saith not the law the same also? For it is written in the law of Moses, Thou shalt not muzzle the mouth of the ox that treadeth out the corn. Doth God take care for oxen? Or saith he it altogether for our sakes? For our sakes, no doubt, this is written: that he that ploweth should plow in hope; and that he that thresheth in hope should be partaker of his hope. If we have sown unto you spiritual things, is it a great thing if we shall reap your carnal things? If others be partakers of this power over you, are not we rather? Nevertheless we have not used this power; but suffer all things, lest we should hinder the gospel of Christ. Do ye not know that they which minister about holy things live of the things of the temple? and they which wait at the altar are partakers with the altar? Even so hath the Lord ordained that they which preach the gospel should live of the gospel. But I have used none of these things; neither have I written these things,

247

that it should be so done unto me: for it were better for me to die, than that any man should make my glorying void. For though I preach the gospel, I have nothing to glory of: for neessity is laid upon me; yea, woe is unto me, if I preach not the gospel! For if I do this thing willingly, I have a reward: but if against my will, a dispensation of the gospel is committed unto me. What is my reward then? Verily that, when I preach the gospel, I may make the gospel of Christ without charge, that I abuse not my power in the gospel. For though I be free from all men, yet have I made myself servant unto all, that I might gain the more. And unto the Jews I became as a Jew, that I might gain the Jews; to them that are under the law, as under the law, that I might gain them that are under the law; to them that are without law, as without law (being not without law to God, but under the law to Christ), that I might gain them that are without law. To the weak became I as weak, that I might gain the weak: I am made all things to all men, that I might by all means save some. And this I do for the gospel's sake, that I might be partaker thereof with you" (1 Cor. 9:1-23).

↑ ↑ ↑

EVERYWHERE the apostle went his steps were dogged by legalistic men who hated the doctrine of grace and who sought in every way possible to shake the confidence of his converts. His commission had been called in question and they denied that he was a true apostle. In order to be an apostle of the Lord Jesus Christ in an official sense, it was necessary that one should have seen the Lord and have been commissioned by Him. More than that the signs

of an apostle, the working of wonders, should be
manifested in him, and these enemies of Paul's
intimated that he could not be a true apostle, for
he had not been connected with the testimony
when the Lord was here on earth; he had not seen
the Lord, they said, and he did not work the
signs of an apostle, having no true commission.
He answered them like this, "Am I not an
apostle? am I not free? have I not seen Jesus
Christ our Lord?"

Certainly Paul had seen the Lord. He saw
Him in the glory that day when he was thrown
to the ground on the Damascus turnpike and he
beheld the risen Saviour seated on the throne of
God. That was the time when he received his
commission, for the Lord said: "I have appeared
unto thee for this purpose, to make thee a minister and a witness both of these things which
thou hast seen, and those things in the which I
will appear unto thee; delivering thee from the
people, and from the Gentiles, unto whom now I
send thee, to open their eyes, and to turn them
from darkness to light, and from the power of
Satan unto God, that they may receive forgiveness of sins, and inheritance among them which
are sanctified by faith that is in Me" (Acts 26:
16-18). That was the time he saw the Lord, and
it was then he received his commission. And had
not the signs of an apostle been manifest in him?

He does not even deign to speak of the miracles. He had wrought miracles as had the twelve, but there was a far greater sign that ever accompanied his ministry, and so he says to those who had been turned to the Lord through the preaching of the Word at his mouth, "If I be not an apostle unto others, yet doubtless I am to you: for the seal of mine apostleship are ye in the Lord." The evidence that he was a truly God-sent servant was found in this, that wherever he went the Spirit of God confirmed the message that he carried, convicted men of their sin, led them to definite faith in Christ, and gave them the assurance of forgiveness and justification, that afterwards by a new life they might demonstrate the reality of the work that had taken place in their souls. And so he says, "Do you listen to men who impugn my apostleship? Are you prepared to believe that possibly the signs of an apostle are not found in me? What about yourselves? Who brought you to Christ? To whom are you indebted under God for the knowledge of His grace?" "My answer to them that do examine me is this."

Others said, "Well, you can see he does not have the same confidence that the rest have, he does not even have a wife, he goes about alone." Many believe those people are mistaken who tell us that Paul was a bachelor and that this possibly

accounts for some things that he has to say in
this letter and elsewhere in regard to the ministry of women. They think this is a mistake
because when the blood of the martyr Stephen
was shed, he gave his voice (or literally, his vote)
against him. That seems to imply that he was a
member of the Sanhedrin, the high council of the
Jews, and that he voted for the death of Stephen.
He could not have been a member of the Sanhedrin if he had not attained the age of thirty
years and if he had not been a married man. So
he may have been married in his earlier life, but
now was a widower and chose to devote his life
in widowhood to the service of the Lord Jesus
Christ, not because he thought it was wrong for a
minister of Christ to have a wife. The idea that
those who preach the gospel should live the celibate life was unknown in apostolic days; that was
a superstitious fiction of after years, when men
came to believe that the unmarried monk and the
childless nun were holier than the Christian
father or mother.

The apostle says, "I have full authority to lead
about a sister in Christ as a wife, I have full
authority to marry a sister in Christ if I desire
to do so. The other apostles did." This of course
shows that the celibacy of the clergy, so-called,
was unknown in those days. "Have we not power
to lead about a sister, a wife, as well as other

apostles, and as the brethren of the Lord, and Cephas?" That is, James and Jude were married men, and Cephas, Simon Peter, was a married man! Some people tell us that he was the first Pope. Well, then, he was a married Pope. "Or," says the apostle, "should only I and Barnabas live this celibate life?" They chose that life that they might be untrammeled in their missionary work as they traveled from land to land enduring hardships one should not expect a wife to endure with them.

Others objected on this ground, "He knows he is not a real apostle for he does not depend on his ministry for his temporal support." I suppose if he were living today, there would be those who would say, "He degrades the cloth by working for a living." He was a tentmaker, and some said ,"He would never soil his hands making tents if he knew that he was a genuinely appointed apostle; he would never stoop to anything like that." But he says, "Oh, no; I have a perfect right to be supported in the same way as others, but I have reasons why I refuse to permit you to support me." He came to them when they were heathens, when they were pagans and living vile ungodly lives, and he did not intend to pass the collection-plate and ask them to contribute toward his support; he would rather go among them and labor, working with his own hands to support himself and his companions and keep the gospel absolutely without charge. I wish the Church of God had never given up that position. It is a great reproach on the Church of God when its representatives turn to a Christless world and beg and wheedle money out of ungodly men to support the work of the Lord. The divine method is that the gospel of God should be supported by the people of God who give out of love for Christ, and when a servant of Christ under certain circumstances is not thus properly supported, he should not be above working with his own hands while he continues to minister the gospel as occasion presents itself.

The apostle here shows that it is quite right and proper that the Lord's servants should be supported by the Church of God. "Who goeth a warfare any time at his own charges?" If a man is a soldier, he is not expected to support himself; the country for whom he is fighting takes care of him. "Who planteth a vineyard, and eateth not of the fruit thereof? Or who feedeth a flock, and eateth not of the milk of the flock? Say I these things as a man? Or saith not the law the same also?" And then he uses an apt illustration from the law of Moses. It is written in the book of Deuteronomy (25: 4), "Thou shalt not muzzle the ox when he treadeth out the corn." The reference is to the old-fashioned way of threshing corn or wheat. The ox goes around and around and treads it out. How inhuman it would be if the ox becoming hungry would not be permitted to munch a little of the grain as he treads it out. The law permitted him to have some for himself. "Doth God take care for oxen? Or saith He it altogether for our sakes? For our sakes, no doubt, this is written." There is an admonition here, something for the people of God to take note of: "That he that ploweth should plow in hope; and that he that thresheth in hope should be partaker of his hope."

And so he lays this down as a principle, "If we have sown unto you spiritual things," that is, if the servant of Christ gives his whole time and energy to the study of the Word of God in order to prepare himself the better to minister the things of the Lord, if he turns from what people call secular life, "is it a great thing if we shall reap your carnal things?" Just as the ox finds its food in the work it is doing, so the Lord has appointed that His servants should be cared for by those who receive benefit from the ministry that they give. "If others be partakers of this power over you, are not we rather? Nevertheless we have not used this power"—we prefer to forego our own rights in order that you may see that our service is an unselfish one and in order that the heathen may not say that we are in the ministry for what we can get out of it. "Lest we should hinder the gospel of Christ."

It is perfectly true that they that minister about holy things should live of them. These words refer to the priests in Judaism for they were sustained by tithes and offerings. "They which wait at the altar are partakers with the altar." In our dispensation while there is no distinct priesthood, and all believers are priests, yet they that give themselves to ministering the Word are to be sustained by the people of God in that work. "Even so hath the Lord ordained that they which preach the gospel should live of the gospel." But if a servant of Christ says, "I choose to forego that privilege, I am able to support myself and still carry on the work of the Lord," he is free to do it. Paul says, "I have chosen that path, I do not want one of you to say that a selfish motive actuated me. I preach the gospel, but I have nothing to glory in; I am a servant. My Master sent me to preach it. He put necessity upon me, yea, I find myself in trouble if I do not preach it." "Woe is unto me, if I preach not the gospel!" I wonder if that word has been forgotten by many who once gave themselves to the ministry of the gospel, but today seldom mention the great truths whereby men and women are saved. Is it not a sad fact that many today who are looked upon as evangel-

ıstic preachers never tell sinners that Christ died
for the ungodly, never proclaim the saving power
of the Lord Jesus, never exalt the cross as the
only means of redemption for poor sinners? What
an account to face before the Lord some day! I
wish that a minister of Christ who gives himself to what he calls a social program, merely
ethical preaching, might be awakened through
these words of the apostle, "Woe is unto me, if
I preach not the gospel!" Our responsibility is
to make Christ known as the only Saviour of sinners. If I do this thing willingly, if I gladly go
forward preaching the gospel for the name's sake
of the Lord Jesus, by-and-by when I stand at the
judgment-seat I shall be rewarded.

Never mind whether people appreciate me now,
never mind whether I get my reward down here,
I can leave it until that day when the Lord will
estimate everything aright. But even if I do not
preach the gospel willingly, still the message is
going out, and God will bless the message, but I
myself will lose the reward. "A dispensation—a
stewardship—is committed unto me," and I must
fulfil it. What is my present reward? That I
make money in preaching it? No! That "I may
make the gospel of Christ without charge, that I
abuse not my power in the gospel." I will not
go to dying men and say, "Give me your money,
and if you do, I will preach to you," but I will go

and preach the Word freely whether I ever receive a penny for it or not. After they become converted it remains with them and the Lord: it is my business to give out the message. The apostle takes a very high and noble position. It is a most obnoxious thing to God when those of us who profess to be ministers of the Word commercialize His truth by setting a price upon our service. Only so much preaching for so much money. Paul says, "It is my joy to preach whether supported by men or not; I make the gospel without charge."

"For though I be free from all men, yet have I made myself servant unto all, that I might gain the more." I am not concerned about what men think of me, but I have deliberately and of my own volition made myself to be the servant of men. What does he mean by that? Simply this, I am the servant of Christ, but Christ has sent me to minister His Word, and I seek to do so in such a way as best to reach men in their need, and in this sense I put myself under bondage to men in order that I may make the gospel clear to all men. "To the Jews I became as a Jew, that I might gain the Jews." When he preached to the Jews, you will find instance after instance in the book of Acts where he turned them back to the Old Testament, to their Jewish ceremonies and laws, and based everything upon the Jews' hope of the Messiah, showing how all has been fulfillea in Christ. On the other hand, when speaking to the Gentiles, men who did not know the law of Moses, he put himself on a level with those to whom he spoke. He talked of God, the Creator of all things, who gives us "rain from heaven, and fruitful seasons, filling our hearts with food and gladness" (Acts 14:17). The God who does all this cannot be an image, an idol made with man's hands, He created the heavens and the earth. And then he undertakes to show how God has sent His Son to save men who have sinned against Him; he puts the gospel in a way that the Gentiles may understand it.

Verse twenty-one is very interesting and should be a help to many who may not quite understand the Christian's relation to the law. Reading from the latter part of verse twenty, "To them that are under the law, as under the law, that I might gain them that are under the law; to them that are without law, as without law." Here we have two classes of men. There are those that are under the law, they are the Jews or, in our day, any to whom the law of God has come. But here is the other class, "To them that are without law, as without law," that is, the Gentile nations, the pagan nations. They have never heard the law of God. If Paul himself were under the law, as some Christians think a believer is, he would not

say, "I *became* as under the law." Where was
Paul? He was not under the law nor was he
without law. He was neither subject to some
legal ritual nor was he lawless. Where did he
stand? Between the two, "Being not without law
to God, but under the law to Christ." He says,
as it were, "I am not under the law of Moses,
neither am I lawless, but I am under law to God,
being legitimately subject to Christ." Do you see
the place of the believer? Neither under law nor
without law, but legitimately subject to Christ.
And where has Christ expressed His mind for
me? In the four Gospels and in the Epistles.
Somebody says, "You do not mean the four Gospels! Do you not know that they are altogether
Jewish?" I know some have said that, but I remember that the Spirit of God has said something
very serious in regard to such. He says in the
First Epistle to Timothy, "If any man teach
otherwise, and consent not to wholesome words,
even the words of our Lord Jesus Christ, and to
the doctrine which is according to godliness; he
is proud, knowing nothing, but doting about questions and strifes of words, whereof cometh envy,
strife, railings, evil surmisings" (1 Tim. 6: 3-5).
Let us be very careful that we do not teach otherwise than in accordance with the words of our
Lord Jesus Christ.

The words of our Lord are found in the four

Gospels, nowhere else excepting in the first part of the book of Revelation and in one or two sentences in the book of Acts; and there the Lord shows us the kind of life Christians should live. Paul says, "I seek to be legitimately subject to Christ." And then the Lord has further given His will in what we call the Epistles. Through the Holy Spirit He has shown us the heavenly calling and the lives that should correspond. We should be very careful if we say we are not under the law, which is true, lest we are found to be lawless, which is antinomianism and repugnant to God. We are to be en-lawed, or legitimately subject to Christ.

"To the weak became I as weak, that I might gain the weak." That is, in ministering the Word of God Paul delighted to enter into the circumstances of the people to whom he spoke. Possibly you make up a sermon in the quiet of your study, working it all out carefully, your introduction, your firstly, secondly, thirdly, and as many other numbers as you like, and then your conclusion, and you say, "There, I have a sermon on such and such a text." And then you go to the pulpit without taking the needs of the people into consideration, and you just pour out the sermon that you have made up for them in the study. That was not Paul's way; he had the needs of men before him and he preached the Word. A minister told me about a difficult position in which he found himself at one time. He always read his sermons, and he had been asked to go and preach to a certain congregation, and so, looking through the barrel, he selected one and shoved it into his brief-case with his Bible. When he got on the platform, he pulled it out, spread it before him, and found that he had brought a different sermon to the one he intended taking. It was a Decoration Day sermon, and this was some time in the fall of the year. So he said, "I am very sorry, dear friends, I have made a mistake, but I am going to give you a sermon I preached on Memorial Day and hope you will get something out of it." Is is any wonder that people get so little edification when they listen to things like that? As a minister of Christ Paul's great object was to get to the hearts of men and give them the Word as they needed it. "To the weak became I as weak, that I might gain the weak." He did not try to astonish people with his eloquence, he gave them the Word to convict and help and bless and cheer and make things plain to them, that he might gain the weak. In fact he says, "I am made all things to all men, that I might by all means save some." This should be the object of all gospel testimony. We have been commissioned to "go into all the world and preach the gospel to every creature."

STRIVING FOR A CROWN

✓ ✓ ✓

"Know ye not that they which run in a race run all, but one receiveth the prize? So run, that ye may obtain. And every man that striveth for the mastery is temperate in all things. Now they do it to obtain a corruptible crown; but we an incorruptible. I therefore so run, not as uncertainly; so fight I, not as one that beateth the air: but I keep my body under, and bring it into subjection: lest that by any means, when I have preached to others, I myself should be a castaway" (1 Cor. 9: 24-27).

✓ ✓ ✓

THERE are two lines of truth running parallel through the Word of God; salvation, which is by grace alone, and reward for devoted service. Salvation is not a reward for anything that you or I may do, nor is heaven a reward for a life of faithfulness here on earth. Salvation is a free gift, eternal life is a free gift, heaven is the home of all the redeemed, open to every one who puts his or her trust in the Lord Jesus Christ. We cannot pay for a place in heaven; we cannot earn it by tears, by sacrifices, by our gifts or by anything that we can do.

"Could my zeal no respite know,
Could my tears forever flow,
All for sin could not atone;
Thou must save, and Thou alone.

"Nothing in my hand I bring,
Simply to Thy cross I cling;
Naked, come to Thee for dress,
Helpless, look to Thee for grace."

That must ever be the confession of every saved soul. "By grace are ye saved through faith; and that not of yourselves: it is the gift of God: not of works, lest any man should boast" (Eph. 2: 8). But while salvation, eternal life, a place in heaven, are all set before us as God's free gifts to believing sinners, the Word of God has a great deal to say about the importance of service and about rewards for faithfulness. "Behold, I come quickly," says our blessed Lord, "and My reward is with Me, to give every man according as his work shall be" (Rev. 22: 12). Manifestly, the reward is not a place with Himself in heaven, but it is the special expression of His satisfaction in the believer because of devotedness, because of faithfulness in the life. The importance of this is brought out in the passage before us.

The apostle Paul has the race course in mind. There is a great deal in the Bible about athletics. One can scarcely help coming to the conclusion that Saul of Tarsus was a thoroughly red-blooded

young man, interested in games and sports and
in everything that would challenge a normal,
clean, decent young fellow such as he evidently
was even before he was converted. What he saw
in the games made a deep impression on his mind,
and the Holy Spirit used all this in after-years to
give us some very striking and remarkable illustrations, one of which we have here. "Know ye
not that they which run in a race run all, but one
receiveth the prize?" What is the prize at the
end of the race? For a young Greek it would
not be citizenship. It was a law with the Greeks
that no young man could contend in the games
unless he could prove that he was of pure Greek
parentage; that had to be settled before he became a contestant. As the people watched the
races they knew that those young men were already Greeks by birth. They were Greek citizens
running a race. For what? To obtain honor, to
obtain glory, to obtain a prize. And so the apostle
here pictures those who are saved as running a
race. We are already heavenly citizens. Of every
Christian it is written, "Our citizenship is in
heaven; from whence also we look for the
Saviour, the Lord Jesus Christ; who shall transform our vile body that it may be fashioned like
unto His glorious body" (Phil. 3: 20, 21). Our citizenship is settled if we believe in the Lord Jesus
Christ. We are not born Christians, but we are

born-again Christians. "That which is born of
the flesh is flesh; and that which is born of the
Spirit is spirit. Marvel not that I said unto thee,
Ye must be born again" (John 3: 6, 7).

It is a great moment in the soul's history when
he awakes to realize that by nature and practice
he is an alien, "alienated and enemies in your
mind by wicked works" (Col. 1: 21), that he does
not belong to the family of God; that ere he can
belong to the family of God a change must take
place, a change which he himself cannot effect,
but which God brings about by His sovereign
power. "Of His own will," says James, "begat
He us BY the word of truth" (James 1: 18). Notice, it is through the Word that we are begotten
of God. Peter says, "Being born again, not of
corruptible seed, but of incorruptible, by the
Word of God, which liveth and abideth forever.
For all flesh is as grass, and all the glory of man
as the flower of the grass. The grass withereth,
and the flower thereof falleth away, but the Word
of the Lord endureth forever. And this is the
word (not the whole Bible as such) which by the
gospel is preached unto you" (1 Pet. 1: 23-25).
Believing the gospel we are born into the family
of God. And now, as in the family of God, we
are running a race, not to get to heaven for, as
far as that is concerned, "It is not of him that
willeth, nor of him that runneth, but of God that

showeth mercy" (Rom. 9:16), but we are running a race for reward for Christian service, Christian responsibility, and if we run our race well, there is a reward at the end. If we fail in the race, we fail in the reward. We do not fail of heaven, of salvation, because our work is not all it ought to be or all we would like it to be. "If any man's work shall be burned, he shall suffer loss: but he himself shall be saved; yet so as by fire" (1 Cor. 3:15), provided he is a Christian.

So the apostle says, "Know ye not that they which run in a race run all, but one receiveth the prize? So run, that ye may obtain." If I am going to run in order to obtain a prize, I must do it in obedience to the Word of God. "If a man also strive for masteries, yet is he not crowned, except he strive lawfully" (2 Tim. 2:5). The 1911 Version translates it, "If a man contend in the games yet is he not crowned if he hath not observed the rules." God has given us instruction in the Word concerning how we are to serve, how we are to run, what we are to do, and we will be rewarded if we go in accordance with the Book.

An incident struck me forcibly some years ago when working among the Indians in New Mexico. It was during the time of the Olympic games in Stockholm, Sweden. One Saturday night I went

to the trader's store. He was a very intelligent
Christian Indian, and was also my interpreter.
He was standing up on a chair with perhaps forty
or fifty Indians crowded around him, and he was
reading from a newspaper and interpreting it for
these Indians. I stepped up behind him, and as
I looked over his shoulder, I saw that he had a
metropolitan newspaper containing an account of
the games in Stockholm, Sweden, telling of the
triumphs of that well-known Indian athlete,
James Thorpe. Many of these Indians knew him
well, and how proud they were to think that one
of their race had gone over there and, contending
with a great number of different athletes, had carried away the greater part of the prizes. Their
enthusiasm knew no bounds when the interpreter
translated the words of the King of Sweden as
he took him by the hand and said, "You, sir, are
the greatest amateur athlete in the world today."
Those Indians were so interested because he was
one of their own, and had beaten the white man
in his own games. A few weeks later I went into
the store again. Once more the trader was reading from a newspaper, but this time the atmosphere was tense. I could feel that something was
wrong. The Indians were scowling and grunting
and I wondered what it was all about, so I stepped behind the interpreter again and looked over
his shoulder, and read that a certain white man

had been indignant that an Indian should have carried off so many prizes, and so made an investigation of his past life and found that some years before when a student at Carlisle, Pa., he had received five dollars a week during the summer months for playing ball with a village baseball team. They unearthed the evidence, sent it to the King of Sweden, and proved to him that Jimmie Thorpe had no right to participate in the games at all because they were entirely for amateurs. He had taken money for playing ball, and that put him out of the amateur class. The king had written to Thorpe and asked him to send back all the papers and medals, and it had nearly broken his heart. He sent all back and wrote to the king, "I hope your majesty will not think too hard of me. Please remember that I am only a poor ignorant Indian boy. I did not know that taking five dollars a week for playing ball on the village baseball team made me a professional. I never meant to deceive." The sequel of that story was that the man who came next in the contests sent them all back to Jim and said, "I won't keep them; you did better than I, and you deserve them." James Thorpe did his work well, but he had not observed the rules, and he lost out accordingly.

I am afraid there is many a one who does a great deal of what we call "Christian work," works early and late, and hard and often, and yet who will fail of the reward at the judgment-seat of Christ because instead of going by the Word of God he has simply been following his own ideas and inclinations. "So run that ye may obtain." How important, fellow-Christians, that we study the Bible and learn what God's mind is, and then work accordingly.

Now notice the importance of self-control. "And every man that striveth for the mastery is temperate in all things." One cannot help but admire some of these splendid young athletes as they look forward to a field day or something of the kind. How self-denying they can be as they train down. They will set a mark and say, "I must enter the field weighing just so much, and before that day I have so many pounds to lose, for I must be at my very best." Some of their friends may say, "Come, now, let us go out and indulge in this and that." But the athlete who means to succeed says, "I cannot do that, I must be at my best when I get into the arena. I cannot, I dare not dissipate." "They do it to obtain a corruptible crown." In this instance it was a wreath of laurel which would fade away in a few hours, and yet how much young men were willing to endure to win that crown, to have it placed upon their brow by the judge among the plaudits of the people. "They do it to obtain a corruptible crown; but we an incorruptible." We have an incorruptible crown in view, and shall we be less consistent, less self-denying, shall we show less self-control than they? For us there stands in the distance the blessed Lord Himself waiting to place upon our brow the incorruptible crown, and alas, alas, many of us are in danger of losing it because we are so self-indulgent, so careless, so carnal, and so worldly-minded. Let us take a lesson from the athlete and be willing to give up present pleasures for future glory.

The crown, you see, is the symbol of reward. It is presented in different ways in the Scriptures. In the second chapter of First Thessalonians the apostle, speaking to his own converts, says, "What is our hope, or joy, or crown of rejoicing? Are not even ye in the presence of our Lord Jesus Christ at His coming?" (1 Thess. 2:19). What is the crown of rejoicing? That is the soul-winner's crown. Oh, to get home to heaven to stand at the judgment-seat of Christ, and see there a great throng that one has had the privilege of leading to Christ! What a crown, what a reward that will be! Think what it will mean for the apostle Paul when surrounded by all his converts he comes before the Lord and says, "Behold I and the children whom Thou hast given me." Are you going in for a crown of rejoicing? It is your privilege if you know Christ.

The apostle says to Timothy, "I have fought a good fight, I have finished my course, I have kept the faith: henceforth there is laid up for me a crown of righteousness, which the Lord, the righteous Judge, shall give me at that day: and not to me only but unto all them also that love His appearing" (2 Tim. 4:7, 8). The gift of righteousness is ours by faith. Every believer has been made the righteousness of God in Christ, but the *crown of righteousness* is the reward given to those who behave themselves in the light of the coming again of our Lord Jesus Christ. Do you love His appearing? How do you show it? By ordering your behavior now in view of His close return. "Every man that hath this hope set on Him purifieth himself even as He is pure" (1 John 3:3).

In James and in the book of the Revelation we have another term used. In Revelation we read, "Be thou faithful unto death, and I will give thee a crown of life" (2:10). And James says, "Blessed is the man that endureth temptation: for when he is tried, he shall receive the crown of life, which the Lord hath promised to them that love Him" (James 1:12). *Eternal life* is ours by faith. "The wages of sin is death; but the gift of God is eternal life through Jesus Christ our Lord" (Rom. 6:23). "He that believeth on the Son hath everlasting life" (John 3:

36). But the *crown of life* is earned by patient suffering, by enduring trial and temptation, taking it all as from the hand of God Himself, even unto death if need be rather than to deny the name of Jesus.

In First Peter we read, "The elders which are among you I exhort, who am also an elder, and a witness of the sufferings of Christ, and also a partaker of the glory that shall be revealed: feed the flock of God which is among you." He does not say, "Fleece the flock," but, "Feed the flock of God which is among you, taking the oversight thereof, not by constraint, but willingly; not for filthy lucre, but of a ready mind; neither as being lords over God's heritage, but being ensamples to the flock. And when the Chief Shepherd shall appear, ye shall receive a crown of glory that fadeth not away" (1 Pet. 5:1-4). I like that, a crown of *glory!* Every believer will be glorified. "Whom He justified, them He also glorified" (Rom. 8:30), but the *crown* of glory is the reward for feeding the sheep and the lambs. In the earliest Chinese translations they had different terms for some of the idioms used. First Peter 5:4 would read like this, "When the Chief Shepherd shall appear, you will receive a bright hat that will never wear out." "A crown of glory that fadeth not away" is to be given by the blessed Lord Himself. My brethren, shall we

allow the things of time and sense to so absorb
us that we shall lose out in that day? Let us
rather gladly say:

> "Take the world and give me Jesus,
>   All earth's joys are but in vain;
> But His love abideth ever,
>   Through eternal years the same."

Let us gladly "lay aside every weight, and the
sin that doth so easily beset us, and let us run
with patience the race that is set before us, looking unto Jesus, the Author and Finisher of our
faith; who for the joy that was set before Him
endured the cross, despising the shame, and is
set down at the right hand of the throne of God"
(Heb. 12: 1, 2).

This was Paul's determination, "I therefore so
run, not as uncertainly; so fight I, not as one that
beateth the air." Some people imagine that Paul
was not quite sure that he would get to heaven,
that he feared that something might happen that
would turn him aside. But he is thinking of the
reward at the end, and he is not afraid of losing
this for he is determined to go through with God.
He says that he is not uncertain; "So fight I, not
as one that beateth the air." I am not engaged
in a sham battle. And then, how important this
is!—"But I keep under my body, and bring it into
subjection: lest that by any means, when I have
preached to others, I myself should be a cast-

away." What does he mean? Is it just a haunt-
ing fear that he may backslide and be lost after
all? Keep in mind what he is speaking of here.
He is speaking of reward for service, and is saying, "I want to so serve that I can have the Lord's
approval in that day. I must not be self-indulgent, I must not let my physical passions master
me, but I must master them and keep under my
body." My body is not to be the lord of me, I
am to be the lord of my body. Sustained by divine
grace I am to keep every physical appetite in its
place, lest if I become careless and self-indulgent
I bring dishonor upon the name of the Lord and
become a castaway.

What does he mean by a castaway? The word
"adokimos" means "disapproved." Lest he be disapproved, lest the Lord shall say to him some day,
"Paul, I had a crown for you, I was counting on
you, and for a while you ran well. What hindered you? You became self-indulgent and careless, and you broke down and brought dishonor
upon My name. I cannot crown you, Paul; you
will have to stand to one side and let some one
else have the crown." To be set to one side when
they are giving out the crowns! God grant that
you and I may not have to endure this great dis-
appointment.

Have you not known of those who ran well for
years and then little by little began to let down?

They were not as prayerful as they used to be, they did not give as much time to the careful study of the Word as they did in the early days, they gave freer rein to the natural appetites, they thought more of their own pleasure and of taking their ease, and one day the whole Christian community in which they moved was startled to hear that there had been a terrible breakdown. They may have confessed it all with breaking hearts and eyes from which the tears were streaming, they may have judged it all and turned from it, yet people never trusted them again as they had before, and possibly they were never able to go on with their ministry. No matter how freely and fully God had forgiven, they never could be what they once were. Some experiences are simply heart-breaking, and so the word to every one who attempts to help others in spiritual things is, be careful of yourselves. "Take heed to thyself," says the apostle writing to Timothy. Keep your physical appetites in subjection, keep your body in its place, do not allow any appetite to master you, and thus you will be able to serve to the glory of the Lord Jesus Christ. If you become careless, He may have to put you to one side, and He who once used you will not be able to do so in the future in the way He did in the past.

The word "disapprove" is also used for com-

plete disapproval. You may be a church-member
taking more or less part in so-called Christian
work, but see to it that there is a real work of
grace in your own soul, or the day may come
when you will be utterly disapproved and you will
find yourself outside the number of those who
enter into the Father's house in that day, not because you were once saved and are so no longer,
but because your life has proved that you were
never truly born of God.

LECTURE XX.

OLD TESTAMENT TYPES OF NEW TESTAMENT TRUTHS

✝ ✝ ✝

"Moreover, brethren, I would not that ye should be ignorant, how that all our fathers were under the cloud, and all passed through the sea; and were all baptized unto Moses in the cloud and in the sea; and did all eat the same spiritual meat; and did all drink the same spiritual drink: for they drank of that spiritual Rock that followed them: and that Rock was Christ. But with many of them God was not well pleased: for they were overthrown in the wilderness. Now these things were our examples, to the intent we should not lust after evil things, as they also lusted. Neither be ye idolaters, as were some of them; as it is written, The people sat down to eat and drink, and rose up to play. Neither let us commit fornication, as some of them committed, and fell in one day three and twenty thousand. Neither let us tempt Christ, as some of them also tempted, and were destroyed of serpents. Neither murmur ye, as some of them also murmured, and were destroyed of the destroyer. Now all these things happened unto them for ensamples: and they are written for our admonition, upon whom the ends of the world are come. Wherefore let him that thinketh he standeth take heed lest he fall. There hath no temptation taken you but such as is common to man: but God is faithful, who will not suffer you to be tempted above that ye are able; but will with the temptation also make a way to escape, that ye may be able to bear it. Wherefore, my dearly beloved, flee from idolatry" (1 Cor. 10: 1-14).

IF I were to choose one verse out of these fourteen as a text, it would be verse 11, "Now all these things happened unto them for ensamples (the word is really, *types*) : and they are written for our admonition, upon whom the ends of the world have arrived."

I learn a number of things from this verse. In the first place, I learn that all that is recorded concerning the nation of Israel in the Old Testament is sober, reliable history. The Word says, "All these things happened." This is the testimony of the Holy Spirit. Therefore, I believe it without a question. The account of the origin of mankind as given in the book of Genesis happened just as we are told it did. It has been given by the only One who was there to know, and that is God Himself. The history of mankind as further unfolded in that early book is all true. "All these things happened." And then after the calling of Abraham and the separation of the Hebrew people from the Gentile world, the story given in the rest of the books of the Old Testament as to God's dealings with these people is true history and nothing imaginary, nothing legendary, but actual history. "These things happened."

The second thing I learn from this verse is that in the preparation of the volume of Holy Scripture, the Spirit of God so guided and directed the human writers that He led them to eliminate anything extraneous, anything not particularly helpful to us, and that the incidents recorded are there for a definite purpose. "All these things happened unto them for types: and they are written for our admonition, upon whom the ends of the ages have arrived." They took place literally just as we are told they did. But there was something beyond the literal. The nation of Israel is a typical nation, the redemption of Israel is a typical redemption, the sacrifices offered under the law were typical sacrifices, the sanctuary of the Hebrew people was a typical sanctuary. David exclaims, "In His sanctuary every whit of it uttereth His glory," and so we may profitably read all of these Old Testament stories with the light of the New Testament shining upon them and see there marvelous pictures, wonderful types of the Person and work of our Lord Jesus Christ and of the people of God today. And so there are both encouragements and warnings for us in the history of Israel.

In the early part of this chapter the apostle particularly deals with some of these narratives. He reminds us how a great multitude went out of Egypt and started ostensibly for the land of Canaan, the land of promise, but many of them failed to reach that land because of unbelief which led them to many other kinds of sin, and so he says, "Moreover, brethren, I would not that ye should be ignorant, how that all our fathers were under the cloud, and all passed through the sea; and were all baptized unto Moses in the cloud and in the sea; and did all eat the same spiritual meat; and did all drink the same spiritual drink; for they drank of that spiritual Rock that followed them; and that Rock was Christ." That is, as that great company of hundreds of thousands of Israelites left the land of Egypt, it would have been impossible for any one to have drawn any distinction between those who were real and faithful and those who because of sin and unbelief would have to be destroyed. And so the warning comes home to us: it is one thing to profess to be a Christian, it is one thing even to participate in the ordinances of Christianity, to have been baptized in the name of the Father and of the Son and of the Holy Spirit, to take part in the Supper of the Lord, to receive the consecrated elements that speak of the precious body and blood of the Lord Jesus Christ given up to death for us; it is one thing to associate outwardly with the people of God and to seem to have fellowship and communion with them, but it is another thing to prove genuine by going on with God, by living for God, and by bearing a faithful testimony right on to the end. Of course, where there is a real work of the Spirit of God in a man's soul, it will be continuous, but alas, there are many of whom it can be said, "Thou hast a name that thou livest, and art dead" (Rev. 3:1).

A number of years ago I was invited by a very godly minister to address his congregation on a certain Lord's Day, and never having preached from his pulpit before, and not knowing what kind of a congregation I might be expected to face, and therefore being rather at sea as to the nature of the message that would be most suitable, I said to him, "Doctor, when I come to speak to your people, what kind of an audience will I address? Will they be mainly your own members, all Christian people, or many strangers and possibly unconverted people?" I can still see the look of sadness that came over his face and the tears that came into his eyes as he said, seriously and solemnly, "Well, my brother, I think that most of them will be our own people; we do not get a great many strangers in our place. But I am afraid that very few of our own members are Christians. After having been with them for a number of years, I greatly regret to say that I fear that the majority of them are like the foolish virgins, they have no oil in their lamps; and therefore I hope you will come to us with a clear, definite gospel message, and I shall be praying that God may use it for the awakening and the salvation of many of our people." What a solemn thing to have to make a confession like that! And yet is it not true in many places to-day? We take too much for granted when we suppose that membership in a Christian church, that participation in Christian ordinances and in outward fellowship, means that one is really a child of God. There must be a second birth, there must be personal faith in the Lord Jesus Christ.

In Israel there were two groups: those who had true faith in God and those who simply had an outward relationship to the people of the covenant. Those who had that outward relationship went with the rest through the Red Sea, and the apostle likens that to baptism. They were sheltered by the pillar of cloud and fire, and he compares that to the gift of the Holy Spirit. They all ate of the manna that came from heaven, and that speaks of participation in Christian fellowship at the table of the Lord. They all drank the water that came from the smitten rock, and that was an outward picture of those who drink today of the water of life that flows from the side of the wounded Christ. But this might all be outward, there might be no reality in the heart, no real work in the soul. Those who were real drank of the spiritual Rock that followed them, and that Rock was Christ. In other words, it was not enough to drink of the water that came from the smitten rock, but of the stream that flowed from another Rock, and wherever there was reality they drank of the "attendant Rock," as one has translated it. It was Christ who led the people of Israel across the desert into the land of Canaan as the Angel of the Lord. Jehovah said, "My name is in Him" (Ex. 23:21), and in every dispensation all who have been saved at all have been saved through the Lord Jesus Christ. All who were genuine in their profession at any time and in any age were saved because they had put their trust in the revelation that God gave concerning the Seed of the woman who was to bruise the head of the serpent. But with many of this company God was not well pleased and they were overthrown. Why? Because of sin. And so the warning comes home to us now to learn from God's dealings with this typical people the importance of being right with God today. Turn from everything unholy, judge every tendency in yourself to that which is impure and unclean, that God may be glorified in you.

"Now these things were types, to the intent we should not lust after evil things, as they also lusted." Christ is the great satisfying portion of the heart. The only way that one can be delivered from the corruption that is in the world through lust is by finding heart satisfaction in the Saviour.

> "O Christ, in Thee my soul hath found,
>   And found in Thee alone,
> The peace, the joy I sought so long,
>   The bliss till now unknown.
>
> "I tried the broken cisterns, Lord,
>   But ah, their waters failed,
> E'en as I stooped to drink they fled,
>   And mocked me as I wailed.
>
> "The pleasures lost I sadly mourned,
>   But never wept for Thee,
> Till grace my sightless eyes received,
>   Thy loveliness to see.
>
> "Now none but Christ can satisfy,
>   None other name for me,
> There's love, and life, and rest, and joy,
>   Lord Jesus, found in Thee."

When people profess to be Christians, outwardly profess to be members of the Church of the Living God, and yet give every evidence that their hearts are still in the world, when there is no separation from the world, no breaking from the things that dishonor our blessed God, when they are still taken up with "the lust of the flesh, and the lust of the eyes, and the pride of life"—one may stand in grave doubt as to whether they have ever really been brought to drink of that spiritual "attendant Rock," that Rock which is Christ.

And then we are warned against putting anything in the place of God. "Neither be ye idol-

aters, as were some of them; as it is written, The
people sat down to eat and drink, and rose up to
play." The reference is to the making of the
golden calf which they set up in the wilderness.
Moses had gone up into the mount. Their leader
who had brought them out of Egypt was no
longer visible, just as our blessed Lord has gone
to the Father's right hand in heaven and our eyes
do not now see Him. Therefore the people
turned to Aaron and said, "We cannot see this
man, he has disappeared from us; now make us
gods that shall go before us, tangible gods that
we can see and worship." And so Aaron told
them to bring all the gold, all the "earrings," and
other ornaments, and he would make a god for
them. And they brought them and he melted
them all down, poured the metal into a mold, and
made a calf of gold, and set it upon a pedestal,
and even gave it Jehovah's name. He said, "Tomorrow is a feast to the Lord." And the people
danced around it and sat down to eat a sacra-
mental meal in the presence of the golden calf,
because of which the judgment of God burned
fiercely against them as Moses came down from
the mount. You remember the dreadful results.
Many of them died under the hand of God, they
that were spared even had to drink the calf!
Moses took the calf of gold that they had made,
and ground it into fine dust and poured this into

the water that they drank. That was the "gold cure" to show them the folly of worshiping any other than the one true and living God, and the lesson for us is that if we dare to put anything else in the place of God, no matter how precious it may seem to be, the time will come when we will rue it. The golden calf is still worshiped. Many worship money, wealth, pleasure, and yet claim to be followers of the lowly Saviour, "Who though in the form of God, thought equality with God not something to be grasped after: but emptied Himself, and became obedient unto death, and such a death, even the death of the cross" (Phil. 2: 6-8, literal rendering). How can I be a consistent follower of Him if I put self or anything that this poor heart of mine can crave on earth in the place of the true and living God? "Little children," says John, "keep yourselves from idols" (1 John 5: 21).

The third is a solemn warning and is against every kind of uncleanness, "Neither let us commit fornication, as some of them committed, and fell in one day three and twenty thousand." We are living in a day when uncleanness is everywhere. Our modern novels are reeking with it, our newspaper stands are filled with vile pornographic literature that came from hell, and men are enriching themselves by poisoning the minds of our young people. The pictures they see, the

songs that come over the radio, many are filled
with suggestions of impurity and uncleanness.
How sternly the Christian Church needs to set its
face against everything of this kind. We should
have no compromise whatever with impurity.
People see the pictures, read the books, listen to
the songs, and they all have their effect upon the
flesh, and before you know it men are drifting off
into unholy, unclean things because of the constant incitation to them in the music and literature of the day. Let us give everything like that
a wide berth. "Ye have been called unto liberty;
only use not liberty for an occasion to the flesh"
(Gal. 5: 13).

I am reminded that this eighth verse is one
that unbelievers and modernists like to point to
as an evidence that the Bible cannot be fully inspired. We read that because of this sin there
"fell in one day three and twenty thousand." And
if you turn back to Numbers 25: 5, you will find
that twenty-four thousand were destroyed because of the sin of fornication. Therefore, these
objectors say, "There is a contradiction in your
Bible; in one place it says twenty-four thousand
were destroyed and in another twenty-three thousand." It is not difficult to harmonize the two
accounts. In Numbers the complete account is
given, there were twenty-four thousand destroyed
during that period in which God was dealing with

His people, but in First Corinthians the apostle is stressing the fact that the very first day that the judgment began twenty-three thousand died. The other thousand, of course, died later on. But he is emphasizing the fact that so indignant was God with His people when they fell into the sin of uncleanness that in one day He destroyed twenty-three thousand.

Notice the fourth warning. "Neither let us tempt Christ, as some of them also tempted, and were destroyed of serpents." How did they tempt Him? When they said, "Can God furnish a table in the wilderness?" they limited the Holy One of Israel. If we say, "Can God undertake for me? I am in very difficult circumstances; is God able to see me through?" we limit God, we limit the blessed God of all grace who gave His Son for us. "He that spared not His own Son, but delivered Him up for us all, how shall He not with Him also freely give us all things?" (Rom. 8:32). Faith believes God and never tempts Him, but goes forward in obedience to His Word.

Then the fifth warning, "Neither murmur ye, as some of them also murmured, and were destroyed of the destroyer." The reference here is to the destruction of Korah, Dathan, and Abiram in the wilderness. They murmured against God and Moses, the servant of the Lord, and Aaron, the high priest of Jehovah, saying, "Ye take too much upon you, seeing all the congregation are holy, every one of them, and the Lord is among them: wherefore then lift ye up yourselves above the congregation of the Lord?" (Num. 16:3). They practically said, "We do not need a mediator, we do not need a high priest, we are good enough for God as we are." They found fault with God's provision for them and destruction was the result.

Let us be grateful to God for the provision He has given through His Word and the Holy Spirit for the salvation of our souls and our building up in Christ. Let us never allow ourselves to become self-confident and imagine we can get along without the daily ministry of our risen, glorified Lord, our High Priest in heaven. "All these things happened unto them for types: and they are written for our admonition, upon whom the ends of the world have arrived." In view of them, let us walk carefully, and, "Let him that thinketh he standeth take heed lest he fall." Let him test his foundation, make sure that he is taking the Word of God as his guide, that he is resting upon the testimony that God has given, and when the hour of trial comes, he can be sure that there is abundant grace to sustain.

"There hath no temptation taken you but such as is common to man; but God is faithful, who will not suffer you to be tempted above that ye are able; but will with the temptation also make a way to escape, that ye may be able to bear it" (1 Cor. 10:13), He did this for Israel of old. As we read the story of His dealings with them, we have instance after instance of His wonderful intervention when they were at their very wits' end, and the God who sustained His people in the wilderness, fed them on manna from heaven and water from the smitten rock, and drove out their enemies from the land of Canaan, is living still. In the measure in which we learn to depend on Him, to count on Him, we too shall find deliverance in the hour of difficulty and trial.

And so the passage closes with the solemn warning, "Wherefore, my dearly beloved, flee from idolatry." These are serious admonitions. Let us take them to our hearts, remembering that it is one thing to have made a profession, but it is another thing to have that profession backed up by a godly life that proves the profession to be real.

THE TABLE OF THE LORD AND THE TABLE OF DEMONS

✓ ✓ ✓

"I speak as to wise men; judge ye what I say. The cup of blessing which we bless, is it not the communion of the blood of Christ? The bread which we break, is it not the communion of the body of Christ? For we being many are one bread, and one body: for we are all partakers of that one bread. Behold Israel after the flesh: are not they which eat of the sacrifices partakers of the altar? What say I then? that the idol is any thing, or that which is offered in sacrifice to idols is any thing? But I say, that the things which the Gentiles sacrifice, they sacrifice to devils, and not to God: and I would not that ye should have fellowship with devils. Ye cannot drink the cup of the Lord, and the cup of devils: ye cannot be partakers of the Lord's table, and of the table of devils. Do we provoke the Lord to jealousy? are we stronger than He? All things are lawful for me, but all things are not expedient: all things are lawful for me, but all things edify not. Let no man seek his own, but every man another's wealth. Whatsoever is sold in the shambles, that eat, asking no questions for conscience sake: for the earth is the Lord's, and the fulness thereof. If any of them that believe not bid you to a feast, and ye be disposed to go; whatsoever is set before you, eat, asking no question for conscience sake. But if any man say unto you, This is offered in sacrifice unto idols, eat not for his sake that showed it, and for conscience sake: for the earth is the Lord's, and the fulness thereof: conscience, I say, not thine own, but of the other: for why is my liberty judged of another man's conscience? For if I by grace be a partaker, why am I evil spoken of for that for which I give thanks?" (1 Cor. 10: 15-30).

✦ ✦ ✦

WE have in this passage a very serious and solemn word regarding the celebration of the Lord's Supper which has been maintained in the Christian Church for the last nineteen hundred years. In the earlier part of the chapter we were warned against compromising with the world. Now Paul continues that warning, saying, "My dearly beloved, flee from idolatry." In civilized lands we do not come in contact with idolatry in the sense that the apostle primarily means it here, but this is still a very live question in pagan lands, where it is found to be very necessary to separate the converts from absolutely everything of a heathenish or idolatrous character, because if there is any compromise, any fellowship with them, the tendency of all these things is to drag one back to the old levels. Here at home we are more concerned about the gay, godless world around us. We have heard the challenge of the Spirit of God, "Come out from among them, and be ye separate, saith the Lord, and touch not the unclean thing; and I will receive you" (2 Cor. 6: 17), and as wise men we will apply the principle of this passage to the conditions under which we live.

As Christians we are linked with the table of the Lord, let us see to it that we "have no fellowship with the unfruitful works of darkness, but rather reprove them" (Eph. 5:11). We are told, "The cup of blessing which we bless, is it not the communion of the blood of Christ? The bread which we break, is it not the communion of the Body of Christ?" In these words he shows us that the Lord's Supper, as we commonly call it, sets forth the very foundation principles of Christianity. It is a rallying center, as it were, where God's people come together to openly confess their adherence to these great fundamental truths. Notice the order given: the cup first, the bread second. When our Lord instituted the Supper, and when we participate in it, thanksgiving for the bread is first, and then for the cup; but the apostle here mentions the cup first because it sets forth the precious poured-out blood of our Lord Jesus Christ, and there can be no relationship with God for those who by nature and practice are lost sinners, until they have been cleansed by the precious blood of Christ. Every time the Communion feast is celebrated, the great fact is emphasized that it is the blood, the blood of Jesus alone, that cleanses from sin and gives access to the presence of God. In this we may see the reason for Satan's antagonism against this ordinance. It suffers in two ways. On the one hand there are those that have added to it a great many unscriptural superstitious practices and have made it a strange and weird mystery, so that many Christians are almost afraid to approach the table of the Lord. On the other hand there are those who pretend to have a deeper spirituality and a greater Bible knowledge than ordinary Christians, and so put the Lord's Supper to one side on the plea that we have no need of ordinances of any kind in the Christian, which is a spiritual, dispensation.

We need to remember that the two ordinances of baptism and the Lord's Supper were given, not so much to be helpful to Christian people as such, though they are helpful to them, but to be a testimony to the world outside and to form as it were a line of demarcation between the Church and the world. We have already seen how baptism does that. I trust the Lord Jesus Christ in my heart, I accept Him as my Saviour, and by my baptism I am saying to the world, "I have identified myself with the Christ that you have rejected; henceforward I am

> 'Dead to the world and all its toys,
> Its idle pomp and fading joys;
> Jesus, my glory be!' "

If baptism does not mean that to me, it is really nothing more than a mere empty form; but if I see that by my baptism I am confessing my

identification with the rejected Christ, it becomes
a sweet and precious ordinance and is a testimony
to the world outside. The Lord's Supper is also a
testimony. Baptism speaks of my death with
Christ; the Lord's Supper speaks of Christ's
death for me as the only ground of approach to
and fellowship with God. And so (chap. 11: 26)
we read, "As often as ye eat this bread, and
drink this cup, ye do show the Lord's death
till He come." The word translated "show" is
exactly the same word which is used on many
other occasions in the book of the Acts and in the
Epistles for "preach." "As often as ye eat this
bread, and drink this cup, ye do *preach*—you
proclaim—the Lord's death till He come," and so
by participation in the Lord's Supper today we
are preaching to the world around the blessed
fact that Christ has died and that His precious
blood alone can cleanse from sin. Therefore the
emphasis on the cup. First, "The cup of blessing
which we bless, is it not the communion of the
blood of Christ?" That is the expression of fellowship which is based upon the blood of Christ.
Therefore, you can readily see that no one has
part nor lot in this ordinance, no one ought ever
to participate in it, who does not put his or her
trust in the precious blood of the Lord Jesus
Christ for salvation. I cannot understand how
any one who denies the atoning efficacy of the

blood of Jesus could even desire to take part in the celebration of the Lord's Supper, and yet I am told that in places where Christ's atoning death is scouted, in places where men ridicule the thought of salvation by His precious blood, the ordinance of the Lord's Supper is still observed in a formal way. It seems to me that is an insult to God, it is an insult to the blessed Saviour whose death is commemmorated in this service. Christ died for sinners, poured out His blood to redeem us to God, therefore from time to time we come together to remember Him in the drinking of the cup.

Then notice that the bread used in the Supper of the Lord has, if I may so say, a double significance. It speaks of the literal body of our Saviour which was offered for us upon the cross, but there is another and wider sense in which it speaks of the mystical Body of Christ to which all believers belong. "The bread which we break, is it not the communion of the Body of Christ?" It expresses our fellowship with the Body of Christ. He said, "This is My body which is given for you." That precious body of His came into being in a different way from any other body. It was the direct creation of the Holy Spirit of God in the womb of the blessed Virgin Mary. Christ says, "A body hast Thou prepared Me" (Heb. 10: 5). It was a human body, a body in every re-

spect like ours excepting that there were in that
body no sinful tendencies whatever, for our Lord
Jesus Christ was, from the moment of His birth
as He had been from all eternity, the Holy One
of God.

In that prepared body He went to the cross
and died for our sins; in fact, He assumed that
body in order that He might die. Deity as such
cannot die. God, no matter how much He loved
us, could not die, but God becoming Man, God
taking humanity into relationship with Deity
could die as Christ has died on Calvary's tree.
And so, every time we participate in the Lord's
Supper we are again announcing the fact, "Christ
died for our sins according to the Scriptures"
(chap. 15: 3). This service preaches, it preaches
loudly, of salvation only through that vicarious
Sacrifice offered upon the cross.

It is evident that the apostle by the Spirit of
God attaches a wider meaning to the use of the
bread in the Communion service. "The bread
which we break, is it not the communion of the
Body of Christ? For we being many are one
bread, and one Body: for we are all partakers of
that one bread." When he says, "we all" he
means, of course, Christians. "We being many
are one bread, and one Body." And again he
means believers. He is not speaking of mankind
in general. Let us never make the mistake of

thinking that all men are included in the Body of Christ, neither is it true that all believers in all ages have been included in the Body of Christ. If I read my Bible correctly, the Body of Christ came into existence on the day of Pentecost. There were believers in the world before that. There were one hundred and twenty of them gathered together that morning, but they were one hundred and twenty individuals, separate units, and the Holy Spirit came according to the Saviour's promise and in a moment baptized those one hundred and twenty individuals into one, and made of them one Body of which the risen glorified Christ is the Head. That Body exists in the world today, and includes every one who all through the years since has put his trust in Christ.

The Body as presented in Ephesians takes in all saints, living and dead, from Pentecost to the Rapture. The Body as presented in First Corinthians takes in all saints upon the earth at a given moment of time. They are all members of the Body of Christ. The Body of Christ on earth is in the place of responsibility; the Body of Christ in heaven, of course, is in the place where praise and thanksgiving alone prevail, for there is no longer the need of prayer because saints have passed beyond the bounds of responsibility. But how blessed to realize when we take the

Lord's Supper that we are doing so as recognizing our unity with every fellow-believer on the face of the earth. There is only one Lord's table in all the world. Wherever bread and the fruit of the vine are placed on a table in commemoration of the death of the Lord Jesus Christ, that is the Lord's table, and Christians are responsible to behave themselves accordingly. The apostle emphasizes that when he points out that there are only two other tables. One is either at the Lord's table on earth, the table of Judaism, which is the fellowship of Israel, or the table of demons which is the fellowship of idols.

"Behold Israel after the flesh: are not they which eat of the sacrifices partakers of the altar?" He is referring to the peace offering. All in Israel had their title to participate when the peace offering was offered; that marked them out as a special communion. On the other hand, "The things that the Gentiles sacrifice, they sacrifice to demons, and not to God: and I would not that ye should have fellowship with devils." Idolatrous feasts and heathen festivals were all expressions of fellowship, just as the Lord's table is an expression of fellowship, or as the peace offering in Israel was an expression of fellowship. But these idolatrous festivals express fellowship with demons whether people realize it or not. I wish that the members of the Laymen's Appraisal

Commission could get the meaning of this. They tell us that we make a great mistake in sending missionaries to heathen lands to draw a line of demarcation between heathenism and Christianity. They say we should go to them and get all the good we can out of their religions, and then share with them what we have. "The things that the Gentiles sacrifice, they sacrifice to demons, and not to God: and I would not that ye should have fellowship with demons." They may not realize it, but behind those idols, those images, there are demon powers controlling the hearts and minds of the people, and Christians are to be separated from everything like that.

"Ye cannot drink the cup of the Lord and the cup of demons: ye cannot be partakers of the Lord's table, and of the table of demons." And, let me say, you cannot be living for the world, the flesh, and the devil, and be a partaker at the table of the Lord. You may sit in a church pew, and when the bread and wine are passed you may eat and drink of them, but you have not partaken of this fellowship, you cannot do it. You may in an outward sense take your place with Christians, but you know there is no real fellowship if you still belong to the world or love the world and its ways. It is the heart that is occupied with Christ that enjoys the sweetness and preciousness of fellowship at His table. "Ye cannot drink the cup of the Lord, and the cup of demons." Did we attempt to do so, it would be as though we would try to provoke the Lord to jealousy.

A young man is engaged to a beautiful young woman. She does not know that his ways are very careless, and by-and-by she learns that while he comes to visit her and treats her with kindness and affection, on other nights he is out with other young women and is just as affectionate and free with them. He comes back to her as though nothing has happened. Do you think she would accept him on the same good terms? No; she would say, "You cannot go on with others if you expect me to be devoted to you alone." And so our Lord has called us to proclaim our whole-hearted devotion to Himself and thus our separation from the world that has rejected our Saviour. Looked at from this standpoint how important the frequent celebration of the Lord's Supper becomes.

The early Christians used to call this "The Sacrament." Where did that term come from? The word "sacrament" was used for the oath of allegiance which the soldiers of the Roman legion took to their emperor. The early Christians said, "In a similar way every time we gather at the table of the Lord we renew our allegiance to our blessed Lord, we are confessing our devotion to Him who in grace gave Himself for us." That is what makes this so precious in His eyes as we thus remember Him.

And so the believer, remembering he is always linked with the Lord's table, that his behavior is to be in accordance with the Communion, should be careful as to how far he participates in things that worldlings think nothing of. "All things are lawful for me, but all things are not expedient: all things are lawful for me, but all things edify not." In other words, the believer is not put under rules and regulations, he is free and is at liberty to do the thing that he believes is right. Let him stop and ask the question in regard to a matter, "Will it edify, will it bless, will it help to make Christ more precious to me? Is there a possibility it may stumble any one else?" If it would not edify, it is something from which I must turn. I am not bound by these things, I am here to seek the blessing of others, not to do my own will.

The apostle says, as it were, "When you go into the market to buy, purchase what you will, take it home and eat it. If you are invited to a meal, feel perfectly free to go and eat what is placed before you. But if when you go to the market and are about to purchase your meat, the butcher should say, 'This has been dedicated to idols,' you say, 'We do not want it.' If you go out to dinner and your host should say, 'We are eating this to-

day as dedicated to such and such a god,'
you say, 'I cannot eat it with you because
I am a partaker at the table of the Lord.' " We
are not to make difficulties unnecessarily, but to
be very careful of the consciences of other people. He does not want the butcher to be able to
say, "I sold that Christian meat dedicated to
Apollo, or to some other god; he evidently recognizes that there are other gods." He does not
want that host to be able to say, "We thought him
very narrow, we thought he recognized only
Christ as God, but you see he partakes with us
in the recognition of all our gods. He has so
much more liberty than we thought." No; the
apostle says, "Flee all that kind of liberty, be out-
and-out for Christ; do not let any one have occasion to speak ill of that which you feel perfectly
free to do."

"If I by grace be a partaker, why am I evil
spoken of for that for which I give thanks?" I
am not to allow myself to partake of anything
that would mislead those who are weak in the
faith. Each believer is to act thus in good conscience toward God.

The conscience of a young person may be more
active than some of the older folk think. Some
of us get in the habit of speaking disparagingly
of the young, and we would like to see them begin
where we have left off. We have had to grow

and they have to grow. Well, then, do not expect too much of young believers. Remember how you had to grow, you had to learn little by little what a poor, wretched thing this world is, and you had to learn how Christ could make up for everything else. They have to learn it too; give them credit for being just as honest as you were. They want to live for God, but they come to me and say, "What do you think of thus and so?" It is generally some kind of amusement. They ask, "Do you think that it is all right for a Christian?" And I always say, "My dear young brother, or my dear young sister, don't you think that you are turning that around? Don't ask the question, 'Is there any harm in it?' but, 'Is there any profit in it? Will it really do me good? Would it be a blessing to me physically, spiritually, and in other ways? Will it help me to be a better testimony for Christ?' If so, do not be afraid of it. But if conscience says, 'It would not be profitable and it would not be a good testimony to others, it may mislead the weak, it will not lead me toward a deeper knowledge of Christ,' then say, 'I cannot, on the principle that the apostle lays down here, and I will avoid it.'" Let Christ be the one supreme Object of the devotion of your heart.

THE JEW, THE GENTILE, AND
THE CHURCH OF GOD

↗ ↗ ↗

"Whether therefore ye eat, or drink, or whatsoever ye do, do all to the glory of God. Give none offence, neither to the Jews, nor to the Gentiles, nor to the Church of God: even as I please all men in all things, not seeking mine own profit, but the profit of many, that they may be saved" (1 Cor. 10:31-33).

↗ ↗ ↗

THESE words form a fitting conclusion to the portion which we considered in our last study. Paul has just emphasized the behavior that should characterize those who are linked with the table of the Lord. A table is the expression of fellowship, there is no place where we enjoy one another's companionship so much as there. We sit down to partake of the good things provided, and there is a feast of reason and a flow of soul, and we find ourselves enjoying fellowship together.

In the spiritual sense there are three tables, representing three great fellowships in this world. First, there is the table of the Lord, and that represents Christian fellowship. As we have seen, the loaf and the cup upon that table speak of the body and the blood of our Lord Jesus, and we being many, all who have been redeemed to God by the precious blood of our Saviour, are members of one Body and so partake together of that one communion feast. Then there is that which the apostle solemnly designates the table of demons. He is referring to heathen festivals, the kind of feasts held in those days, and that are still being held in pagan lands where devotees of idolatry gather together for fellowship in their abominably mysterious and unspeakably evil rites and ceremonies. Behind all this is the power of Satan. "The things which the Gentiles sacrifice, they sacrifice to demons, and not to God." In the third place there is what might be called the table of Israel. "Are not they that eat of the sacrifices partakers of the altar?" (ver. 18). That was called the table of the Lord, but when the Lord Jesus was forsaken these forms and ceremonies became empty. Yet today we recognize that there is that fellowship in the world, a fellowship which is neither Christian on the one hand nor pagan on the other, the fellowship of the house of Israel. And now the apostle shows us that as Christians we are to live in this world having due regard to these different fellowships, seeking to bless all in each of these various circles.

First, we have our individual responsibility to order our lives to the glory of God. "Whether therefore ye eat, or drink, or whatsoever ye do, do all to the glory of God." How far-reaching is this commandment. I wonder whether we always bear it in mind as we should. I am quite certain that many of us as Christians would live very different lives if we kept this admonition in mind, "Whether therefore ye eat, or drink, or whatsoever ye do, do all to the glory of God." That takes in my entire life. A great many people try to live their lives in sealed compartments; there is one compartment for the church, there is another for the family, another for business, and another for pleasure and recreation, and the same man may seem to be an altogether different person in each one of these. When he comes to church he is the essence of sanctimoniousness, he has a long face and reverent mien as he sits in his pew. You would not think an unholy thought ever passed through his mind. His eyes are either uplifted to heaven or closed as if in rapt meditation. But see that same man during the week when he goes out into the world in business. Now his eyes are never closed, they are never lifted heavenward, but he is looking about him furtively in a most anxious way, and he is always interested in how he may make a dollar honestly or dishonestly. In fact, he sometimes does not "make" the dollars at all, he simply gets them. There is a great deal of difference between making money and getting money. We *make* money when we give a legitimate return for it; we *get* money without giving a legitimate return for it, and even professing Christians often engage in various nefarious schemes that would not bear the test of the Word of God nor even a close application of the law of the land, in their efforts to get money. When they are questioned they say, "Well, you know what the Bible says, 'Not slothful in business.'" That is a scripture that has made a great impression upon many minds. And then again this same man goes to his home, and there he is an altogether different person. In business he is so affable, at church so reverent and so solemn, but in his home where he feels he is best known he is sometimes anything but affable and solemn, he shows a miserably bad temper and is a kind of boor and makes everybody around him uncomfortable. You have possibly heard the story of the wife who said of her husband who was a preacher, "When I see him in the pulpit, I think he never ought to come out of it, and when I see his behavior at home, I think he never ought to go into it." There are many people like that, they live one way at home and altogether another outside. John Bunyan speaks of a man as a "devil at home and an angel abroad."

These same people have another compartment
in their lives, and that is the one that has to do
with their leisure time, their pleasure. It is
amazing to see the very person who looks so
serious on a Sunday morning make his way into
some ungodly moving-picture show, or some other
unholy place of amusement, on a week-night. I
wonder how people can attempt to combine the
two, how there can be any respect whatever for
the things of God if they go on with the vile,
wicked amusements that so many are running
after today. We are not to live our lives in these
air-tight compartments, but are to do everything
to the glory of God. If we gather with the people
of God in the church services, it is that He may
be glorified; if we go out to take our place in the
business world, it is that we may bring glory to
His name. A straightforward, upright godly-
living Christian business man may be a far
greater testimony for God than a preacher. Men
expect the preacher to unfold the Word of God,
but it often comes to them as a wonderful surprise
when they see a business man living out the Word
of God, and it appeals to them, it gives them to
know that what the preacher declares is the right
thing.

The home is the place where perhaps above
every other a man may show what a Christian
really should be, as in the presence of his wife

and his children he manifests the grace of the
Lord Jesus Christ and seeks to lead those who are
young in the ways that be in Christ. And then
we come to his recreation, for a Christian needs
recreation, a Christian has a body and a mind to
be thought of, and needs to get out in the open
and give a certain amount of time to that which
is not so serious. But in his recreation he will
say to himself, "I am still to have this in view,
that I am to live to the glory of God, and whatever I do I must be careful that I do not allow
in myself anything, under the plea that it is simply pleasure or recreation, that would not have
the approbation of the Lord Jesus Christ." We
can easily make the test by saying, "If I do thus
and so, would it disconcert me in the least if the
Lord Jesus would suddenly appear, if He would
look down upon me and say, 'What are you doing?'"

During my unconverted days I had never been
in a theater, but some seven years after my conversion I got into a low backslidden state and I
said, "I am going to find out what the theater is
like." I felt like Moses before he killed that man,
when he looked this way and that way to see if
anybody was watching. I looked to the right and
to the left, but I forgot to look up, for there was
One watching me, the blessed Lord Jesus Himself.
I paid for my ticket and went in and the miser-

able thing began. I had not been sitting there long until I seemed to hear a voice say, "What doest thou here, Elijah?" and I thought, "Where does that come from? Oh, yes; I remember, that is in the Bible." It stirred me so I got up and ran from the place. If you cannot enjoy things with the Lord's approbation, then you had better avoid them.

If you want to be the kind of Christian who grows in grace and in the knowledge of the Lord Jesus Christ, you must order your life according to His Word. We have a similar verse to this in the Epistle to the Colossians (3: 17), "Whatsoever ye do in word or deed, do all in the name of the Lord Jesus Christ, giving thanks unto God and the Father by Him." If you call yourself a Christian, the next time you think of going to some ungodly place of worldly amusement, get down on your knees first and say, "Blessed God, in the name of the Lord Jesus I am going down to the moving-picture show—or whatever it may be—to see some of those ungodly Hollywood divorcees cavorting on the stage, and I pray that it may be for my spiritual blessing and that I may be enabled to glorify God." If you can pray that way without biting your tongue for being a hypocrite, you may go; but if you find you cannot pray like that, you had better give the place a wide berth.

I have heard Pastor D.H. Dolman tell that he
was giving some addresses, before the world war,
in a palace in Russia. He had been invited over
from Germany by a Russian princess who was an
earnest evangelical Christian. She had gathered
together many of the old Russian nobility and
it was to them Pastor Dolman was speaking.
At one of his meetings he was talking of the
Christian's attitude toward the world. A Grand
Duchess was there and she was a professed
Christian. At the close of the meeting, being a
strong-minded lady, she spoke up and said, "I do
not at all agree with some things that Pastor
Dolman has said today."

He turned to her and said, "Your Imperial
Highness, what have I said with which you dis-
agree?"

"You said a Christian should not go to the
theater, and I do not agree with you. I go to the
theater, and I never go but what I get down on
my knees first and say, 'I am going to the theater
today, and I want Thee to go with me and protect
me from all evil,' and He always does."

"Your Imperial Highness, may I ask you a
question? Where did you get the authority to
decide what you were going to do or where you
were to go, and then ask the Lord to go with you
in it? Why do you not wait until the Lord says
to you, 'Grand Duchess, I am going to the theater

tonight and I want you to come with Me,' and then follow Him to the theater?"

She threw up her hands and said, "Pastor Dolman has spoiled the theater for me, for if I wait for the Lord to bid me go, that time will never come!"

That is true of a great many other worldly places. Give the Lord the opportunity to guide you and He will lead your steps in the right way. You may say, "Oh, well; whose business is it how I behave?" That is something like the question Cain asked, "Am I my brother's keeper?" If you profess to be a Christian, there are a great many eyes fixed upon you, people are watching you to see what a Christian should be and they are judging your Master by your life, and if your life is worldly, mean, and ungodly, they decide that your Master is not the blessed, glorious, holy Christ that your lips tell them He is.

And so the apostle reminds us that there are three great classes of people who are looking on and he says, "Give none offence, neither to the Jews, nor to the Gentiles, nor to the Church of God." "Give none offence." He does not mean that we are not to offend any one, for it is impossible to keep from offending somebody. For instance, if I preach the Lord Jesus Christ, I offend my unbelieving neighbor. If I try to live for God, I offend people who do not want to live for God. If I stand against the liquor traffic, I offend all those engaged in that abominable business and who are interested in it from the standpoint of revenue. It is impossible for a Christian to live as he should without offending somebody, but the old English word "offend" has an altogether different meaning. The admonition may be translated, "Give no occasion to stumble," do not allow yourself in anything that would give another occasion to stumble because of your inconsistency.

"Neither to the Jews, nor to the Gentiles, nor to the Church of God." Here are the three classes into which the world is divided. The Jews of old, God's covenant people, the people to whom He gave the revelation of His Word and who preserved that revelation for us down through the centuries, the people to whom the Saviour came—in fact, He was one of them, "Of whom as concerning the flesh Christ came" (Rom. 9:5). But that people reading their own Scriptures fulfilled the predictions of the prophets in condemning and rejecting that Saviour, and because they condemned and rejected Him God has set them to one side. He went out to die, sadly saying to Israel, "Your house is left unto you desolate. For I say unto you, Ye shall not see Me henceforth, till ye shall say, Blessed is He that cometh in the name of the Lord" (Matt. 23:38, 39). And so

because of their awful sin in rejecting their promised Messiah they are scattered everywhere
among the Gentiles today. It may be that I am
addressing sons or daughters of Israel. Let me
assure such that every honest Christian heart
goes out in tender sympathy toward Israel, with
yearning and longing for their salvation. We
realize that Israel having been set to one side,
great blessing has come to the Gentiles, the nations outside to whom we belong, but we desire
that God's ancient people may share these blessings with us.

A Jewish lady once said to me, "If Jesus was
the Messiah, the One predicted by our prophets,
why is it that it is you Gentiles who seem to enjoy the blessings that Jesus brings while we are
bereft of them?" I said, "My dear friend, the
blessed Lord came and spread a table laden with
all good things and said, 'I am not sent but to
the lost sheep of the house of Israel,' and He invited the people of Israel to come and partake of
these good things, but they turned away and did
not come; they rejected the Saviour and the blessings He brought. It was then He threw open wide
the door to the Gentiles and said, 'Come in, and
take of the good things that Israel refused,' and
that is why we have come in; but we still recognize
Israel as God's ancient covenant people and know
from the Word of God that the day is coming

when their eyes will be opened and 'They shall look upon Me whom they have pierced, and they shall mourn for Him, as one mourneth for his only son, and shall be in bitterness for Him, as one that is in bitterness for his firstborn' (Zech. 12:10). Meantime blindness in part has happened to Israel until the fulness of the Gentiles be come in."

We as Christians are to live our lives consistently, carefully, before the Jew, we are to have consideration, we are to remember that judicial blindness has come upon him and are to commend our Christ to Israel by the godly lives that we live. I am afraid that some Jews might well be excused for rejecting Christ Jesus because of the behavior of those who profess to belong to Christ. Shame that it ever should be so.

Perhaps there never was a day when it was more important that real Christians should confirm their love toward Israel than the present one. There seems to be a rising tide of anti-semitism sweeping all over the civilized world. To follow the writings of some, one might think that the Jew is responsible for all our national and political ills. But we know who is responsible. Professing Christian people have turned away from the living God, have spurned His Word, have rejected His Son, have dishonored His Holy Spirit, and so God is giving the Christian nations of the world to feel that it is an evil and a bitter thing to forsake the Lord their God. But Israel we know is blinded, and many of them have turned away from the God of their fathers, and instead of being a blessing to the world they are a curse. However, the great majority of them today are simple, kind, earnest people. How dare we try to blame on them the ills of the nations? We as Christians should show them that our hearts are toward them, and that we desire to have them share with us the blessings which we have found through the One who came from them, Jesus of Nazareth, the rightful King of the Jews.

But the apostle says, "Give no occasion to stumble, neither to the Jews, nor to the Gentiles," the Christless nations all about us. Most of us are Gentiles by birth and at one time we were outside the covenants of promise, we were aliens to the commonwealth of Israel, and today the great part of the Gentile world still remains in its ignorance and darkness and sin although nineteen hundred years have elapsed since the Lord Jesus said, "Go ye into all the world, and preach the gospel to every creature" (Mark 16: 15). There are over a billion persons in this world today who are still without God and without hope. What a tremendous responsibility rests upon us as Christians to give the gospel to the Gentile world. You do not need to go across the sea to do that, you work with them day by day, these Gentiles are all about you. How careful we should be to give no occasion to stumble.

I have said to some, "Are you a Christian?" They have answered, "No." "Wouldn't you like to be?" I have asked. "Well, I have sometimes thought so, but I have seen so many hypocrites among people professing to be Christians that I have not much interest." That is, of course, a very foolish excuse to make. It is as if I were to offer a man a ten-dollar bill and he said, "Thank you, but I have seen so many counterfeit bills I don't like to touch it." It would be a very foolish way of reasoning. I do not excuse any one for reasoning like that, for no one will talk that way in the day of judgment. When the Lord says, "Why didn't you trust Me?" no one will dare to look up and say, "I would have, but I saw so many hypocrites among those professing to be Christians." But on the other hand you and I are to be careful that there be no possibility of people getting a wrong conception of Christianity because our lives are not what they should be.

"Give none offence, neither to the Jews, nor to the Gentiles, nor to the Church of God." What is the Church of God? This is a third company. There was a time when the Church of God had no existence. You remember when our Lord

Jesus was on earth after Peter made his confession, He said, "Upon this rock I *will* build My Church; and the gates of hell shall not prevail against it" (Matt. 16:18). There was no Church of God existing on the earth in the four Gospels, but when you come to the book of the Acts after the descent of the Holy Spirit on the day of Pentecost, you find a new company. The apostle Paul when speaking of what he was in his unconverted days says, "I persecuted the Church of God and wasted it." And speaking to the Ephesian elders he says, "Feed the flock of God, over which the Holy Ghost hath made you overseers," and he calls it, "The Church of God, which He hath purchased with His own blood" (Acts 20:28). Writing to Timothy long years afterward, he tells him how he ought to behave himself in the house of God and adds, "Which is the Church of the living God, the pillar and ground of the truth" (1 Tim. 3:15). What is the Church of God? In the first place, it is not a building in which we meet. When we speak of a church in that sense, we use the word colloquially. The Church is the company of people who have been redeemed to God by the precious blood of His Son. At one time some of these people were Jews, in the beginning the great majority of them were Jews, and then God began to work in power among the Gentiles and the two together constituted the Church of God, as it is written in Ephesians 3: 6, "That the Gentiles should be fellowheirs, and of the same Body, and partakers of His promise in Christ by the gospel." It was the Jew first and then the Gentile, and now all who believe form this wonderful company called the Church of God. Let me ever remember as I walk down the street that I am a member of the Church of God; as I meet with fellow-Christians I am a member of the Church of God; in my home life, in my business life, I am a member of the Church of God. I cannot get out of the Church, so I always have to behave as in Church. Some people have one manner of behavior in what they call a church building and another outside. Parents will say to their children, "You must be good in church." Let me say to every Christian, You and I must always "be good," for we are always in Church! We are members of the Church of God, and we are to behave ourselves accordingly. "Giving none offence, neither to the Jews, nor to the Gentiles, nor to the Church of God."

Now see how the apostle says, as it were, "I am not asking you to do something that I do not ask myself to do." He was not one to say, "You do as I say and not as I do." "Even as I please all men in all things." Of course he uses the word "please" in the sense of seeking to profit all

men. You cannot please them in the sense of
doing that which every man wants you to do. If
you did, you would not please God, but we are
to behave ourselves properly toward others.
"Even as I please all men in all things, not seeking mine own profit, but the profit of many, that
they may be saved." Why is it so important
that I should behave myself aright as a Christian? Because others who are not saved are
watching me, and if I am not careful my behavior
will perhaps be such that they will never be saved.
They will say, "No; I have no use for God, for
Christianity. I have no use for the Bible, for I
have been watching that man who professes to
love God, to love Christ, and to honor the Bible,
and I do not see anything in his life to commend
either God or Christ or the Bible." We want to
behave ourselves so that people looking at us will
see Christ.

"That they may be saved." Well, then, there
are some people not saved. "If our gospel be hid,
it is hid to them that are lost: in whom the god
of this world hath blinded the minds of them
which believe not, lest the light of the glorious
gospel of Christ, who is the image of God, should
shine unto them" (2 Cor. 4: 3, 4). Scripture
divides all mankind into two classes, the lost and
the saved. Who are lost? Those who reject the
gospel, those who live on in their sins and never

come to Christ. Who are saved? Those who put their trust in Jesus, those who believe the gospel, those who come to Christ. My friend, are you lost or are you saved? Notice, it is, *"are* lost," not merely in danger of being lost, but you are lost now if you have not trusted Christ. If you are lost, you may be saved, and you may be saved now.

THE VEILED WOMAN

✔ ✔ ✔

"Be ye followers of me, even as I also am of Christ. Now I praise you, brethren, that ye remember me in all things, and keep the ordinances, as I delivered them to you. But I would have you know, that the head of every man is Christ; and the head of the woman is the man; and the head of Christ is God. Every man praying or prophesying, having his head covered, dishonoreth his head. But every woman that prayeth or prophesieth with her head uncovered dishonoreth her head: for that is even all one as if she were shaven. For if the woman be not covered, let her also be shorn: but if it be a shame for a woman to be shorn or shaven, let her be covered. For a man indeed ought not to cover his head, forasmuch as he is the image and glory of God: but the woman is the glory of the man. For the man is not of the woman; but the woman of the man. Neither was the man created for the woman; but the woman for the man. For this cause ought the woman to have power on her head because of the angels. Nevertheless neither is the man without the woman, neither the woman without the man, in the Lord. For as the woman is of the man, even so is the man also by the woman; but all things of God. Judge in yourselves: is it comely that a woman pray unto God uncovered? Doth not even nature itself teach you, that, if a man have long hair, it is a shame unto him? But if a woman have long hair, it is a glory to her: for her hair is given her for a covering. But if any man seem to be contentious, we have no such custom, neither the churches of God" (1 Cor. 11:1-16).

IN our study of this epistle we have noticed that in the first six chapters the apostle brings before the Corinthian church certain matters that require correction and instruction. We can be very thankful that God providentially permitted so many things to come up in the early Church in order that they might be corrected by apostolic authority during that first century of the Christian era, because similar things come up continually in the churches of God down through the years. The remarkable fact is that there are no circumstances that can arise, no sins that may cause trouble and distress, no irregularities that may appear, that are not already met and provided for right here in the epistles of the New Testament. Because these things were rife in the beginning of the Church's history they were met by the Holy Spirit through inspired man, and all we need to do today is to walk in obedience to the Word.

In those first six chapters the apostle deals with such questions as divisions among Christians, schisms of various kinds, immorality getting into the Church of God, Christians going to law one with another, and other things that disturb the peace of the Church.

Beginning with chapter seven and going right on to the end of the epistle, Paul takes up certain things concerning which the Church wrote for in-

struction and help. He says in the opening verse
of chapter 7, "Now concerning the things whereof
ye wrote unto me," and he deals first with the
question of marriage and divorce, the relationship
of a Christian wife to a heathen husband or a
Christian husband to a heathen wife. And then
in chapters 8 and 9 he takes up the question of
meats offered to idols and the Christian's relationship to idol temples. He carries that on over
into chapter 10 and shows how carefully the
Christian ought to walk apart from everything
that savors of idolatry.

And now in chapter 11 he touches on another
problem that was disturbing the early Church.
In order to properly understand this portion we
need to try to visualize conditions existing in
those distant days. Corinth was a very loose, a
very dissolute city. I question if any of the great
cities in which the apostle preached the gospel
were worse in character in this respect than the
city of Corinth. We are rapidly getting into the
same condition, for we are living in a day when
everything like purity and chastity is looked upon
as a joke, and people are utterly cynical and indifferent in regard to personal morality. The literature of our day reeks with filth and impurity,
pictures are vile and lewd, theaters and picture-
shows, they tell me, are characterized by the same
thing. Low ideas of morals and behavior

are prevalent. Corinth was a city in which this could be seen at the very worst.

In that city looseness of every kind had to be faced by the early Church, and the apostle was desirous that Christian women should not permit anything in their behavior that would allow the least cloud upon their purity. Loose women in those days went bareheaded, and were found in the streets unblushingly seeking those who might be companions with them in their sin and wickedness. Women who sought to live in chastity and purity were very particular never to appear in public unveiled. The unveiled woman was the careless woman, the immoral woman; the veiled woman was the careful wife or mother who was concerned about her character and her reputation. It would seem that after Christianity came to Corinth and converted women rejoiced in a liberty they had never known in the old pagan days, that some of them were inclined to be rather careless and indifferent as to the customs of the day and were saying perhaps, "We are all one in Christ; Paul himself has taught us that in the new creation there is neither male nor female, and so there is no reason now why Christian women should be subject to any of the conventionalities of the day. We can go unveiled and bareheaded in public places, and we need not be concerned about it." The Corinthians wrote to

Paul to get his judgment in this matter and this is his answer, "Be ye followers of me, even as I also am of Christ." In other words, I am about to give you instruction, instruction which I have a right to give as a divinely appointed apostle of the Lord Jesus Christ. I seek in all things to be subject to Christ. When He speaks, I endeavor to obey. Now, in what I am going to put before you I trust you will have the same spirit, that you will seek to follow me in this, to be led by me as I seek to be led by the Lord Jesus Christ. In all matters in which you have been obedient to the instructions formerly given, I praise you— "I praise you, brethren, that ye remember me in all things, and keep the ordinances, as I delivered them to you." He was the one who under God had founded the Church at Corinth. He had given instruction ere leaving them as to how things should be carried on, and though now he had to touch on a rather delicate subject and one which some among them might resent, he first of all gave them credit for all their past obedience to the instruction they had received.

When he says, "And keep the ordinances, as I delivered them to you," he is not simply referring to the two Christian ordinances, baptism and the Lord's Supper, though these would certainly be included. It is unthinkable that any subject Christian should ever set to one side these ordinances of the Christian Church, but the word here has a much wider meaning than that. It refers to the instruction given to them regarding a great many things which have to do with the happy fellowship of saints. A little while ago these people had been idolaters, led by Satan, captive at his will; now they were redeemed and seeking to walk together in Christian fellowship. There must be subjection to the revealed will of God in order to have happy fellowship in the Church.

He now takes up this question of woman's place in nature and in the Church, and I wish you would bear in mind that he is not speaking, as he does elsewhere, of woman's place in the new creation. In the new creation, as already intimated, there are no distinctions. "There is neither Jew nor Greek, there is neither bond nor free, there is neither male nor female: for ye are all one in Christ Jesus" (Gal. 3:28). We are all one in Christ. We were all sinners alike, we have all been redeemed alike, we are all indwelt by the Holy Ghost alike, we have all been baptized into one Body alike, and so all these distinctions vanish and we think of one another as members of Christ. But this does not alter the fact that we still have our place in nature and must maintain that place. The Christian is not to be careless as to his responsibilities. You will see how important this is if I illustrate in this way: According to the Word of God I am a heavenly citizen. Suppose I say, "Inasmuch as I am a heavenly citizen, I have no responsibilities to any country here on earth," I will soon have to reckon with the income tax collector and other authorities. I will soon find out that though I may pride myself on being a citizen of heaven only and may say that I have no responsibilities here, the governors of this world are not satisfied to have it so and I shall have to learn by experience that I have responsibilities, I have earthly relationships that must be maintained. Just so, although there is neither male nor female in the new creation, yet we have our places to fill in nature and in the Church.

"I would have you know, that the head of every man is Christ; and the head of the woman is the man; and the head of Christ is God." Somebody may say, "But is not Christ the head of every woman?" Yes; in the new creation Christ is the Head, and men and women are members of His Body, of His flesh, and of His bones; but this verse emphasizes the fact that it is not that of which he now speaks. In creation the Head of every man is Christ. When God made man He said, "Let Us make man in Our image," and He had Christ in view, and when the first man came into the world, he came as the type of Him which was to come. And so the Head of every man is Christ, and man is to be subject to Christ and to represent Christ. But God did not leave man alone in the world; He said, "Let Us make him an helpmeet," and so He created woman and said to the woman, "Thy desire shall be to thy husband, and he shall rule over thee" (Gen. 3: 16). He gave Eve to Adam, and she saw in Adam her head, and that relationship still exists. The head of woman is the man. I suspect there are some women in our modern day who would resent that, they would like to make the head of the man the woman. They resent the thought that God has given to woman anything that looks like a subject or inferior place. Let us put aside any thought of inferiority. The point is that it is the responsibility of the husband to care for and to protect the wife—"Giving honor unto the wife, as unto the weaker vessel" (1 Pet. 3: 7). The woman, when she agrees to take a man's name, tacitly consents to what we have here. Some extremely modern women do refuse to take their husbands' names. They say, "We will not subject ourselves in any way, as we would in taking a man's name." I would say to you, young women, if you have any thought of getting married, do not marry a man until you are willing to accept him as your head and take his name. Otherwise it is far better that you should remain single where you can run things to suit yourself!

"The head of the woman is the man; and the head of Christ is God." Why does he bring Christ in here? I take it that some one might say, "But I refuse to take that place of subjection," and he would say, "Remember, the Lord Jesus took that place. He humbled Himself, but it is His glory to be in that place." When the Son of God became Man, He took the place of subjection which He will keep for all eternity—"The Head of Christ is God."

And then he says, "Every man praying or prophesying, having his head covered, dishonoreth his head. But every woman that prayeth or prophesieth with her head uncovered dishonoreth her head: for that is even all one as if she were shaven." Notice how he meets their difficulty. If a man should stand up in public to pray or to preach (the word "prophesieth" really means "preach"), wearing a covering on his head, he would be dishonoring his Head. Not that which is above his neck, but dishonoring his Head which is Christ. If I stood in this pulpit preaching with my hat on, every one of you would rightfully say, "Has he no respect for the Master whom he professes to serve?" I come into the presence of God and Christ and of the angels who are learning the wisdom of God in the Church, and I remove my hat. For the same reason when a woman comes into the Church, she keeps her hat on. "Every woman that prayeth or prophesieth with her head uncovered dishonoreth her head." Who is her head? The man. She shows by uncovering her head that she wants to be like the man; she dishonors her head when she says, "I am not going to take any subject place, I have as much right to have my hat off in a public meeting as a man." It does not say that she dishonors the Lord Jesus Christ. She may be quite unconscious of dishonoring any one, but I am giving what the Word of God says.

Concerning this and other matters it has well been said, "Some things are commanded because they are right, other things are right because they are commanded." "Thou shalt not steal." The commandment did not make it wrong to steal, it was always wrong to steal. "But every woman that prayeth or prophesieth with her head uncovered dishonoreth her head: for that is even all one as if she were shaven. For if the woman be not covered, let her also be shorn: but if it be a shame for a woman to be shorn or shaven, let her be covered." This is right because it is commanded. God has spoken and it is very often in little things like this that we test our state, whether there is self-will working or whether one is ready to be subject to the Word of God.

In that pagan city it would have been a great

shame and disgrace for a woman to have appeared in public with her head uncovered; it would have marked her out as an immoral person. Of course we must recognize that customs change, but nevertheless the principle of this chapter abides. God is calling Christian women to modesty of deportment, that in this way they may be distinguished from worldly women. Here he says, "If the woman be not covered" (the word is really "veiled"), if she does not have a veil covering her hair, let her come out and be just like a man. Let her go to the barber shop and have her beautiful locks all shorn, as many do today. I do not understand why women want to be so manlike. I think a womanly woman is one of the sweetest and most beautiful creatures God ever made. I like a womanly woman and a manly man, but I wonder if any one really admires a manly woman or a womanly man! Let each one hold to his proper place in creation, but if not willing to cover her head, let the woman come out and be shorn and shaven.

"For a man indeed ought not to cover his head, forasmuch as he is the image and glory of God." God had said, "Let Us make man in Our image." "But the woman is the glory of the man." She is of so much finer character than the man, she is so superior to the man in many ways that he feels ashamed to see her getting out of her place and lowering herself by trying to take the place of a man. I wonder sometimes whether women have any idea how even worldly men express their disgust in the days in which we live at the manlike behavior of women in public places. I have been on railroad trains, in hotels or restaurants, and when women have, for instance, taken out a cigarette and begun to smoke, I have heard even unsaved men say, "What are we coming to? I am glad I did not have a mother like that." Even unsaved men hate to see women aping men, and Christian women should be absolutely above reproach.

"For the man is not of the woman; but the woman of the man." The woman was taken from man. An old writer says, "When God created man, He made him of the dust of the ground; when He created woman, He took her from the man. He did not take her from his head in order that she might lord it over him; He did not take her from his feet that he might trample upon her, but He took her from his side, close to his heart, in order that she might be his companion and that he might love and care for her." And so we read, "Neither was the man created for the woman; but the woman for the man."

Passing over the tenth verse for a moment and continuing with the eleventh, we read, "Nevertheless neither is the man without the woman, neither the woman without the man, in the Lord. For as the woman is of the man—through creation—even so is the man also by the woman—through birth—but all things of God." So every one has his place to fill in creation and none can take the place of the other.

What about that tenth verse which comes in parenthetically? "For this cause ought the woman to have power on her head because of the angels." This is admittedly a somewhat difficult verse. In the margin of our Bibles we have, "power—in sign that she is under the power or authority of her husband." I think that marginal note was probably put in by some worthy brother in years gone by who may have had a little difficulty in maintaining his position as head of the house! I question that this is what it means. You see, if a woman in a city like Corinth appeared in a public place with uncovered head, it would at once expose her to insult. Therefore, when going shopping or visiting her friends or going to the Christian services, she put the veil, the covering, over her head and walked down the street unmolested. Her covering was her power. I spent the first six years of my Christian experience as an officer in the Salvation Army. In those days I often had occasion to see how that beautiful little blue bonnet was the power of the Salvation Army lassie. I remember going into a saloon on the Barbary

Coast in San Francisco seeking the lost. Two of our Salvation Army lassies appeared, and I noticed that everybody treated them respectfully and nicely excepting one man, a half-drunken sailor. When the Salvation Army girl approached him with her paper, he turned toward her and made a movement as though he would have kissed her, and in a moment as she drew back five of those ungodly men sprang to their feet, knocked him down, thrashed him within an inch of his life, and then threw him out into the gutter for the police. Her bonnet was her power on her head. There were lots of other girls there, God help them, that nobody would have fought for or protected. There they were with their brazen faces and uncovered heads, but this little lassie's power was her bonnet, and so the apostle is saying, "Women, you are not belittling yourselves, you are not degrading yourselves when you show proper respect by appearing in public places with your heads covered. You are simply availing yourself of that which is your protection against insult."

But what does the expression, "Because of the angels" mean? It is a little difficult to know, after nineteen centuries, just what was in the mind of the apostle. Did he mean, as many think, that whenever the Christian company are gathered together, God's holy angels in heaven are looking down with delight upon the scene, and that they note everything that savors of subjection and obedience to the Word of God, note it with approval, but also observe with disapproval everything that savors of self-will and insubjection? We are told that angels are learning the wisdom of God in us, that is, in the Church, and so the apostle may be saying, "Let the angel hosts see in Christian women a reverence, a modesty, and a respect for holy things which is not found in the women of the world." If that is the meaning, it is very beautiful. We read of one class of those holy angels called the seraphim. Every one had six wings, "with twain he covered his face, with twain he covered his feet, and with twain he did fly." Angels cover their faces in the presence of God and the angels looking down see the covered women sitting in reverence and modesty in the presence of God, and approve. That may be the meaning.

William Thomson in his volume, "The Land and the Book," points out that ever since the days of the apostle John the word "angel" has been used for a minister in the Church, and in some eastern churches the ministers are still called the angels of the churches. In those oriental lands even until very recent times the women and men were segregated as they gathered together that there might be nothing to disturb the equanimity of the men. But the "angel" stood on a platform and saw both groups, and Dr. Thomson points out that practically none of these angels had ever looked upon the uncovered face of a woman except his mother or sister or some other near relative, and he says that no one who has not seen for himself conditions under which they work can understand why the apostle should tell Christian women that they should keep their faces veiled because of the angels or ministers. He would be so disconcerted by looking into the unveiled faces of so many women that he might get his mind off from his message! This is at least most suggestive.

"Judge in yourselves: is it comely that a woman pray unto God uncovered?" Should she not take that reverent attitude? It is perfectly right for me to pray with my head uncovered, but a woman is to cover her head as a sign of reverent subjection.

And now he goes back to nature and says, "Doth not even nature itself teach you, that, if a man have long hair, it is a shame unto him? but if a woman have long hair, it is a glory to her: for her hair is given her for a covering." Somebody says, "That settles the question. Her hair is her covering." But the apostle says that if she is not veiled she is to let her hair be shorn. She has that natural covering which distinguishes her from man and over that she puts a veil. Why? Because her hair is her glory. Is not that most striking? In the presence of God she covers her chief beauty in order that no mind may be turned from Christ to her beautiful hair. It is precious to think of Mary of Bethany and of the poor woman in Luke 7 who washed the feet of Jesus and wiped them with their hair. They cast their glory at His feet.

In closing he says, "If any man seem to be contentious, we have no such custom, neither the churches of God"—if people are going to make a fuss about a matter of this kind, all I have to say is we have no such custom. If women will persist in being disorderly in this way, you cannot discipline them, you cannot put them out of the Church. I have laid down God's Word, now let women settle it themselves as to how far they will subject themselves to the Word of the living God.

What is the real importance of this? It is the test of whether our wills are subject to God or whether we are going to be subject to the fashions and order of the day in which we live. The Christian is one who has forsaken the world for Christ's sake, has turned his back on the fashion of this world that passeth away in order that he may subject himself to Another, even the Lord from heaven, and I do beg of you, my brother and sister, remember the word, "Happy is he that condemneth not himself in that thing which he alloweth." You settle it with God as to just how far a passage like this, having to do with customs of long ago, still has authority over your conscience at the present time, but do not go beyond conscience. Seek to be obedient in all things to the Word of the living God, for this is the path of blessing.

LECTURE XXIV.

THE LORD'S SUPPER

✓ ✓ ✓

"Now in this that I declare unto you I praise you not, that ye come together not for the better, but for the worse. For first of all, when ye come together in the church, I hear that there be divisions among you; and I partly believe it. For there must be also heresies among you, that they which are approved may be made manifest among you. When ye come together therefore into one place, this is not to eat the Lord's supper. For in eating every one taketh before other his own supper: and one is hungry, and another is drunken. What? have ye not houses to eat and to drink in? or despise ye the Church of God, and shame them that have not? What shall I say to you? shall I praise you in this? I praise you not. For I have received of the Lord that which also I delivered unto you, That the Lord Jesus the same night in which He was betrayed took bread: and when He had given thanks, He brake it, and said, Take eat: this is My body, which is broken for you: this do in remembrance of Me. After the same manner also He took the cup, when He had supped, saying, This cup is the new testament in My blood: this do ye, as oft as ye drink it, in remembrance of Me. For as often as ye eat this bread, and drink this cup, ye do show the Lord's death till He come" (1 Cor. 11: 17-26).

W E have here perhaps the fullest instruction concerning the correct observance of the Lord's Supper that is given us in Scripture. It is very evident that it was intended to occupy a very large place in the hearts and minds of Christians during the dispensation in which our blessed Lord is absent in body, sitting on the right hand of the Majesty in the heavens. It was intended to call Him very vividly to mind in order that His people might be so occupied with Him that, as they went forth afterwards in service, Christ Himself might be the joy of their hearts. Apparently at a very early day Christians began to misunderstand the Lord's Supper.

It is rather a sad commentary upon our fallen human nature that everything God has given us has been abused by man. No physical appetites that He has given have not been abused, and there are very few privileges we have that have not often been misused. Under law, God gave Israel the Sabbath, and you would think that men would have recognized in that a part of His gracious provision for the comfort of His creatures when He said, "Six days shalt thou labor, and do all thy work, but the seventh day is the sabbath of the Lord thy God" (Ex. 20: 9, 10). But the Sabbath became a loathing to many people because they connected with it all kinds of laws and prohibitions which God Himself had not put upon it, so that our Lord Jesus had to reprove the men of His day by saying, "The Sabbath was made for man, and not man for the Sabbath" (Mark 2: 27). And so it is with other observances in Old Testament times.

The same is true in connection with the two ordinances of the Christian Church, the Lord's Supper and baptism. They were designed to continue in the Church until the end of the present age, until the coming of the Lord Jesus Christ and our gathering together unto Him. But people either go to the extreme of making these ordinances saving sacraments or are inclined to become very careless about them. The fact is that neither baptism nor the Lord's Supper has anything to do with the salvation of our souls, except that they picture the way in which we are saved —through the death and the resurrection of our Lord Jesus Christ. And yet they are of great importance because they help to draw our hearts out to Him and to give us a more vivid realization of our identification with Him who loved us and gave Himself for us.

In the early Church the Lord's Supper was observed very frequently; for a time at least it was observed every day. In the early chapters of Acts it is set forth that they daily participated in the breaking of bread. Afterwards it was observed on the first day of the week, as Acts 20:

7 would seem to show. I am sure that the oftener we gather together "to show the Lord's death until He come" the greater blessing comes to us and the greater glory to the Lord Jesus Christ, and yet in the early Church they fell into ways in which this ordinance was abused. The apostle, for instance, writing here says he cannot praise them for the way they attempted to celebrate the Lord's Supper—"I praise you not, that ye come together not for the better, but for the worse." It is possible then even to assemble to celebrate the Lord's Supper and go away not benefited but rather harmed. How was it that they were celebrating it for the worse rather than for the better? In the first place there was a spirit of faction working among them. Instead of recognizing that the Lord's Supper speaks of the unity of the whole Church of God, and that all alike participate in that one loaf and cup which set forth the body and blood of our Lord Jesus Christ, the Corinthians were grouping together, in one place, it is true, but under various heads. Some said, as it were, "I am of Paul, the teacher; I am of Apollos, the preacher; I am of Cephas, the exhorter," and some said, "We do not recognize these gifts at all, we are only of Christ." It is just as bad to make Christ's name the head of a party as any other name. Christ is the Head of all believers and not merely of some little group.

"When ye come together in the church, I hear that there be divisions among you; and I partly believe it. For there must be also heresies among you, that they which are approved (of your-selves) may be made manifest among you." You are making a great deal of leaders instead of be-ing taken up with Jesus Christ.

Then too they were linking the "Agape," the love-feast of which Jude speaks, with the Lord's Supper. Many of these early Christians were slaves and could not get away from their duties very often. When they came together, they evi-dently put in just as many hours as they could, and so brought their food with them and between gatherings they would spread it out and partake together. They fell into the habit of linking the Lord's Supper with this fellowship. Some had a great deal to partake of while others had nothing; some drank even to inebriation, and some were left without sufficient for their needs. "When ye come together therefore into one place, this is not to eat the Lord's Supper. For in eating every one taketh before other his own supper: and one is hungry, and another is drunken. What? Have ye not houses to eat and to drink in? Or despise ye the Church of God, and shame them that have not?" The rich spread feasts while the poor were left without anything, and so he says, "It is far better to do your eating at home." He is not insisting that it is wrong for Christians to come together for love-feasts, for Jude speaks of these, but if it is a question of separating believer from believer, it is far better to eat at home. "What shall I say to you?" he asks; "Shall I praise you in this? I praise you not."

Having reproved them for their misbehavior at the Table, he lays down clearly the revelation that the risen Christ gave him from Heaven concerning the proper observance of this service. First, "For I have received of the Lord that which also I delivered unto you." Paul never knew the Lord here on earth, he was not with the twelve in the upper room when Jesus instituted this ordinance; therefore, he must have received this as a direct revelation from Heaven. That is very significant, for there must be something extremely precious to our risen Saviour about the frequent observance of the Lord's Supper if He, the glorified One, gave to His apostle a special declaration from the glory regarding it. And this is what He told him: "That the Lord Jesus the same night in which He was betrayed took bread." Why does the apostle slip in the expression, "In which He was betrayed," if not for us to realize that the Lord's Supper was meant to appeal to the hearts of His people and so to remind them that in that very night when our blessed Saviour was to know to the fullest the untrustworthiness, the wickedness, the treachery, the perfidy of the human heart, He gave this feast in order that His people might have before them the continual expression of His loving heart in giving Himself for them.

There is something very tender here. "The Lord Jesus the same night in which He was betrayed took bread." Judas evidently was not present when He did this. There is a question as to that, but if you follow carefully through the accounts in the different Gospels, I think you will see that Judas was present at the Passover Feast, but when that was concluded, the Saviour said, "That thou doest, do quickly...and he went immediately out: and it was night" (John 13:27, 30). Jesus had said before, "The hand of him that betrayeth Me is with Me on the table" (Luke 22:21). But Judas went out, and in his absence the Saviour gave this memorial feast to His own. That is very suggestive, for it is only for those who have been redeemed by His precious blood that the Lord's Supper is given. It is not for the unsaved, it is not for those who are hoping to be saved; it is for those who are in the joy of accomplished redemption, who know Christ as Saviour. To them the Lord spake when He took that bread and gave thanks and said, "Take, eat: this is My body, which is broken for you: this do in remembrance of Me."

Some tell us that the Lord meant that the bread and the wine are changed into the actual body, blood, soul, and divinity of Christ when we give thanks to God for it. Others say this is not true, but that when you receive the bread in some special sense you are actually receiving the body of Christ. I do not think it necessary to go into these various views, for the Lord sat at that table in His complete human body and did not divide that among the disciples. When He took the loaf and said, "This is My body," His own hands held that loaf, so it seems to me the simple and clear meaning is that it in the bread on the Lord's table we have set forth in picture the precious, holy body of our Lord Jesus Christ. But it certainly is true that as we receive that bread with honest sincere hearts, with minds occupied with Christ, we do receive our blessed Lord in faith in a sense that is not true at other times. Thus far we are willing to go with the sacramentalists. It is a memorial, and it is one that makes Christ very real to us and gives a very definite sense of His presence.

A member of a great church in Christendom said to me at one time, "We believe in the real presence of the Saviour in the sacrament, and you believe in His real absence." "Oh, no;" I said; "you are mistaken. We simply do not believe that the bread and the wine are actually changed into the body, blood, soul, and divinity of Christ, but we do believe in the real presence in Spirit of our blessed Lord, for He has said, 'Where two or three are gathered together in My name, there am I in the midst of them'" (Matt. 18: 20). And there is no time when Christ's presence is so definitely realized and so distinctly felt as when remembering Him in the breaking of bread. He said, "Take, eat: this is My body, which is broken for you: this do in remembrance of Me." The Lord's Supper is a continual reminder of the vicarious character of His death, and that is one reason why our blessed Lord is so desirous that it should be celebrated frequently.

Then we read, "After the same manner also He took the cup, when He had supped, saying, This cup is the new testament in My blood: this do ye, as oft as ye drink it, in remembrance of Me. For as often as ye eat this bread and drink this cup, ye do show the Lord's death, till He come." On every table where there stands a glass of wine (I do not speak now of whether it be fermented or unfermented), the fruit of the vine, partaken of by the people of God, it is a standing testimony to the fact that redemption is alone through His precious atoning blood. If people deny the vicarious character of the death of our Lord Jesus Christ, I cannot understand how with consistency they can participate in the celebration of the

Lord's Supper for, "As often as ye eat this bread and drink this cup, ye do proclaim (the word translated 'show,' is elsewhere in the New Testament translated 'preach') the Lord's death till He come." Wherever Christians eat this bread and drink this cup, participating in the Lord's Supper, they are preaching a sermon. By their very actions they are declaring that His death was not merely that of a martyr for righteousness' sake, but that it was death as a sacrifice, that He died for sinners, that He shed His blood for sinners.

A dear Japanese who attended some of our meetings in Sacramento, California, was troubled about his soul, but it seemed impossible to bring him to Christ because of his love for money. He would say, "If I accept this Jesus as my Saviour, I do not see how I can make money."

So we told him he would have to make the choice of being rich on earth and poor in eternity, or poor on earth and rich in eternity. When I use the pronoun "we," I refer to a Japanese evangelist who was associated with me at the time, and through whom I met this man. A year went by, I returned to the city of Sacramento for meetings, and one night was preaching the gospel on the street corner. In the audience I saw this little Japanese. There was an expression of concern on his face that stirred my heart. At the close of

the meeting he stepped up and shook my hand
and said, "I so glad to see you again."

I said, "And so am I glad to see you. Have you
accepted Christ as your Saviour yet?"

Tears filled his eyes and he said, "No; I fight
against Him. I cannot give up. If I accept Him,
I cannot make money. Do you have some meetings here where you are speaking?"

I said, "Yes," and told him where the meetings
were being held.

He said, "Do you have a meeting on Sunday
where you eat the bread and drink the wine showing how Jesus died?"

I said, "Yes, next Sunday morning."

"I come," he said.

So on the Sunday morning we had gathered together to participate in the Lord's Supper, and as
the meeting commenced this Japanese came in
and sat close up in the front. I was praying that
God might speak to him, and as the meeting went
on it was evident that he was greatly perturbed.
Finally the people of God partook of the bread
and the fruit of the vine, and this heathen Japanese sat and looked on. Just as the elements
were replaced on the table, he rose and said, "I
like to pray."

I thought, "My! I wish I had told him that he
would not be expected to take part in the meeting!"

But he prayed like this: "O God, I all broke up. For one whole year I fight You. I fight You hard. Your Spirit break me all to pieces. O God, today I see Your people eating the bread, drinking the wine, tell how Jesus died for sinners like me. O God, You love me so You give Your Son to die for me. I cannot fight You any more. I give up, I take Him as my Saviour."

It did not spoil our meeting at all to have him take part with such a prayer. We realized that this simple ordinance had preached to him for, "As often as ye eat this bread, and drink this cup, ye do *preach* the Lord's death till He come." At the close of the meeting we gathered about him to rejoice with him, and then he turned to me and said, "Jesus say before He go away, when you believe Him, you bury in water, show old life gone, new life begin. I like bury."

"You want to be baptized?" I asked. "I will see you during the week and perhaps we can do it next Sunday."

Referring to the Japanese evangelist, he said, "A year ago he tell me Jesus Christ coming back again, so?"

"Yes," I said; "that is true."

"He coming soon?"

"He may."

"He not come before next Sunday?"

"Well, I couldn't say, He might come before then."

"Then I no like to wait till next Sunday, I like show I no fight any more, I like be buried today."

I said, "Forgive me for trying to put it off; we will go down to the river this afternoon."

And so in the afternoon he came dressed in his best with the Japanese mayor, as we called the richest man in the Japanese settlement, and forty other Japanese merchants behind him. We preached the Word and he gave his testimony, and then he was buried in the waters of baptism.

The Lord's Supper, if given the place our Saviour intended it to have, will constantly preach to the world, and will say more than any words of ours can say: "As often as ye eat this bread, and drink this cup, ye do *preach* the Lord's death till He come."

You may have known the Lord Jesus Christ for years, but I wonder whether this ordinance is precious to you. I am afraid to some it is just a legal thing, a feeling that one ought to come and take the Lord's Supper because He has commanded it. Let me suggest that it is not so much a command as a request. When our Saviour says, "This do in remembrance of Me," He does not mean, "You must do this," but rather, "I would like to have you do this." It is as though a loved one were dying and before slipping away should call the children around the bed and handing each one of them a photograph would say, "Here are pictures of myself; I am going to leave you, you won't see me again for a little while, but I would like each of you to take one of these pictures. I wish you would cherish it and from time to time take it out and look at it, and as you do, remember me." Would it be a task to do that in response to the request of a loving mother or a precious father or possibly a darling child? Surely not. If you loved that one, you would be delighted again and again to take down that picture and as you looked at it, you would say, "There is the one who loved me and is now gone from me, but I am so glad in this way I can call my dear one afresh to mind." That is the place the Lord's Supper has in the Church of God. There is nothing legal about it, you do not have to participate in the Lord's Supper if you do not want to. You can go to Heaven by trusting the Saviour even if you have never once partaken of the cup that speaks of His suffering and death, but if your heart is filled with love for Him, you will be glad from time to time to gather with His people to remember Him.

If you are unsaved, you may have thought of the Lord's Supper as a means whereby you might obtain salvation. Perhaps you have come to the Communion Table and hoped that thereby you might obtain the evidence that your sins were ᶠorgiven. My dear friend, the message of the Lord's Supper is this, "Christ died for our sins according to the Scriptures, and was buried, and rose again" (1 Cor. 15: 3). What you need is not an ordinance, for the sacrament cannot save you, but you need the blessed Saviour Himself; you need to trust the One whose death is pictured in the Lord's Supper, the Saviour who gave Himself for you.

LECTURE XXV.

THE IMPORTANCE OF SELF-JUDGMENT

✐ ✐ ✐

"Wherefore whosoever shall eat this bread, and drink this cup of the Lord, unworthily, shall be guilty of the body and blood of the Lord. But let a man examine himself, and so let him eat of that bread, and drink of that cup. For he that eateth and drinketh unworthily, eateth and drinketh damnation to himself, not discerning the Lord's body. For this cause many are weak and sickly among you, and many sleep. For if we would judge ourselves, we should not be judged. But when we are judged, we are chastened of the Lord, that we should not be condemned with the world. Wherefore, my brethren, when ye come together to eat, tarry one for another. And if any man hunger, let him eat at home; that ye come not together unto condemnation. And the rest will I set in order when I come" (1 Cor. 11: 27-34).

✐ ✐ ✐

WE have in the two Christian ordinances, baptism and the Lord's supper, two witnesses to the death of our Lord Jesus Christ, His vicarious atoning death, which our Lord has set in His Church to be observed until the end of the age, until He shall return. In these ordinances we have constant testimony to the

356

death that our Saviour died on Calvary. Baptism
is the initiatory ordinance of the Christian faith;
the Lord's Supper is to be observed frequently
throughout the believer's life until he shall see
his Saviour face to face.

We come now to consider the portion beginning
with verse twenty-seven which deals with the
state and condition of believers as they approach
the Table of the Lord. "Wherefore whosoever
shall eat this bread, and drink this cup of the
Lord, unworthily, shall be guilty of the body and
blood of the Lord." Very solemn words these.
They should surely put a check upon the carelessness and the levity of our hearts. How often
some of us have been guilty of approaching the
Table of the Lord in a very careless spirit, and
perhaps with considerable levity, forgetting that
we have here something which in the eyes of God
is most sacred, most holy.

What does it mean to eat the bread and to drink
the cup unworthily? A misapprehension of this
term, "unworthily," has kept some conscientious
people from ever approaching the Table. They
reason like this, "I never can be sure that I am
worthy. I know my Saviour is worthy, that all
holiness, all purity, all goodness are His, but I
am so conscious of the impurities that surge up
from my own evil heart, I am so conscious of my
frequent failure in thought, word, and deed, that

if it is a question of worthiness I dare not come to the Table of the Lord, I dare not receive those sacred elements, for I am very far from being worthy." Let me say to you, my conscientious friend, that the word here is not "unworthy," but is rather "unworthily," referring not to the person, but to the state of mind in which one comes to the Table of the Lord. Of course in ourselves we are altogether unworthy, but we have found acceptance in the worthy One, and in Christ every believer is worthy to approach the Table of the Lord. I remember reading of an aged saint oppressed by a sense of his unworthiness. He bowed weeping as the sacred emblems were going around and refused to touch the bread. When the deacon offered it, he sobbed, "I am too great a sinner to receive that which is so holy;" and the aged Highland minister exclaimed, "Take it, mon, take it; it is for sinners and for none else that Jesus died." Oh, yes; my very acknowledgment of my sinnership is that which gives me the right to come because, "This is a faithful saying, and worthy of all acceptation, that Christ Jesus came into the world to save sinners" (1 Tim. 1:15). If I truly feel my sinfulness, confess it, and put my trust in the Saviour of sinners, then in Him I find my worthiness.

But here it is not an adjective, it is an adverb, "unworthily." It refers, you see, to manner or behavior. What is the meaning? If I come to the Table of the Lord in a light, frivolous, careless way; if, as the bread and the wine are being prayed over, I am thinking of a thousand and one other things, perhaps occupied with the business of the week, or recalling the latest foolish story I have heard; if when the bread and the cup are actually passed to me, I am not thinking of the Saviour of whom they speak, but perfunctorily participating in it as a religious ordinance, I am taking the loaf and the cup unworthily. Or perhaps I come altogether unprepared, I have spent no time with God in the morning thinking of the solemnity of all this, I rush into His presence bringing strange fire, as it were, and I fail to recognize that in the loaf and the cup we have set forth the precious body and blood of the Lord Jesus Christ. To partake in such a spirit is to do so unworthily. "Whosoever shall eat this bread, and drink this cup of the Lord, unworthily, shall be guilty of the body and blood of the Lord." It is as though I crucify Him afresh and put Him to an open shame in forgetting that it was my sins that caused His death upon the cross. I act as though He had never yet died. I fail to realize what these symbols set forth.

Then am I to remain away from the Table? Not if I am a Christian. "Let a man examine himself, and so let him eat of that bread, and drink of that cup." Observe, it does not say, "Let a man examine himself, and so let him refrain from participating," but, "Let a man examine himself, and so let him eat." No matter what he sees in himself of that which is evil and unholy, if he judges himself before God and confesses his own unholiness, he is in a state of soul where he is free to participate in this sacred service. In other words, he is to come into the presence of God with self-judgment. He who does not do this "eateth and drinketh damnation—or judgment— to himself, not discerning the Lord's body." He only exposes himself the more to divine judgment because of his frivolous behavior.

You say, "In what sense does he fail to discern the Lord's body?" Let me illustrate in this way. How frequently we have gone to a funeral service and have seen before us the casket containing all that was mortal of some loved one. What a solemn time it was. What would you think of some light, flippant person coming into such a service and perhaps hardly taking his seat before he leans over to the person next to him and says, "By the way, I heard a most amusing story; let me tell it to you while we wait for the minister to begin." Every respectable person would look upon him with indignation and say, "What is the matter with the foolish man? Does he fail to discern the body of our dear one lying there?" The

bread and wine upon the Table of the Lord set
forth the precious body and blood of the Lord
Jesus Christ and any one coming into such a
scene carelessly, failing to discern the Lord's
body, does not recognize that this is a memorial
of death, this is a remembrance of the One who
died for our sins.

Because these Corinthians had allowed themselves to become very careless in this matter the
apostle says, "For this cause many are weak and
sickly among you, and many sleep." Just what
does he mean? What does the word "sleep"
mean? If you go through the Epistles of Paul
carefully, you will see that it is a term used over
and over again for the death of the believer. It
is not the sleep of the soul, but the sleep of the
body. When the believer dies, the spirit is absent
from the body and present with the Lord. Let me
direct your attention to that lovely word in the
third chapter of the Epistle to the Ephesians
where it says, "For this cause I bow my knees unto
the Father of our Lord Jesus Christ, of whom the
whole family in heaven and on earth is named."
Notice this, "the whole family." By this he
means all of God's children, the entire redeemed
family. And where does he locate the family? Part
of it in Heaven and part on earth. If Saint Paul
were a "soul sleeper," he would have said, "Of
whom the whole family in the grave and on earth

is named." But he did not think of our departed
loved ones in Christ as being in the grave, but in
Heaven. Elsewhere in Scripture we find that
death for the believer is "to depart and be with
Christ, which is far better," and yet the word
"sleep" is used many times, but only in reference
to the body. The tired, weary bodies of believers
are put to sleep to rest until awakened on the
resurrection morning.

It is a blessed thing to sleep in Christ, and yet
there is such a thing as a believer being put to
sleep before his due time. We read, "The ungodly
shall not live out half their days," and it is quite
true that even godly persons may so fail, so fall
into sin, that God may not permit them to live on
to a green old age, but may take them Home in
youth or in middle life. I would not say that
when a young believer dies it is always an act of
discipline, for many a young saint has been taken
away from the evil to come, in grace rather than
in judgment. Some ripen earlier than others,
some of us develop so slowly it will take fifty or
sixty or seventy years to bring us to spiritual
maturity, but there are others like Borden of
Yale who ripen so young that the Lord can say,
"I am going to pluck that fruit and take it Home
to Heaven, it is ready early." On the other hand,
very frequently early death is an evidence of the
Lord's discipline. That is what Paul is saying to

the Corinthians, "You have been dishonoring me
at the Table of the Lord, approaching it in a light
frivolous manner; you have been given to levity
and have misused this sacred ordinance and
mingled it with a feast for yourselves. Therefore, many of you are weak, many of you are
sickly, and many of you sleep." Sickness is one
way by which the Lord often chastens His people.
Chastening is not necessarily punishment, but it
is educational, and the Lord uses sickness in order
to bring us to realize our littleness, our insuffi-
ciency, and the importance of living only for
eternity. Many a young or middle-aged Christian
has gone on perhaps for years without much recognition of the Lord's authority over his life, and
then sickness has come, and for long weary weeks
or months and sometimes years that dear one has
been laid aside. At first very restlessly he has
asked, "O God, why do I have to suffer? Why
cannot I go out to enjoy things with others?"
But little by little there comes a change, and by-
and-by there is a chastened spirit, and the sick
one says, "Lord, perhaps Thou hast lessons to
teach me which I would not learn while in health
and strength; make me a ready pupil in Thy
school," and God uses the chastening to lead that
believer into deeper fellowship with Himself. It
is a very serious thing to be under the hand of
God in chastening. I am afraid that some of us

are more or less under it almost all our days because we are so slow to learn our lessons, so self-
willed; it takes us so long to get to the place
where we judge ourselves in the presence of God
so that His hand may be lifted.

"If we would judge ourselves, we should not be
judged." This is a call to self-judgment. But
how am I to judge myself? By bringing my inmost thoughts, my ways, my outward behavior
into the light of the Word of God and asking
myself, "Are these thoughts of mine, is this behavior of mine, in accordance with what is here
written?" And if I find that there is something
in which I am continuing, certain ambitions I am
cherishing that are contrary to the Word, if I find
that this Word has something to say to me personally about my thoughts and ways, then I am
to turn to God and confess my failure, acknowledge my sin, and seek by His grace to walk in
obedience to His Word. And as I thus judge myself I come out from under the place of discipline.
"For if we would judge ourselves, we should not
be judged."

In regard to this matter of self-judgment, God's
Word should always be the standard of judgment.
He says something in His Word and I say, "Oh,
yes; I see it there on the page of the Bible, but
certainly it has no application to me." Yet it is
God's direct Word to my soul, and I am putting

away a good conscience, and so I need not expect
to hear Him speak to me again until I am ready
to listen to Him in this matter. Why should He
reveal other things to me when I refuse to bow
to Him in this? When you read the Bible, do you
read it to become acquainted with it as literature,
to become familiar with its history, its philosophy, to derive help from its comforting passages,
or do you read it in order that you may obey it,
make it the Man of your Counsel?

Let me give you a word of personal testimony.
For the first six years of my Christian life I was
largely dependent upon what I called the Spirit's
guidance. I knew very little of the guidance of
the Word. When perplexed, I would say, "I will
ask the Lord what His will is," and as I felt
impressed I would act. But I found as I read my
Bible that I was often going contrary to the written Word. I shall never forget the night I knelt
before God, and opened my Bible to a passage of
Scripture on the subject of baptism, which I had
been avoiding for years. I would say, "I am going to ask the Lord about it," and then I thought
I had an inward feeling that baptism of the Holy
Spirit was all I needed, and every time I read a
scripture and saw baptism before me I dodged it.
I had a lot of dodging to do, for there were a
great many scriptures that had to do with that
subject, but finally before the open Word I said,

"Blessed God, by Thy grace from today on I will never try to dodge one thing that is written in Thy Word for Thy people in this age. If Thou wilt make it clear to me, by Thy grace I will walk in obedience to it," and from that time I had blessing I had never experienced before. Two weeks after that I went down to the sea-side and was buried with Him in baptism, and a week later I sat at the Table of the Lord. I had said, "All you need is to feed mentally upon the body and blood of Christ, you do not need the outward symbols." One by one many things came before me that I had tried to make myself believe were all right, but I found they were contrary to His Word. I have sought conscientiously now for many years to yield obedience when God speaks. I do not always understand why He tells me to do certain things, but it is not necessary for me to understand, the thing for me is to obey, to do what God has asked me to do, and it is as we obey the Word that we are kept clean. "Christ loved the Church, and gave Himself for it; that He might sanctify and cleanse it with the washing of water by the Word" (Eph. 5: 25, 26). And so, as we judge ourselves, as we obey the Word and confess our failures, we come out from under the judgment of the Lord.

"But when we are judged, we are chastened of the Lord, that we should not be condemned with the world." When we are judged, when we become the objects of divine discipline, when God has to deal with us because we will not judge ourselves, it is in order that we may not be condemned with the world. The unsaved man is going to be dealt with in the day of judgment, the child of God is judged by the Father in this life. "Whom the Lord loveth He chasteneth, and scourgeth every son whom He receiveth" (Heb. 12:6). Every bit of pleasure and enjoyment that the worldling is going to know he has in this life. Sometimes people say, "I do not understand it, I am a Christian, and yet it seems to me I have nothing but trouble. I look at the people of the world and they seem to take things so easily." You do not need to be surprised at that, the worldling gets all his heaven right here.

The Christian gets all the sorrow, all the trouble, all the tears he will ever have right here. When he is chastened of the Lord, and comes under the rod and is beaten for his naughtiness, when God has to deal with him here, that is in order that he "should not be condemned with the world." And when he gets to Heaven there will be no more punishment. Yonder, "God shall wipe away all tears from their eyes;" and they will be "forever with the Lord." But until we get Home, let us remember we are here to glorify our Lord. That is the only thing worth living for, there is nothing else that matters, just to live for Jesus, to glorify Him. We have only a little while to do it and I do not want any thought of ease or pleasure or having a good time in this world to keep me from being one whom God can use until called to Himself.

The apostle closes this portion by saying, "Wherefore, my brethren, when ye come together to eat, tarry one for another." That is very sweet, for the Lord's Supper is a matter of fellowship, that is why we observe it together, that is why we read, "Where two or three are gathered together in My name, there am I in the midst of them" (Matt. 18:20). And so we tarry and together show the Lord's death until He come. This is not something to gratify appetite. "If any man hunger, let him eat at home." Just a morsel of bread, just a sip of wine will do. It is only a reminder. We are to come together, not to condemnation but in a serious manner, so truly occupied with Christ that we will have the Lord's approval.

We come now to the last words of the chapter. I like to think of them as not merely the words of the Apostle Paul to the Corinthians but as the words of our blessed Master to the whole Church. "And the rest will I set in order when I come." There is so much that we can never regulate, so much that will never be right down here, so many things that are out of gear in our individual lives, in our families, and in the Church of God. We may try to set them in order, but we readily blunder. He says, "Walk in obedience to My Word, and the rest will I set in order when I come. I will be back soon, and what a day it will be!"

I have searched this old Book for a great many years and have never found in it one scripture that would intimate that I must put one moment between this present hour and the coming of the Lord Jesus Christ. He may come today, but I rejoice to know that all who have put their trust in Him are ready to meet Him when He returns.

SPIRITUAL MANIFESTATIONS

✐ ✐ ✐

"Now concerning spiritual gifts, brethren, I would not have you ignorant. Ye know that ye were Gentiles, carried away unto these dumb idols, even as ye were led. Wherefore I give you to understand, that no man speaking by the Spirit of God calleth Jesus accursed: and that no man can say that Jesus is the Lord, but by the Holy Ghost. Now there are diversities of gifts, but the same Spirit. And there are differences of administrations, but the same Lord. And there are diversities of operations, but it is the same God which worketh all in all. But the manifestation of the Spirit is given to every man to profit withal. For to one is given by the Spirit the word of wisdom; to another the word of knowledge by the same Spirit; to another faith by the same Spirit; to another the gifts of healing by the same Spirit; to another the working of miracles; to another discerning of spirits; to another divers kinds of tongues; to another the interpretation of tongues: but all these worketh that one and the selfsame Spirit, dividing to every man severally as He will" (1 Cor. 12: 1-11).

✐ ✐ ✐

WITH this chapter we come to the beginning of a new division of the epistle. From verse one of chapter twelve to the end of chapter fourteen the subject is the gifts of the Spirit, and the exercise of those gifts in the

Church, or the assembly of God. When the apostle gives instruction as to behavior in the Church he means behavior in the assembly, and that takes in all who are redeemed, grouped into local assemblies.

In the churches of God there are spiritual gifts given for the blessing of all. In the Epistle to the Ephesians we read, "When He ascended up on high, He led captivity captive, and gave gifts unto men" (Eph. 4: 8). The Lord desires that His gospel should be preached, that His Word should be expounded, that His people should be builded up in their most holy faith, and to this end He has imparted certain spiritual gifts. He has not given the same gifts to everybody, but to all He has given some gift for the blessing of the whole company.

"Now concerning spiritual gifts, brethren, I would not have you ignorant." You will notice that the word "gifts" is in italics, and yet it appears farther down in verse four, so we are perhaps justified in using that word. If it were proper to speak of "spirituals" in English, that would seem to be what he wrote in the Greek. The meaning is, concerning spiritual manifestations; there are different ways in which the Spirit of God is manifested, and we should not be ignorant of these. They are called "gifts" because they are given freely by the ascended Christ for the edification of the Church and to assist in the proclamation of the gospel.

These Corinthians in their unconverted days knew nothing of this gospel. "Ye were Gentiles, carried away unto these dumb idols, even as ye were led." "Carried away" suggests satanic power, and there is satanic power behind all idolatry. "The things the Gentiles sacrifice, they sacrifice to demons, and not to God" (chap. 10: 20). There is a terrible demon power working in every idolatrous system, and nothing can deliver from this power but the gospel of the grace of God. Our mission is to "Go into all the world and preach the gospel to every creature." We do not go necessarily to antagonize people, we do not go to find fault with their religion, but we do go to preach Christ and Him crucified, and as the gospel is preached it delivers people from the satanic power that is working in these false religious systems. There is something that absolutely distinguishes them all from Christianity. They have no place for Jesus Christ, they all unite in calling Him, "Anathema," accursed.

"Wherefore I give you to understand, that no man speaking by the Spirit of God calleth Jesus accursed: and that no man can say that Jesus is the Lord, but by the Holy Ghost." Thus the apostle marks the clear-cut dividing line between Christianity and every system of man's devices.

Christianity exalts Jesus Christ as Lord, these other systems deny His Lordship and rather think of Him as accursed. Even such a system as Mohammedanism recognizes Jesus Christ to a certain extent as a prophet of God, but sees Him as the accursed one, and so with every pagan system and so also with Judaism: it has counted Jesus Christ as an accursed one. Therefore the necessity of deliverance from those systems if people would know the truth. "No man speaking by the Spirit of God calleth Jesus accursed: and no man can say that Jesus is the Lord, but by the Holy Ghost." It is by the Holy Spirit that we recognize His Lordship. I wonder whether you have ever taken the trouble to go through this Epistle to the Corinthians and count the number of times the apostle uses the title of "Lord" as applied to our blessed Saviour. This is the Epistle of the Lordship of Christ, and we are called upon to ever recognize His Lordship, that is, His absolute authority over our hearts and lives. When He speaks, we have only to obey. It is not ours to question, it is not ours to reason, it is not ours to ask why, it is ours to do what we are commanded to do, for we are His servants and He is our Lord.

We here read of the entire Trinity in connection with the giving and using of gifts. In verse four we have the Holy Spirit, in verse five, the

Lord Jesus Christ, and in verse six, God the Father. We read in verse four, "Now there are diversities of gifts, but the same Spirit." The one Holy Spirit manifests Himself through the Church of God in different ways. We do not all have the same gift, we are not all constituted alike even from the human and intellectual standpoint, and when it comes to spiritual things we do not have the same ministry committed to us. A great many people in our day would be saved from the wildest fanaticism if they realized this. Efforts are made to recognize some one or more of these gifts, and everyone is urged to seek them, and told that if one does not possess them, he does not have the Holy Spirit dwelling in him at all. "Now there are diversities of gifts, but the same Spirit." We shall see presently what they are, but the one Spirit operates in each case.

Second, "And there are differences of administrations, but the same Lord." The gift and the manifestation are all of the Spirit of God within the believer, and when it comes to using those gifts all must be in subjection to the Lordship of Christ. If, for instance, God has given me some particular gift, I am not to use that gift whenever and as I think fit, but only in subjection to the Lord Jesus Christ Himself. At a funeral service some time ago I was put in a rather peculiar position. I was called upon to officiate at the

burial of the mother of one of our State Senators
in California. The mother had been a very devoted Christian woman, but I did not know
whether her son was a Christian or not. There
were present a great many of his friends, perhaps
seventy-five or more men from the legislature,
and naturally I was anxious to use that opportunity to the best of my ability in subjection to
God, not only to seek to comfort those who were
bereaved, but to present clearly and definitely that
precious gospel message which had been the joy
of that mother's heart who had gone Home to be
with the Lord, for I was not sure that these poli-
ticians had heard the gospel for a long time. I
was told that this dear lady who had passed away
had a number of friends given to the use of a
peculiar gift which was designated as "speaking
in tongues," though certainly not that which the
Bible speaks of as the gift of tongues. They had
a habit of going off into a semi-trance condition
and uttering weird sounds. Somebody said,
"Now just as you stand up to preach, these
women will immediately begin with this weird
gift of theirs." So I said to the undertaker,
"There are four people back there by the door.
I wish you would keep an eye on them. If you see
their jaws begin to work in a peculiar way (I had
heard that for a few minutes before they began
to make this noise, their jaws would work very

peculiarly), you might suggest that they go outside and not remain for the funeral service." So I began to speak and, sure enough, in a minute or two I saw the jaws begin to work, but the undertaker was on the job and immediately suggested to them that they all leave. In a moment they straightened up, but said with indignation, "This is a gift of God and we are free to use it where we will." But the undertaker said, "Not here in my undertaking parlor," and so they were quiet. One might have the most marked gift of God, but that does not mean that he is at liberty to use it wherever he will. "The spirits of the prophets are subject to the prophets" (1 Cor. 14: 32), and if any are gifted by God, they are to hold that gift in subjection to the Lord Jesus Christ and not make spiritual nuisances of themselves. Our blessed Lord's authority must be recognized in the use of gifts.

Then we read, "There are diversities of operations, but it is the same God which worketh all in all." There are different ways by which the Word of God is given out, but it is the same God, and here of course it is God the Father "that worketh all in all." He may have given to some of you very modest gifts. Your voice may never be heard in public, but you are to use your gift in subjection to the Lord Jesus Christ, if only in the quiet place of your home, just as truly as though you were called to preach or to teach in the assembly.

"The manifestation of the Spirit is given to every man to profit withal." That is, it is not given for show, it is not given in order that a man may attract attention to himself, but for the edification of others. This in itself is very important. If God gives me any little gift at all, He gives it not that I may gather people about myself, but He gives it to me for the blessing of others, for the salvation of sinners and for the edification of saints. In John the Baptist we have a lovely picture of what every gifted servant of Christ really ought to be. John says, "I am the voice of one crying in the wilderness, Make straight the way of the Lord" (John 1: 23). And pointing to the Saviour, he says, "He must increase, but I must decrease" (John 3: 30). John found his delight in lifting up Christ, not in directing people's attention to himself. All gifts are given that Christ may be exalted, and in that way others find blessing.

In verse 8 we have these gifts definitely specified. We may not see them all in evidence today, probably there are some of them that we never see. That does not say that they are not in the Church. Some insist that some of these gifts have absolutely disappeared, but I do not know of any scripture that tells us that. I do not know of

any scripture that says that the age of miracles
has passed, and I would not dare to say that the
sign gifts all ended with Paul's imprisonment. I
know from early Church history that this is not
true. As the early servants of God followed up the
work of the apostles, gifts of healing and other
signs were frequently manifested, and if the gift
of tongues had fallen into disuse, marvelous help
was given to the servants of God to preach in
languages of the people that they had never
known before. So I do not think it correct to
take the ground that these gifts have necessarily
disappeared from the Church. I do, however, believe that many of them are not often seen today,
and I think there is good reason for that.

In the beginning the apostle writes to these
very Corinthians, "I have espoused you as a
chaste virgin to Christ." It was a separated
company, the affianced bride of the Lamb, and as
this Church went forth it was the delight of the
blessed risen Lord to lavish upon her gift after
gift. These Corinthians "came behind in no
gift," we are told, but it seems to me we can see
in the book of Acts that as time went on and the
Church began to drift a little, and as dissension
and other things came in that grieved the Lord,
there was more reserve on His part in bestowing
gifts. That, I believe, explains the lack of many
of these gifts today. The Church has gotten so

far away and there is so much strife, division, worldliness, and carnality that He no longer delights to lavish His gifts upon her as He did in the beginning.

Let me illustrate it this way. Here is a young man who is engaged to be married to a beautiful young woman. They have plighted their troth each to the other, and he seals that engagement by giving her a beautiful diamond ring. But now suppose that he has to be away from her for some time before the marriage; we will say he is going over to Manila or to Shanghai to earn enough money to build a home for his bride and send for her. Every little while what a joy it is to him to pick out some beautiful thing, and send this gift back to her, and she in turn is proud and happy to know that she is constantly remembered by him. But suppose that absence instead of making the heart grow fonder on her part should make her careless. She thinks, "Well, he is away from me so long, and he cannot expect me to forego the pleasures of the other young folk," and so she allows other young men to take her out and to pay a great deal of attention to her. By-and-by word comes to him, perhaps from his mother or his sister, "Your fiancée is playing you false; she is not as true to you as she promised to be, you had better come home if you want to win her heart again." Perhaps he can-

not get home, and writes a letter to her which
provokes a rather indignant answer on her part.
He no longer finds the same delight in sending
gifts to her as before, when he believed her to
be true to him. He loved to bestow his gifts upon
her once, but now he becomes more reticent in
his own expressions of love and is more careful
in what he spends on her. This illustration may
be a very inadequate one, but it expresses one
reason why our blessed Lord does not now give
to His Church all the sign gifts that He did when
she was walking with Him in holiness and separation from this godless world. Another is that
since we have a whole Bible, the New Testament
as well as the Old, the sign-gifts are not needed
as at the beginning.

What are those gifts? Let us look at them.
"For to one is given by the Spirit the word of
wisdom; to another the word of knowledge by the
same Spirit." Here are two gifts intimately
linked together. What is the difference between
them? Let me speak of knowledge first. The
blessed Lord gives to some the knowledge of His
Word, insight into the Holy Scriptures, in a remarkable way. I have known men who filled me
with holy envy, for they seemed to know this
Book from Genesis to Revelation. They could
turn unerringly to almost any portion, and I have
prayed, "O Lord, make Thy Word to me what it

is to them; give me the gift of knowledge; open Thy Word to me." You do not get this in some sudden miraculous way, but if you wish it, there is a way by which you can seek for it that is in perfect accordance with the Word of God. In Proverbs 2: 1-5 we read, "My son, if thou wilt receive My words, and hide My commandments with thee; so that thou incline thine ear unto wisdom, and apply thine heart to understanding; yea, if thou criest after knowledge, and liftest up thy voice for understanding; if thou seekest her as silver, and searchest for her as for hid treasures; then shalt thou understand the fear of the Lord, and find the knowledge of God." The gift of knowledge is given to those who earnestly study the Word of God in dependence upon the Holy Spirit. But one might have the gift of knowledge and yet fail greatly because of the lack of ability to use that knowledge aright, and so we have here the gift of wisdom. This is the ability to use what God has revealed to us in a way that helps and blesses others. How many a one knows a little of the Word of God, but uses it in such a way that he drives people from him. Everything he says may be scriptural, but you can say scriptural things in such an unwise way that you upset people instead of helping them. Of course, I know there are some people who are upset, no matter what you do.

Some one came to a preacher and said, "I don't like to hear you preach, because you always rub the fur the wrong way." He answered, "Not at all, sister; just turn around." Very often, no matter how carefully you use the Word of God, you seem to rub people the wrong way, but that is because they are going the wrong way. The gift of wisdom is the ability to use the Word of God wisely, so that you will edify people and build them up instead of driving them from you.

In the next verse we read, "To another faith by the same Spirit." This, of course, is not the faith by which we are saved, otherwise many might say, "I would like to believe in the Lord Jesus, but I have not the gift of faith and so cannot believe." So far as you are concerned, my unsaved friend, "Faith cometh by hearing, and hearing by the Word of God" (Rom. 10: 17), and if you open your heart when the Word of God is preached, He will give you faith. When we read, "All men have not faith," it is because some men turn from the Word of God, but here God gives to His own people the gift of faith and this refers to special faith for a special service.

George Mueller, in that great work of the Bristol Orphan Houses, was, I believe, the outstanding man of faith in the nineteenth century. God called him to open the orphanage to care for homeless boys and girls, but he had no money, and so he said to the Lord, "Thou wilt have to supply the means." And so in the name of the Lord he went forward and spent every cent he had in opening the first building. The Lord sent more money, the children came, and the work went on. In fifty years he received $6,500,000 for that work; and he never asked people for it, he did not beg for money, the Lord sent it in. I have met a number of people who told me that they were going to do the same kind of a work as George Mueller. They started a home, announced that it was a faith work, but there is only one instance that I know of where the whole thing has not ended in failure. Why? Because they were trying to do George Mueller's work without George Mueller's gift of faith. When God calls a person to do a certain work, He gives him the gift of faith. The same thing is true in connection with missionary work. When God raised up Hudson Taylor to start the China Inland Mission, he knew that he was not to ask for money, but to trust the Lord. Every little while I have known some one else to say, "I am going to start a mission and run it on faith like Hudson Taylor." They have gone on for a while, and then we have read of starving missionaries, and the whole thing has gone to pieces. They tried to do Hudson Taylor's work without Hudson Taylor's faith. This faith is a special gift for a special work.

Then we read, "To another the gifts of healing by the same Spirit." The gift of healing is the ability to lay one's hands upon the sick in the name of the Lord Jesus Christ and call them back to life and to health. I do not know whether any today have that gift. I have never seen it exercised. I have gone in with other brethren and prayed for the sick, and we have seen the Lord graciously raise them up, but I have never felt that any of us had the gift of healing. I have heard of this sort of thing, but I must have been unfortunate in my investigations, for whenever I made any, I found the people who were supposed to be miraculously healed were either dead or worse than ever. I thought at one time that one dear man of God had this gift, but I was with him one day when he was praying for a sick woman and she did not get healed, and he turned on her and scolded her soundly because she did not have more faith, and told her she must have some hidden sin in her life. If that brother had had the gift of healing, her faith would not have made any difference. If there are such people in the world today—and there may be—we can thank God for them. Personally, I have never known one.

"To another the working of miracles." God gives to certain servants the ability to work miracles. A miracle is anything that is not ac-

counted for by mere natural law. God has often
wrought wonderful things not to be accounted for
naturally. When in Africa there was a terrible
drought, and the natives had cried and cried to
their false gods, but no relief had come, a missionary felt called upon to bring them all together
and said, "Now I am going to cry to the God of
Heaven to give rain." He stood before them and
offered a prayer, and as he began to pray there
was a cloudless sky above him, but he had not
finished praying before there was a terrific clap
of thunder. The thunder and lightning continued
and in half-an-hour the rain was pouring down.
That was a miracle.

"To another prophecy." In the New Testament sense prophecy is not the foretelling of
future events. Prophecy is preaching in the power
of the Holy Spirit of God that meets the actual
need of the case.

"To another discerning of spirits." That is
the ability to see through people. That is a gift
I fear I do not have. I am too apt to believe every
story that anybody tells me, at least until I have
proven it to be false.

"To another divers kinds of tongues." The
gift of tongues was the ability to preach the gospel in languages that people had never learned.
The preacher, in the power of the Spirit, was able
to stand up and preach in the language of the

people without having a course of schooling to learn the language. I do not know of this gift in the world today.

"To another the interpretation of tongues." That is the ability to interpret a language that one has never learned. God gave those gifts in the beginning.

Then we read in verse 11, "All these worketh that one and the selfsame Spirit, dividing to every man severally as He will." If it is His will for us to have any of these gifts, He will give them to us; otherwise, He will not. Therefore, the folly of any one insisting upon having one or more of these gifts as the definite manifestation of the indwelling of the Spirit of God. In Ephesians we read of certain gifts that will abide to the end, that is, teaching and preaching for the edification of the saints.

BAPTIZED INTO ONE BODY

✓ ✓ ✓

"For as the body is one, and hath many members, and all the members of that one body, being many, are one body: so also is Christ. For by one Spirit are we all baptized into one Body, whether we be Jews or Gentiles, whether we be bond or free; and have been all made to drink into one Spirit. For the body is not one member, but many. If the foot shall say, Because I am not the hand, I am not of the body; is it therefore not of the body? And if the ear shall say, Because I am not the eye, I am not of the body; is it therefore not of the body? If the whole body were an eye, where were the hearing? If the whole were hearing, where were the smelling? But now hath God set the members every one of them in the body, as it hath pleased Him. And if they were all one member, where were the body? But now are they many members, yet one body. And the eye cannot say unto the hand, I have no need of thee: nor again the head to the feet, I have no need of you. Nay, much more those members of the body, which seem to be more feeble, are necessary: and those members of the body, which we think to be less honorable, upon these we bestow more abundant honor; and our uncomely parts have more abundant comeliness. For our comely parts have no need: but God hath tempered the body together, having given more abundant honor to that part which lacked: that there should be no schism in the body; but that the members should have the same care one for another. And whether one member suffer, all the members suffer with it; or one member be honored, all the members rejoice with it" (1 Cor. 12:12-26).

SEVEN things are brought before us in the section, but that which is first emphasized is the unity of the Body of Christ. In verse 12 we have the unity of the human body as a figure of that of the Church. "For as the body is one"—that is, your body and my body. We have a great many different members, each one having special functions, and yet the body is one; it is under one central control, one heart, one circulatory system, one mind dominating and controlling everything. "As the body is one, and hath many members, and all the members of that one body, being many, are one body; so also is *the* Christ." The definite article is found in the original, although we do not see it on the page of our Authorized Version. When the apostle uses the term, "The Christ," it is just the same as if he said, "The Church," for as the context shows, he is thinking of the entire Church as linked with the Lord Jesus Christ, its Head in heaven. As the human body is one, so also is the Christ. "Christ" means "the Anointed," and our Lord Jesus is The Anointed. God anointed Jesus of Nazareth with the Holy Ghost and with power, that is why He is called Christ. But we read of all believers, "He which hath anointed us, is God" (2 Cor. 1:21) so we too have been anointed— "Christed"—by the same Spirit with whom God anointed Jesus. **Therefore**, our risen Head in heaven and the members of the Body everywhere on earth constitute the Christ, the anointed One.

We cannot break the link that joins the believer to his Head in heaven. "For by one Spirit are we all baptized into one Body." Notice, it is not by the possession of divine life that we become members of the Body of Christ. All believers from Abel (and we can go back to Adam, for Adam believed God when the promise came that the Seed of the woman should bruise the seed of Satan, and God declared His satisfaction in that faith by clothing Adam and his wife with coats of skin) down to the end of time have life from Christ. There is no other source of life, and no natural man in any dispensation was ever a child of God. The only way a man can become a child of God is through a second birth, through the reception of Divine life, and this is given through believing the gospel. I know that people sometimes say, "But we must have life first before believing the gospel." We have life before we believe a great many particulars in the gospel, but the Apostle Peter says, "Being born again, not of corruptible seed, but of incorruptible, by the Word of God, which liveth and abideth forever. ...And this is the Word which by the gospel is preached unto you" (1 Peter 1: 23, 25). Therefore, by believing the gospel, whatever form it takes in the various dispensations (for God's message to man has differed in the various ages, but it has always had to do with Christ), men are born again.

However, to be born again is not the same thing as being baptized into the Body of Christ. No one is baptized into the Body of Christ until the Spirit of God dwells in him, and the Spirit comes to dwell only in people who have been born again. There is as much difference between being born by the Spirit and being indwelt by the Spirit as between building a house and moving into it. New birth is by the Word of God and the Spirit of God. The Holy Ghost builds the house, and then He comes to indwell the believer, He comes to take possession. In our dispensation there is no appreciable difference in time between a man's being born again and being baptized into the Body of Christ, but there was a time when there were numbers of people who were born again by the Spirit, but were not indwelt by Him.

On the day of Pentecost the Holy Spirit came to indwell believers and to baptize them into one Body. The Spirit of God now dwells within us and makes all believers one. That is what is meant by, "For by one Spirit are we all baptized into one Body." I like the good old translation of the word "baptized," to which some people object. I take this Greek word to mean "immerse;" "For by one Spirit are we all *immersed* into one Body."

We who were so many individuals before have
now been immersed into one, and in this Body
there is neither Jew nor Greek. Some used to
be Jews, some used to be Gentiles, before they
were born of God and indwelt by His Spirit. Now
they have lost their old standing in the flesh.
When we meet our Hebrew Christian brethren,
we do not think of them as Jews any more, we
think of them as fellow-members of the Body of
Christ, and when they look upon us, their Gentile
brethren, they do not think of us as unclean Gentiles, but as fellow-members of Christ's Body.
That is what took place on the Day of Pentecost,
and has been going on ever since.

In this Body there are neither bond nor free.
It is not a question of master or servant. In the
world outside we meet one another on that basis.
If I am employed by another I am to render
proper service to my master, but when we come
into the Church of God, we come together as
fellow-members of Christ's Body.

A Christian worker once told of her visit to the
beautiful palace of an English Duchess, a very
humble Christian. On the Lord's Day morning
the Duchess took the visitor to a meeting of a
little group of Christian people gathered together around the table of the Lord, and as they
sat there, a man got up and expounded the Word
to them. The Duchess whispered to the lady,

"That is my coachman." The Christian worker was a little surprised that this lady should go and listen to her coachman expound the Word, and said to her later, "Isn't it hard on your pride to have to listen to your coachman open the Scriptures to you?" The Duchess replied, "In the Church of God there is neither Jew nor Greek, bond nor free, we are all one in Christ Jesus." All these earthly distinctions are wiped out in the presence of God.

So the apostle adds, "We have all been made to drink into one Spirit." Just as by water baptism a line of demarcation has been drawn between the Christian and the world, so in this way we are definitely linked with the one Body and enjoy fellowship in Him. Everything that you enjoy of a spiritual character in fellowship with your brethren, you do as in fellowship with the Holy Spirit who now indwells you.

Then we have a passage that is really a warning against discontent as to position in the Body of Christ. In verses 14 to 17 we read, "For the body is not one member, but many. If the foot shall say, Because I am not the hand, I am not of the body; is it therefore not of the body? And if the ear shall say, Because I am not the eye, I am not of the body; is it therefore not of the body? If the whole body were an eye, where were the hearing? If the whole were hearing, where were the smelling?" As men and women not yet glorified we still possess that old carnal nature. Even though set apart to God in Christ with new natures, we so often still find working within us envy and jealousy, and there is the tendency to say, "Well, as I cannot do what so and so does, I will not do anything," and so discontent is engendered. Remember that every member of your physical body has its own special function. Just imagine a foot going on strike, and some morning when you are getting out of bed and you go to put your foot on the floor it should say, "I do not like being a foot, I do not like always being shut up, having a stocking pulled over me and then a shoe, I have just as much right to be in the open as that hand. I do not like it that the hand does all the writing, the painting, and the playing of the piano while i have to be hidden away all the time. I do not like that kind of a thing, and I am not going to function unless you train me to write and to play the piano. I refuse to work any longer as a foot." I have seen folks just like that, folks that won't play unless they can do things that other people do. I heard of a man born without arms who had been so wonderfully trained that he could hold a pen between his toes and write and paint on a board, but he was a freak in a side-show. A normal person does not do that. The foot cannot do

the work of a hand. If the foot is content to do its
own work, what a splendid thing it is, but if it
tries to do the work of a hand, what a failure it is.

If every member of the body does its own work
and does it well, the whole body is benefitted thereby. Just so in the Church or assembly of God.
He does not gift every one in the same way; some
have special public ministry, others have quiet,
private service for the Lord, but all are important. I think I shall never have the least inkling
until I get to Heaven and stand at the judgment-
seat of Christ, how much I have owed to quiet
saints shut away in hidden places who have
bowed down on their knees before God and asked
His blessing upon my ministry during these
forty-three years that I have been preaching the
gospel. I have had the public place, but I am sure
that the greatest amount of the credit for work
done goes to those hidden saints who have thought
enough about me to bear me up in prayer, that
God might keep me from sin and use my testimony for the glory of His name. So let us be
content to labor on in the place God has given us.

"If the ear shall say, Because I am not the
eye, I am not of the body; is it therefore not of
the body?" Fancy the ear going on strike and
saying, "I refuse to hear; if I cannot be the eye,
I am not going to do anything." What a foolish
thing! And yet there are people like that. The

apostle says, and I imagine he smiled as he said it, "If the whole body were an eye, where were the hearing?" Just imagine a body a great big walking eye. Or, "If the whole were hearing, where were the smelling?" If the body were one immense ear, would it not be a peculiar thing? And so each member has its place, and each is to act for God in that place.

In verse 18 the apostle shows that there should be no discontent, that there is no place for natural ambitions. "But now hath God set the members every one of them in the body, as it hath pleased Him." When I think, "I should like to do so much that I cannot," is it not blessed to realize that He has set me right here where I am, that I am in the place where He has put me, and He will give me grace to live for Him here?

"But now are they many members, yet but one body. And the eye cannot say unto the hand, I have no need of thee: nor again the head to the feet, I have no need of you." What a rebuke to that sense of disdain that some of us cherish at times for other members of the Body of Christ. Our Christian fellowship would be ten thousand times more precious if every one of us would settle it with God that by His grace we would never let an unkind criticism go out of our lips against any of His people. I find that the people who are the most sensitive to criticism are the most ready to criticize, those who get all broken up and upset if some one makes the least derogatory remark about them are those who will speak in the most cruel, unkind, and critical way of others.

I speak to you as a preacher, and I fear we are more guilty of this than anybody else. We often think and speak of one another in the most unkind way. Is it not a shame that men who have been set apart by God for the proclamation of His truth, who ought to stand shoulder to shoulder and be very jealous of each other's reputation, should try to climb up on the failures of others? We who try to minister the Word, shall we not set an example to our brethren by covenanting with God that we will always say the thing that is good, the thing that is kind and helpful of our fellow-servants; and if we see faults in them shall we not go to them personally and seek to help them; and when we speak to others of them, tell about the good things? In a restaurant I once saw a sign which read, "If you like our food, tell others; if you don't, tell us." I think that would be a good sign for a church of God. If you do not like things, you come and tell us about it, and let us seek to put things right. We need one another and we ought to be helpers of one another. The tongues of some of us are so vitriolic, we can say such unkind things, and forget that these people are souls whom Jesus loved enough to die

for, so dear to God that He gave His Son for their
redemption.

> "Oh, that when Christians meet and part,
> These words were graved on every heart—
> > They're dear to God!
> However wilful and unwise,
> We'll look on them with loving eyes—
> > They're dear to God!
>
> Oh, wonder!—to the Eternal One,
> Dear as His own beloved Son;
> Dearer to Jesus than His blood,
> Dear as the Spirit's fixed abode—
> > They're dear to God!
>
> "When tempted to give pain for pain,
> How would this thought our words restrain,
> > They're dear to God!
> When truth compels us to contend,
> What love with all our strife should blend!
> > They're dear to God!
>
> When they would shun the pilgrim's lot
> For this vain world, forget them not;
> But win them back with love and prayer,
> They never can be happy there,
> > If dear to God.
>
> "Shall we be there so near, so dear,
> And be estranged and cold whilst here—
> > All dear to God?
> By the same cares and toils opprest,
> We lean upon one faithful Rreast,
> We hasten to the same repose;
> How bear or do enough for those
> > So dear to God!"

Let us remember that "God hath set the members
every one of them in the body, as it hath pleased
Him."

"Nay, much more those members of the body, which seem to be more feeble, are necessary." Sometimes perhaps we discount some one's gift because it does not appeal to us, and yet that very person may be God's messenger to others. Years ago when I was in the Salvation Army we had a girl who was certainly imbued by the Spirit of God, but she had worked in the open air so much that her throat was spoiled. I remember listening to her once as she tried to sing a song, but she could not sing. I felt so sorry for her, and somebody standing next to me said, "Why does she make such a fool of herself by trying to sing?" And on the other side some one said to me, "Oh, it does me so much good every time I hear that girl sing; it comes from her heart and she is doing it for love for Christ." Remember, the people whom you do not appreciate may be God's messengers to other folk. Be careful that you do not do anything to spoil the effect of their testimony.

I went to the dinner-table in a home, and the people said, "We wish you would pray for our sons and daughter. We have tried to bring them to Christ. We do get them to come to meeting with us, but they are getting less and less interested." I said, "I am sorry; we must pray for them." There had just been a change of pastors in that church, and I had come to help the new pastor in some meetings, and as the dinner was passed around I said, "This new pastor of yours seems a fine godly man." The mother said, "I haven't any use for him; he doesn't know how to dress for one thing, and he murders the king's English." The father said, "Yes, we are most disappointed in him." And then the two boys and the girl went for them and said, "We would like to know why you expect us to go to church." After the meal I said to the father, "How do you expect your boys and your girl to be interested in spiritual things when you tear the messenger of Christ to pieces over the dinner-table?" Let us be careful, let us value one another, and remember that we each have our place to fill, and let us seek to fill it to the glory of God.

"And those members of the body, which we think to be less honorable, upon these we bestow more abundant honor; and our uncomely parts have more abundant comeliness." You heard that man testify in the mission, and his grammar was so bad you said, "Oh, I wish he would sit down," but yonder a poor wretch listened and said, "What! Did God save a man like that? Maybe He can save me. I am about as bad as he was when God saved him." He was not a very handsome nor a very brilliant member of the Body, but *you* never could have reached that poor down-and-outer as he did.

"And those members of the body, which we think to be less honorable, upon these we bestow more abundant honor; and our uncomely parts have more abundant comeliness." The Apostle Paul was a very observing person. Here is a woman who has a rather badly-formed ear. Upon that member she bestows more honor. Her beautiful hair is drawn over the ear, and that very uncomely part has become the most beautiful thing about her. People try to cover up the things in themselves that they do not think are pleasing, and try to make them more beautiful. I wish we would learn to cover up the uncomely things in our brethren. You never saw a perfectly beautiful woman yet who tried to cover her face with a dark heavy veil, unless she was about some nefarious business.

"For our comely parts have no need: but God hath tempered the body together, having given more abundant honor to that part which lacked." He has done this in order that there should be no divisions in the body, no strife, "That there should be no schism in the body; but that the members should have the same care one for another." Now honestly, if you had loved that brother or that sister as much as you love yourself, would you have said that thing the other day? Remember, "The members should have the same care one for another."

A brother came to the late Leon Tucker and started telling him quite a little about another preacher. Mr. Tucker asked, "Is it because you love this brother so much you are telling me this?" He turned very red and did not know how to answer him. Test yourself by that. "The members should have the same care one for another."

And then it is a practical thing, "Whether one member suffer, all the members suffer with it." We know how it is in the human body. When you have had a festered finger, did you ever say to yourself, "That affects only my thumb or finger, and I am not going to let the rest of the body bother about it." But the whole body was affected because of it. Let me say something serious and solemn: Your entire local assembly is affected if there is one member that is not living for God in it. The whole Body of Christ is affected if there is one member playing fast and loose with holiness and purity and righteousness, because we are so intimately linked together.

"Or one member be honored, all the members rejoice with it." One member is selected for some position of honor, and all the members are jealous of that one. Is that it? No, if "one member be honored, all the members rejoice with it." If a member suffer, I suffer with him; if a member be honored, I rejoice with him.

LECTURE XXVIII.

CHRIST'S PROVISION FOR HIS CHURCH

✓ ✓ ✓

"Now ye are the Body of Christ, and members in particular. And God hath set some in the church, first apostles, secondarily prophets, thirdly teachers, after that miracles, then gifts of healing, helps, governments, diversities of tongues. Are all apostles? are all prophets? are all teachers? are all workers of miracles? Have all the gifts of healing? do all speak with tongues? do all interpret? But covet earnestly the best gifts: and yet show I unto you a more excellent way. Though I speak with the tongues of men and of angels, and have not charity, I am become as sounding brass, or a tinkling cymbal" (1 Cor. 12:27-13:1).

✓ ✓ ✓

IN this particular portion we have Christ's gracious provision for the edification of His Church in this scene. In summing up, the apostle says, "Ye are the Body of Christ, and members in particular." That is, you Christians are the Body of Christ.

Recently I read a book on a political theme in which the writer said, "It is important for us to remember, as Scripture says, we are all members of one body and therefore should work for the

good of every nation." Scripture is not talking
about nations when it speaks about members of
the Body of Christ, nor does it use the word
"body" as we use that term. We speak of a body
of troops. a body of soldiers, etc., and mean a
company, a collective company, but that is not
what is meant by the term "Body" when it is used
in the New Testament for the Church of the living God, the Body of Christ. The illustration, as
we have seen, is taken from the human body. As
the human body is one but has many members,
so also is the Christ, and every member joined together and linked with the Head is to work for
the good of the whole. And so it is Christians
that the apostle has in view when he says, "Ye
are the Body of Christ," and then he adds, "and
members in particular." Looked at in one sense
we have lost our former identity, we are not just
so many units as once we were, having no special
relationship each to the other, for we are now
united to one another. We who are saved, we
who are indwelt by the Holy Spirit, are thus baptized into one and are members of the Body. But
on the other hand we have our individual responsibility as members. Just as the various
members of my body have their part in the building up of the whole, so every Christian has his
special responsibility for the blessing of the entire Body of Christ.

God has given to the Church special gifts which are for the edification of the rest, and in this we may see Christ's gracious provision for His Church. In Ephesians 4:8 we read, "When He ascended up on high, He led captivity captive, and gave gifts unto men," and (verse 11) we are told what some of these gifts are: "He gave some, apostles; and some, prophets; and some, evangelists; and some, pastors and teachers." Then we are told why He gave them (ver. 12). If we should read it exactly as in our Authorized Version, we would think it was for three purposes. Let me read it emphasizing the punctuation, "For the perfecting of the saints, for the work of the ministry, for the edification of the Body of Christ." From this you would gather that Christ had given these gifts, evangelists, pastors, teachers, etc., for three things: to perfect the saints, to do the work of the ministry, to edify the Body of Christ. But let me point out that these punctuation marks are put in by our English editors, and have no real place in the Greek text. Now let us read it omitting the punctuation marks. "He gave some apostles and some prophets and some evangelists and some pastors and teachers for the perfecting of the saints for the work of the ministry for the edifying of the Body of Christ." He did not give these special gifts to certain ones to do everything for the rest that they might sit back and be perfected and helped and blessed through them, but that they through the ministry of the Word might perfect the saints, in order that the saints might go out and do the work of the ministry and thus edify the Body of Christ. It never was the mind of the Spirit of God to have any drones in the gospel hive.

Now notice, the gifts that men most highly esteem are apparently the least valuable. For instance, we hear a great deal today and have heard for the last twenty or twenty-five years, about the gift of tongues, and some people imagine that this is the most important gift of all. Often people say to me, "Brother, have you the Holy Spirit?"

I say, "Yes, I have. I believe the gospel, and that tells me that upon believing I was 'sealed with the Holy Spirit of promise'" (Eph. 1: 13).

"Well, then," they say, "can you speak in tongues?"

"Well, I speak a little English, and a very, very little Chinese, but I had to study very hard to get those."

"But that is not it," they say; "can you speak in tongues in the power of the Spirit?" and they mean some strange language that I have never learned, and they tell me that is the supreme evidence of the gift of the Holy Spirit.

Instead of that being the greatest of all the gifts, it is apparently the least. for notice the order in which these are given, "And God hath set some in the Church, first apostles." And where do we have their ministry today? Right here in the blessed Word of God. Their voices have long since been silenced, but the witness still goes on and through their written ministry they abide in the Church until the end of time. Linked with them we have the prophets, and they too have long since been silenced in the primary sense. Luke and Mark were prophets, and they gave us their written ministry and went Home to Heaven. And so we are told that the Church of the living God is built upon the foundation of the apostles and prophets.

Then notice in the third place, "teachers." The teacher then is one of the special gifts that God has given to the Church, and—may I say?—if I had my choice of all the gifts there are two that I would find very difficult to choose between. If the Lord were to say to me, as He did to Solomon, "Ask what I shall give thee;" if He should say, "I am going to give you any gift that you want to be used for the blessing of a needy world and for My people." I would have difficulty in choosing between the gift of an evangelist and that of a teacher of the Word. My heart yearns to be able to preach the gospel in a way that will grip dying

men and women and bring them face to face with
the realities of eternity. The gift of an evangelist
is one of the greatest of all, but on the other hand
when I see how the people of God today are bewildered and misled, are carried about by every
wind of doctrine, I realize how much they need
careful, thoughtful Biblical instruction, and my
heart cries out, "O God, help me to feed Thy people; give me the gift of teaching in order that I
may open up Thy Word to Thy people." For after
all, "Man shall not live by bread alone, but by
every word that proceedeth out of the mouth of
God" (Matt. 4: 4). And so I crave the gift of
the teacher. The teacher is the one who comes
to men giving them, not his own thoughts, not
making up beautiful essays which he calls sermons, but he opens up, expounds, the Word of
God. Our Lord Jesus, I think, describes the
teacher in a wonderful way when He says, "Every
scribe which is instructed unto the kingdom of
heaven is like unto a man that is an householder,
which bringeth forth out of his treasure things
new and old" (Matt. 13: 52). The treasure-house
is the Word of God.

I listened to a widely-advertised man the other
day who was said to be one of the outstanding
religious leaders of our day, and for nearly an
hour he was telling ministers how to preach. I
listened carefully, but I did not hear him quote

one verse of Scripture. He quoted from Shakespeare, from George Bernard Shaw, and a number of trashy novels, and he drew his illustrations from ancient and modern literature. Yet he was supposed to be a teacher of preachers. If preachers have to listen to that kind of a teacher it is no wonder they deliver sermons that never could convert one poor sinner.

Scripture says, "The entrance of Thy words giveth light, it giveth understanding unto the simple" (Ps. 119: 130), and the apostle writing to Timothy says, "Preach the Word...For the time will come when they will not endure sound doctrine; but after their own lusts shall they heap to themselves teachers, having itching ears" (2 Tim. 4: 2, 3). The teacher is the man who calls the people of God back to the Book and opens up the Word of God to them. One of our very well-known American pulpit orators stated some time ago that expository preaching is the poorest type of preaching in the world because it leaves so little scope for the imagination. Thank God for any kind of preaching that leaves little scope for man's imagination, for the Word of God says, "And God saw that the wickedness of man was great in the earth, and that every imagination of the thoughts of his heart was only evil continually" (Gen. 6: 5). It ought to be the earnest desire of the real minister of Christ to subject himself to the Word in order that all unholy imaginations might be cast down, and only the solemn serious truth of God brought to bear upon the minds of people. God give us teachers of the Bible!

Then we read, "After that, miracles." Some people may have thought it was, "First of all, miracles." I am not a miracle worker and do not pretend to be. I have gone in and prayed with a great many sick people and some of them have been healed very quickly, but I did not have the gift of healing. To go in and pray for people is one thing; to have the gift of healing is another. If a lame man were here and I could turn to him and say, "In the name of Jesus, rise up and walk," and in a moment he would spring to his feet and become whole, that would be the gift of healing, that would be working a miracle. I have seen some people throw away crutches, but I have heard that they came back for them a week or two later. And so I say of the next gift, the gift of healing, what I say of miracles. The Lord may give these gifts, and if He does, we will thank Him for them, but we do not know of any at the present time.

But in the next one, "helps," is something we can all understand. Here are two terms, "helps, governments," linked together. In these we have pretty much what we find elsewhere in Scripture where we read of the officers of the church, its deacons and elders. A true deacon is a help; he is one who can help in all the temporal and business affairs of the church, and a true elder is one who has spiritual discernment and can govern in the Church of God. What a wonderful thing it is when men are really thus gifted of the Lord as "helps" and "governments!" What a pitiful thing it is when a church is bereft of this kind of gifts! There are too many deacons who are deacons in name only. The word "deacon" means "servant," a ministering servant. There are too many elders who are elders in name only, who are not really guides and helps to the Church of God, but it is a blessed thing when God gives to a church true "helps" and "governments."

Last of all in this list we have "diversities of tongues," as though it is the gift least of all to be accounted of. And why is that? Because anybody can with a little intelligence learn a new tongue, and in most instances it is better that he should do that than to receive it miraculously. One may say in regard to this the same about receiving the truth of God. God could give every one a sudden illumination that we might have an amazing insight into His truth, but He does not choose to give it in that way. He says, "Study to show thyself approved unto God." There are too many Christians today who would like to have everything pre-digested. This is the day of this

kind of thing, and many Christians would like
to have the truth presented in a pre-digested way
so that it would not require any trouble to get it
into their inmost systems. But God wants us to
study His Word, and does not give us His truth
in that easy way.

"Are all apostles?" Admittedly, no. We do
not know of any such today in the full sense. "Are
all prophets?" Again we have to answer, "No."
There may be prophets today, but they are very
few, and as far as I know there are none in the
full sense. "Are all teachers?" Again we have
to answer, "No," and yet there are teachers that
God has thus gifted. If you as a minister are
troubled with the question of empty pews, begin
to dig into the Book and teach the Word, and you
will soon draw the people. I know two young
ladies who after they were graduated from col-
lege, did not know what to do in order to support
themselves. So they came to my old home city,
Oakland, California, and in a little side street
opened up a wee restaurant. It was so small that
only about seven people could sit down at one
time. I went over to sample their cooking, and I
found that the coffee was very different from
what I was used to in most lunch-rooms and so I
went back to my book-room and said to the other
workers, "If you want a good cup of coffee, go
to such and such a place." The next day people

were standing on the outside walk waiting for the seven inside to finish their lunch. Soon the girls had to rent the place next to them. When I was in Oakland the last time, they had a great big restaurant serving hundreds of people. The word had gone out over the city, "You can always get a good cup of coffee and excellent things to eat there." Let the word go out, "You can always get the Word of God in that church, for that minister gives you the truth of God to refresh your soul," and you won't have any problem about empty pews. I heard a minister say to a group of pastors, "There is one thing that is a great help; you can do a great deal with different colored lights. You can get up wonderful effects with colored lights, and people will come from far and wide to see. Then, you can do so much with rhythmic dancing." And then he added, "One of the finest things I have found is moving pictures for the night service."

The Church of God does not exist for the amusement of people. What we need is the Word of God presented in simplicity and power. Get your own mind filled with the truth of God and then give it to others. This minister said to the pastors, "You know, some of you may not approve of these modern methods, but I say you have to take your choice between empty pews or up-to-date methods." Oh, no; we do not have to make any such choice; if you just give people the Book in the power of the Spirit they will come, for they are really ready to listen to the Word of God.

"Are all workers of miracles?" We know of very few indeed, if any. "Have all the gifts of healing?" No; and whether there are any we cannot say. "Do all speak with tongues?" Not in the Bible sense. "Do all interpret?" They do not. But now the apostle says that we are not to be concerned if we do not have all these gifts, "but covet earnestly the best gifts," seek those that are for the edification of the Church of God. Suppose it does not please God to give you any of these, "Yet show I unto you a more excellent way."

There is something more excellent than signs and wonders. What is that? "Though I speak with the tongues of men and of angels, and have not love, I am become as sounding brass, or a tinkling cymbal." This leads us right into the wonderful "Love Chapter," the thirteenth chapter of this epistle. The greatest gift of all is to have the Spirit of God dwelling in you shedding abroad the love of God in your heart so that you manifest the love of Christ.

There used to be a little mission in the lower part of Manhattan in New York. A poor little Irish boy started going there and got a great deal out of it. By-and-by his folks made a little more

money and moved from that section and said,
"Now, Patsy, you must attend one of the more
stylish churches." And so they took him over
and entered him in the Sunday School. The little
fellow put in two Sundays there, and the third
Sunday he was found away down near the Bat-
tery sitting in this little mission Sunday School,
and when he got back home, the folks said, "O,
Pat, why weren't you in the nice Sunday School?"

"I wanted to go back to the other Sunday
School," he said.

"But why did you want to go back to that one?"

He hesitated, and they said, "Come, tell us
why."

"Well," he said, "they love a fellow down there."

That is what took him miles and miles down to
the simple little mission. It is a great testimony
for any church, assembly, mission or Sunday
School when people can say not alone that the
Word of God is preached there, but that "they
love a fellow there."

This divine love is not something that is pump-
ed up out of the natural heart; it is divinely given.
"The love of God is shed abroad in our hearts by
the Holy Spirit which is given unto us" (Rom.
5:5), and that is why men and women need to
be born again. That is why we need to have a
definite dealing with God about the sin question.
That is why we have to come to the place where

we put our heart's trust in the Lord Jesus Christ as our own Saviour. Trusting in Him we are born of God and the Holy Spirit comes to dwell in us, and thus the love of Christ will be manifested in our ways.

LECTURE XXIX.

THE LOVE CHAPTER

1 1 1

"Though I speak with the tongues of men and of angels, and have not charity, I am become as sounding brass, or a tinkling cymbal. And though I have the gift of prophecy, and understand all mysteries, and all knowledge; and though I have all faith, so that I could remove mountains, and have not charity, I am nothing. And though I bestow all my goods to feed the poor, and though I give my body to be burned, and have not charity, it profiteth me nothing. Charity suffereth long, and is kind; charity envieth not; charity vaunteth not itself, is not puffed up, doth not behave itself unseemly, seeketh not her own, is not easily provoked, thinketh no evil; rejoiceth not in iniquity, but rejoiceth in the truth; beareth all things, believeth all things, hopeth all things, endureth all things. Charity never faileth: but whether there be prophecies, they shall fail; whether there be tongues, they shall cease; whether there be knowledge, it shall vanish away. For we know in part, and we prophesy in part. But when that which is perfect is come, then that which is in part shall be done away. When I was a child, I spake as a child, I understood as a child, I thought as a child: but when I became a man, I put away childish things. For now we see through a glass, darkly; but then face to face: now I know in part; but then shall I know even as also I am known. And now abideth faith, hope, charity, these three; but the greatest of these is charity" (1 Cor. chap. 13).

416

WE have noticed that in the twelfth chapter of this epistle we have the gifts which the risen Christ gave to His Church. In chapter fourteen we have the use of the gifts; but in between the two chapters we have the spirit in which they are to be exercised. Someone has said that the thirteenth chapter of First Corinthians is "the divine smithy," alluding to the furnace in the blacksmith's shop, where the tools of chapter twelve are heated red-hot to be properly used in chapter fourteen. Gift without love is a poor thing. One might preach with great clarity and even eloquence, but if there is no love behind it, it would be almost wasting words. The word translated in the A. V. as "charity" is not the thought of the good works, the kindness, that we attach to the word, but the root and source of those good deeds, that which pleases God—love. So here the apostle emphasizes the importance of love, not only in the life of the servant of God, but in the lives of all Christians.

There are three well-known Greek words for "love": *eros, phileō,* and *agapē.* *Eros* you will recognize at once as the name we are familiar with in Greek mythology, as the god of love, the son of Aphrodite. *Eros* is the word ordinarily used in classical Greek for love between the sexes, the love of sweethearts, the love of husband for wife and wife for husband. *Phileō* is a broader word,

generally used for the love of friends. It speaks
of a kindly friendly affection, and is also used for
the love of parents to children and children to
parents, and the love of citizens for the state to
which they belong. Then the other word, *agapē*,
is used for a higher type of love, a love that is
all-absorbing, that completely dominates one's
whole being. This is the word that we have in
this chapter.

It is very significant that in the writing of the
New Testament the Spirit of God seemed to
utterly forbid the use of the word *eros*. It is very
freely used in the writings of the Greek poets
and philosophers, but is never found in the New
Testament. This word representing the love between the sexes had been so abused, so degraded
by the Greeks that God, as it were, stood over His
Book and said to those who were writing, "Do not
put that word in here; it is too capable of being
utterly misunderstood. I do not want that word
in My Book, for so many vile things have been
linked with it." It had become so misused that
it was not even right to think of it as expressing
the true love of a chaste wife and a good husband.
So God did not allow it any place in the New
Testament.

The word, *phileō*, is used in its verbal form in
many places in the New Testament, but always
for friendliness, kindly feeling one toward an-

other, and brotherly love, or fraternal affection.
When it comes to a question of that which is
divine, the Holy Spirit has chosen most carefully,
and He uses this word, *agapē*. "God is *agapē*"—
"God is love"—in this highest, most utterly unselfish sense. It is used in the New Testament for
God's love to us and our love to God, and for the
love we have for anything we put in place of God.
When we are warned against the love of the
world, this word, *agapē*, is used, for men devote
themselves wholly and completely to the things
of the world and to obtaining money, and so make
a god of the world and of money. We can readily
see how beautifully this should bring before us a
love that is absolutely holy, and ought to be complete and supreme in our lives.

The love of this chapter then, this divine love,
is not that which is in the heart of the natural
man; it is not a love that you can pump up out of
your heart if you are not a child of God, because
it is not there. You may have *"phileō."* Take that
poor heathen mother, she loves her child, and she
may even love her husband. That unsaved man
and woman love their country, they love those
that love them in this lower sense, but it is only
when one has been born of God that he loves in
the high sense represented in this chapter. That
is why we read, "Every one that loveth is born
of God." If the word *phileō* had been used there,

you might say that every mother who loves her children, every patriot who loves his country is born of God. But that is not true; this completely unselfish divine love is the portion of only those who are regenerated. This is the word that the Holy Ghost uses when we read, "The love of God is shed abroad in our hearts by the Holy Spirit which is given unto us" (Rom. 5:5). It is He, dwelling in the believer, who sheds abroad this love in our hearts.

We shall divide this chapter into three parts for our purpose. In verses one to three we have the unique value of love. "Though I speak with the tongues of men and of angels, and have not love, I am become as sounding brass, or a tinkling cymbal." Here you see, the warning is against substituting mere talent for love. A man might preach and be so talented that he could stir his audience to deepest emotion, but there might be nothing there for God, nothing that would reach the needy hearts of men. To speak with the eloquence of an angel apart from divine love will accomplish nothing.

"And though I have the gift of prophecy, and understand all mysteries, and all knowledge." You say, "Is it possible to have the gift of prophecy and not have love?" Oh, yes! They said of Saul, and he was not a child of God, "Is Saul also among the prophets?" When associating with prophets, he talked like a prophet; when associating with the world, he talked like a worldling. And then you have the tragic case of Balaam to whom God actually gave the gift of foresight. He was able to look on down through the years and utter marvelous prophecies, yet his heart was exercised by covetous practices; he wanted Balak's money and therefore desired to curse Israel, but the Lord forbade him, and he said, "How shall I curse, whom God hath not cursed?" (Num. 23: 8). Think of this marvelous prophecy coming from a man whose mere intelligence had been illuminated by the Spirit so that he could say, "The people shall dwell alone, and shall not be reckoned among the nations" (Num. 23: 9). Since those words were spoken 3500 years have elapsed and they have proven true ever since. The people, God's earthly people, the covenant people, Israel, have lived alone, and they are not reckoned among the nations. So one may have the gift of prophecy and yet not have love. What an empty thing! Think of Balaam, able to look down through the centuries and utter those prophecies recorded in Numbers 23 and 24. He prayed, "Let me die the death of the righteous," but instead of that he died under the judgment of God because he was never regenerated.

"Though I have all faith, so that I could remove mountains, and have not love I am nothing." Of course he is not speaking of saving faith here, but rather the gift of faith spoken of in chapter twelve. And though it were possible for God to give me faith that would scatter the hills from their places, yet without love I am nothing. How solemn the words of our Lord Jesus, "Ye must be born again," for it is absolutely impossible for any man to produce such love in himself apart from divine grace. The apostle is not speaking of mere sentiment.

A pastor was leaving his church to go to another. He was one of these modern, up-to-date preachers who could say a lot of sweet nothings that would not hurt a flea, and on the other hand would do no one any good. A young man came up to him and said, "Pastor, I am so sorry we are going to lose you. When you came to us three years ago, I was a young man who did not care for God, man or the devil, but since listening to your beautiful sermons I have learned to love them all." That is the kind of sentiment that passes for love in these days. The apostle was speaking of the manifestation of divine life in the soul, a love that is absolutely unselfish.

"Though I bestow all my goods to feed the poor, and though I give my body to be burned, and have not love, it profiteth me nothing." You may say, "But I can't give my goods to feed the poor apart from love; can I?" Oh, yes; I may do all that from a desire to be seen of men. The

Pharisees of old did their charity that way, and
they sounded trumpets before them so people
could see them. "Verily, they have their reward."
There was no love there. It was merely hypocrisy. And then we read, "Though I give my
body to be burned, and have not love, it profiteth
me nothing." I may be a religious zealot, so
wedded to an idea that I am willing to die for it,
and yet there may be no real love behind it all.
Of course it took the love of Christ in the soul
to enable the Christian martyrs to go to the stake
singing for Jesus' sake, it took the love of Christ
to cause those devoted believers to go forth to the
lions, ready to die with a song of love in their
hearts. But it is quite possible to die for an idea,
to yield your body to the stake because of some
great principle, and yet have no real love in the
heart. So we see the uniqueness of love; it stands
alone, and is distinct from mere "charity," as we
call it.

In verses four to seven we have the character
of love. What is this love of which he is speaking?
How may we know it? How may we recognize
it when we see it? As we examine these verses
phrase by phrase, I wish you would think of one
blessed Person. If the apostle Paul had tried to
give us a pen portrait of the Lord Jesus Christ,
he could not have done better than to use the
words that we have here. As you read these

verses you can see the blessed Saviour of men moving about in this world on His mission of love. So true is this that you could substitute the word "Christ" for the word "love," or "charity" here. Let me show you. "Christ suffereth long, and is kind; Christ envieth not; Christ vaunteth not Himself, is not puffed up, doth not behave Himself unseemly, seeketh not His own, is not easily provoked." Was He ever provoked? Oh, yes. About what? About the wickedness, the sin, the hypocrisy of men. When they would have hindered His healing the poor woman in the synagogue because of their pretended regard for the sanctity of the Sabbath, Jesus looked round about upon them and was angry. There is an anger that is divine, but, "Love is not *easily* provoked." "Christ thinketh no evil; rejoiceth not in iniquity, but rejoiceth in the truth; beareth all things, believeth all things, hopeth all things, endureth all things." This is indeed a character sketch of the Lord Jesus Christ. It tells me that it is only as Christ dwells in me that I will manifest these characteristics, and then I can truly say with Paul, "I am crucified with Christ: nevertheless I live; yet not I, but Christ liveth in me: and the life which I now live in the flesh I live by the faith of the Son of God, who loved me, and gave Himself for me" (Gal. 2:20). If I take this as a divine picture of what every man ought to be, if I dare to say that not until this is true of me am I really fit for a place with God in Heaven, I might sink into utter despair if it depended upon me, for I never could measure up to this. There is so much in my heart of self, of evil, of unholiness, but as I receive Christ as my personal Saviour, as I put my trust in Him, the One who died because of man's selfishness, sin, and unholiness, I am born again of the Holy Spirit and the Word of God, and Christ comes to dwell in my heart by faith. Now in the measure in which I yield myself to Him, He lives out His wonderful life through me, and thus I am able to manifest the love that is revealed in this chapter.

"Love suffereth long." It does not become impatient when tried, when wronged, and when it has to face misunderstanding, and when people disapprove. Love moves on just as sweetly and graciously as when people do approve, and "Love suffereth long, and is kind." How much we need to realize that! Ella Wheeler Wilcox has said something that is not altogether true:

> "So many gods, so many creeds,
> So many ways that wind and wind,
> While just the art of being kind
> Is all this poor world needs."

That is a very pretty sentiment, but it is not altogether true. The world needs a great deal more than that; it needs God, it needs Christ. But the world does need people who can be kind. I am afraid many Christians are not always very kind.

I remember hearing of an old Scotch preacher in whose congregation were a number of folks who fancied they had attained a spiritual experience far beyond the majority of the members, a state of perfect holiness wherein all inbred sin had been removed from their very being, and because they were so holy they were extremely critical of other people and harsh in their judgments. The old minister was not much of a theologian, and was not able to meet their arguments in regard to the doctrine, but when he heard them censoring others, he would lean over the pulpit and say, "Remember, if you are not very kind, you are not very holy, because holiness and kindness cannot be separated." "Love is kind." Oh, the kindness of God as seen in the Lord Jesus Christ!

And then, "Love envieth not," or really, "Love is never jealous." Did it ever occur to you that jealousy implies selfishness? Love delights to see another honored and esteemed. Of course there is a holy jealousy. The Lord is a jealous God. He would have us altogether for Himself. But this is a very different thing to a carnal jealousy which makes us unhappy when others are preferred before us. Jesus ever took the lowest place and was content to be despised and rejected.

"Love vaunteth not itself." In plain English, love never brags. Love never exalts itself or its ability; it never tries to draw attention to itself. And love "is not puffed up." There is a scripture that says, "Knowledge puffeth up, but love edifieth," or buildeth up (1 Cor. 8:1). I think I know a great deal more than other people and so become conceited, puffed up over it, but real love does not puff up, it builds up.

"Doth not behave itself unseemly," or literally, "is never boorish." The finest gentleman in the world is the man who knows Christ best. I remember reading a history of the world written by an English writer, completed about the year 1600. In the course of his history he came down to the early years of the Christian era, and he said, "It was in these days that there appeared in Judea that Knightly Gentleman, Jesus Christ," and I was so taken aback, I thought, "I do not know whether I like that." I stopped to analyze it and then I thought, "Could words have been used that more truly described the life of my Lord here on earth?" What is a gentleman? Is it somebody born heir to some vast estate and perhaps having the right to put a title to his name? Not necessarily. A man might be heir to millions but be a perfect boor. A man might be the poorest of the poor and yet be controlled by divine love and so be a perfect gentleman. Have you never noticed the refining influence of the Lord Jesus Christ? Take a man brought out of the gutter and saved by grace, see how the Spirit of God quiets him, changes him, until his whole character becomes different. Love never behaves in a boorish way.

"Love seeketh not her own." The apostle's word to those quarreling women in Philippi was, "Look not every man on his own things, but every man also on the things of others" (Phil. 2:4). When divine love controls the heart, it will be others first instead of self first.

"Love is not easily provoked." We read, "Be ye angry and sin not." A Puritan once said, "I am determined so to be angry as not to sin; therefore to be angry with nothing but sin." Sin may well stir my indignation but, "Love is not easily provoked."

"Love thinketh no evil." How apt we are to make snap judgments of people. One says, "I think everything she does is done ostentatiously." What business have you to be thinking those things? Love credits people with the best possible motives, and therefore because of that, "Love hopeth all things." Love may see something upon which a very bad construction may be put, but it waits a moment and says, "Could I put a better construction upon that? I will not put the wrong

one if I can possibly find a good one. I will hope
for the best. I will never be guilty of marring a
brother's or a sister's reputation because of
something said or done that looks unwise to me
and yet might be innocent." That is love. And
so, "Love endureth all things"—it is willing to
suffer, for that is just the character of love.

In verses eight to thirteen we have the *perma-
nence* or finality of love. Everything else may
disappear but love abides. "Love never faileth."
We read of prophecy, "Whether there be prophecies, they shall fail." Prophecy will be fulfilled
eventually, but love will continue forever.
"Whether there be tongues, they shall cease." We
do not know exactly when they passed away from
the Church, but we have no evidence that there
are men today who have the ability to preach in
languages never learned, and the apostle uses a
very strong word here, "Whether there be
tongues, they shall *cease.*" It is an altogether
different word from the word translated "fail".
He knew that the day would come when the gift
of tongues would no longer be seen, but love
would remain. "Whether there be knowledge, it
shall vanish away." Knowledge, in the sense that
we have it now, only a partial thing, will vanish
away in the light of the coming of our Lord Jesus
and our gathering together unto Him.

"For we know in part, and we prophesy in

part. But when that which is perfect is come, then that which is in part shall be done away." And now he uses a little illustration comparing the present with the days of our childhood, our glorious future with the years of maturity. "When I was a child, I spake as a child, I understood as a child, I thought as a child: but when I became a man, I put away childish things." I wonder whether that is actually true of every one of us. I am afraid some of us are quite childish still. I know full-grown men and women who profess the name of the Lord Jesus Christ, but still have a great many characteristics of children. Let them have their own way and they are perfectly delightful to get along with, but cross them and they pout like little children. The apostle says, "When I became a man, I put away childish things." In other words, I was through with childish ways.

May I make a plea for true Christian manhood and womanhood? Let us put away these little childish things that so often characterize us. One thing that often grieves my own heart is that there are so few Christian people content to do their duty as God shows it to them without human praise. As men and women in Christ we have put away childish things, and we are here to do the right as He shows it to us, and whether men praise or blame, what difference does it make?

But in another sense, this is still the time of our childhood as compared with the glorious maturity that is coming when our Lord shall return and we shall be fully conformed to His blessed image. Some day we will put all these things away and will be just like Him.

"For now we see through a glass, darkly." There were no glass windows in those days. They had a crude kind of glass, but it could not be used for windows. Sometimes they used a very thin horn which had been pressed out, and sometimes almost a transparent crystal was used. That may be what was referred to, but in all likelihood it is the brass mirror. You can see enough in a brass mirror to know whether your hat is on straight, but you cannot see what your complexion is like, and so the apostle says that we are just like folk looking at themselves in a brass mirror. We see nothing as we shall see it by-and-by. "But then face to face: now I know in part"—I know through the revelation that God has given, and thank God for that! How little I would know without that, but there are still many things concerning which He has not yet given me information. How many questions there are that even the Bible does not answer. "But then shall I know even as also I am known." The exact tense, I believe, would be, "Even as also I have been known." I will know others and will know all mysteries in that coming day, even as God knows me now and has known me all down through the years.

"Now abideth faith"—because "faith is the substance of things hoped for, the evidence of things not seen" (Heb. 11:1). "Hope"—because I am living in hope of the coming of the Lord Jesus and our gathering together unto Him. "Love"—for this is the manifestation of the divine life. "These three; but the greatest of these"—even at the present moment here on earth, before I enter eternity—"is love."

May God give us to manifest the love of Christ through yielding ourselves wholly to Him, that He may live out His life in us and then by-and-by when faith has changed to glad fruition, when our most wonderful hopes have all been accomplished, when we stand face to face with our blessed Lord, love will abide throughout all the ages to come, and we shall understand then what we cannot understand now, the love that moved the heart of God and led Him to send His only begotten Son into this dark world that we might live through Him. What a wonderful thing to know Christ. Let us go out and live Him before men!

THE BEST GIFTS

✓ ✓ ✓

"Follow after charity, and desire spiritual gifts, but rather that ye may prophesy. For he that speaketh in an unknown tongue speaketh not unto men, but unto God: for no man understandeth him; howbeit in the spirit he speaketh mysteries. But he that prophesieth speaketh unto men to edification, and exhortation, and comfort. He that speaketh in an unknown tongue edifieth himself; but he that prophesieth edifieth the church. I would that ye all spake with tongues, but rather that ye prophesied: for greater is he that prophesieth than he that speaketh with tongues, except he interpret, that the church may receive edifying. Now, brethren, if I come unto you speaking with tongues, what shall I profit you, except I shall speak to you either by revelation, or by knowledge, or by prophesying, or by doctrine?

"And even things without life giving sound, whether pipe or harp, except they give a distinction in the sounds, how shall it be known what is piped or harped? For if the trumpet give an uncertain sound, who shall prepare himself to the battle? So likewise ye, except ye utter by the tongue words easy to be understood, how shall it be known what is spoken? for ye shall speak into the air. There are, it may be, so many kinds of voices in the world, and none of them is without signification. Therefore if I know not the meaning of the voice, I shall be unto him that speaketh a barbarian, and he that speaketh shall be a barbarian unto me. Even so ye, forasmuch as ye are zealous of spiritual gifts, seek that ye may excel to the edifying of the church. Wherefore let him that speaketh in an unknown tongue pray that he may interpret. For if I pray in an unknown tongue, my spirit prayeth, but my understanding is unfruitful.

433

"What is it then? I will pray with the spirit, and I will pray with the understanding also: I will sing with the spirit, and I will sing with the understanding also. Else when thou shalt bless with the spirit, how shall he that occupieth the room of the unlearned say Amen at thy giving of thanks, seeing he understandeth not what thou sayest? For thou verily givest thanks well, but the other is not edified. I thank my God, I speak with tongues more than ye all: yet in the church I had rather speak five words with my understanding, that by my voice I might teach others also, than ten thousand words in an unknown tongue.

"Brethren, be not children in understanding: howbeit in malice be ye children, but in understanding be men. In the law it is written, With men of other tongues and other lips will I speak unto this people; and yet for all that will they not hear Me, saith the Lord. Wherefore tongues are for a sign, not to them that believe, but to them that believe not: but prophesying serveth not for them that believe not, but for them which believe. If therefore the whole church be come together into one place, and all speak with tongues, and there come in those that are unlearned, or unbelievers, will they not say that ye are mad? But if all prophesy, and there come in one that believeth not, or one unlearned, he is convinced of all, he is judged of all: and thus are the secrets of his heart made manifest; and so falling down on his face he will worship God, and report that God is in you of a truth" (1 Cor. 14: 1-25).

✓ ✓ ✓

HERE we have love in exercise for the edifying of the Body of Christ. We have considered already the many diverse gifts of the Spirit as set forth in chapter 12. He divides to every man severally as He will. In this the

Holy Spirit is sovereign. No one has the right to demand that he be given any certain gift or gifts as an evidence of the Spirit's baptism. What He gives will be for the edification of the Church as a whole, not for the enjoyment or aggrandizement of some individual. While we are not told of any special limit, so far as time is concerned, yet we know both from Scripture and Church History that most of the so-called miraculous gifts passed away shortly after the Bible was completed. They are not needed now as they were at the beginning. Yet, if the Spirit so wills, He might give them today under special circumstances. But we need not be surprised because we do not see them in exercise. They served their purpose, a very useful one, in authenticating the message as divine, when these signs followed the proclamation of the truth. Now with God's complete revelation in our hands, we do not require signs to manifest it as the Word of the Lord. When preached in power, it authenticates itself.

Then in chapter 13 we have love, the manifestation of the divine nature, and this we know is shed abroad in our hearts by the Holy Spirit, who is given unto us. Apart from love the gifts are useless.

Now in chapter 14 we are told, "Follow after love and desire spiritual gifts, but rather that ye may prophesy." As a member of the Body of

Christ I should desire to be a means of blessing to my brethren and sisters in the Lord, and to be used of God in giving the gospel to a lost world. I can only do this right as I am filled with the Spirit and gifted by Him in some special way.

It is therefore quite in keeping with my Christian profession to seek to be at my best for God. Worldly ambition is obnoxious and unholy, but, on the other hand, there is a laudable ambition which I can consistently entertain, and that is to desire spiritual gifts. But I must be sure that I do this in love. Every gift is given for the blessing of the whole assembly, and not in any sense for the glory of the individual possessing that gift.

In the Church of God as a whole and in the assembly of believers gathered together as a worshiping company, there is no place for mere fleshly display. If I am gifted of God in a measure in preaching the gospel, I am not to take advantage of that to exhibit my abilities ostentatiously or to gather people about myself. If I have been gifted of God to sing the fine old gospel songs that people enjoy hearing so much, I am not to use that talent to attract attention to myself or my voice, but I am to use it to give out a message which, winged by melody, will move human hearts that the spoken word might not reach. If I should be gifted of God to teach the Holy Scriptures, I am not to take advantage of that gift in order to exercise people's minds about strange and perplexing problems, which would make them think, perhaps, that I am a more deeply-taught man than most, but I am to make things as plain and simple as possible, in order that the saints may receive edification. This is the standard for using the gifts that God has given. All are to be exercised in love.

The apostle singles out one gift as that which we should earnestly covet, "Desire spiritual gifts, but rather that ye may prophesy." Take the great prophets of the old dispensation: read carefully the entire seventeen prophetic books of the Old Testament, and you will be surprised to find how small a portion of those writings is devoted to foretelling future events. There are, indeed, many most remarkable predictions which have been fulfilled with the utmost particularity down through the centuries. There are many more that are yet to be fulfilled. But, on the other hand, the greater part of the prophetic books is taken up not with future events, but with endeavoring to bring home the truth of God to the hearts and consciences of His people. There is a difference between the teacher and the prophet. The teacher expounds the Scriptures and illuminates the mind and understanding. The prophet brings the truth home to the conscience in order that it may exercise people before God. I might take this letter of Paul to the Corinthians and perhaps through divine help be able to expound it so that my hearers may thoroughly understand just what it is that the Spirit of God is teaching, and yet their consciences might not be exercised in the least degree. Their hearts might not really be lifted unto God, though they were edified intellectually. But if I had the gift of prophecy, I might take exactly the same scripture and, as the Spirit of God enables, I will press it home to heart and conscience, so that those who hear will go away into a secret place, kneel down and search themselves and ask God to enable them to go out to live the truth that they have been learning. That is the highest form of ministry.

This is brought out very clearly in the two verses that follow, where you have what may be called one of the show gifts, the gift of tongues. We read: "He that speaketh in a tongue speaketh not unto men, but unto God: for no man understandeth him; howbeit in the spirit he speaketh mysteries." Suppose I had the ability, divinely given, without going to school to learn it, to speak the Chinese language in at least one of its many dialects, and suppose I should endeavor to exercise the wonderful gift the Spirit of God had given me and I should pour out my heart in public in Chinese. At once you would say, "We cannot understand a word that he is saying." Yet I myself might be quite happy and perfectly self-satisfied to think I was able to use such a remarkable gift. But others would not understand, unless Chinese were present. So you see the gift of speaking in tongues is not for the Christian; it is for the heathen. Let that gift be exercised where that tongue is spoken. Do not get up in a Christian assembly and take the time of God's people giving out something they cannot understand.

"But he that prophesieth speaketh unto men to edification, and exhortation, and comfort." It is this gift upon which the apostle lays so much stress. Notice the three aspects of real spiritual ministry:

First, the man who is divinely gifted to give a message from God speaks unto men for edification. They get something from him that is for their spiritual good. If I am able to open up the Word of God to you in a way that instructs and feeds your soul, then you are edified. It is a great thing to build up God's people.

Then, in the second place, the prophetic message is for exhortation. How you and I need the message of exhortation! We are so apt to slumber in our spiritual lives. That is the very meaning of the word "exhortation," something to awaken, to arouse the one who has gone to sleep or become apathetic. How the Word of God comes home to the conscience in that way, to arouse people! I know some folks do not like that kind of Bible teaching. But the true servant of God will bring things home in a way to exercise the hearts of men to seek after God, and to show them their true state as He Himself sees it.

In the third place, true spiritual ministry is for comfort and encouragement, and how much you and I need comfort! Dr. Joseph Parker, the great London preacher, in addressing a group of young theologues, said, "Young gentlemen, always preach to broken hearts, and you will never lack for an audience." How many broken hearts, and how many bereaved ones there are! Trouble and distress of financial circumstances, all those things that come home so cruelly to the heart— trouble in one's own family! How much God's people need the word of comfort and the word of exhortation. "He that prophesieth speaketh unto men to edification, exhortation, and comfort."

"He that speaketh in a tongue edifieth himself." He enjoys it, but no one else does. You would understand this if I should try to sing a solo. If I get into the woods or out on the mountainside I just let myself out. I just love to sing. I delight in it there. If I were to do that in a crowd I might put someone else out of tune. Well, if I were to sing a solo, I might enjoy it thoroughly,

but you would not, and there would be good reason. So, if one speaks in tongues he edifies himself, but others are not edified. Do not covet a
gift that makes you as selfish as that. "But he
that prophesieth edifieth the Church." So the
apostle says he would not slight the gift of
tongues. If anyone has it, let him use it to the
glory of God; but he wishes "rather that ye prophesied: for greater is he that prophesieth than
he that speaketh with tongues, except he interpret, that the Church may receive edifying."

So we conclude that we should desire spiritual
gifts; and the gifts of the Spirit are not for anyone's individual enjoyment or glory, but for the
edification of the entire Church.

And now let me point out that the word "unknown" before "tongues," as found many times in
this chapter, is in italics, and so does not represent anything in the original text. Strictly speaking, the apostle was not thinking of unknown
tongues, but of definite languages. The miracle
of Pentecost consisted in the eleven apostles being
empowered to preach the gospel in languages
they had never learned, so that all who heard
were able to understand them "in their own
tongue wherein they were born." We know of
nothing like this today.

The next eight verses, as you see, are all very
intimately connected, and in them the apostle re-

sumes the subject which he began in the early
part of the chapter. The Corinthians were very
anxious for what may be called the "showy" gifts
of the Spirit, the gifts that would attract wide-
spread attention, particularly the gift of speaking in tongues. Through this remarkable gift the
gospel was spread in a wonderful way in the
earliest period of the Church of God. It was
nothing like the rhapsody which people give way
to when they utter strange, weird sounds, which
may in truth be called *unknown* tongues, for they
are unknown to heaven or earth. But the tongues
here referred to were definite languages, and one
can see at once why the apostle should rebuke display of such a gift when there were no people
present who could understand the language. The
man himself would get a great thrill in speaking
in a language that was strange and incompre-
hensible to others; but there would be no blessing
to the Church.

In the public assembly of the people of God
everything should be done unto edifying. So the
apostle says: If I myself should come speaking in
tongues, speaking in various languages, "what
shall I profit you, except I shall speak to you
either by revelation, or by knowledge, or by
prophesying, or by doctrine?" We have no record
that he ever had to learn the languages in which
he spoke to the people. He spoke to the Greeks

in their own language, to the Romans in theirs, to the Hebrews he spoke in their tongue, and to the various barbarians in the tongues to which they were accustomed.

Suppose I should come before the Church and speak in those tongues, what would I profit you unless I should give you the interpretation of what I had said, or unless the Spirit of God should enable someone else to interpret it in order that you might understand? "What shall I profit you, except I shall speak to you either by revelation, or by knowledge, or by prophesying, or by doctrine?" If he is able to reveal the language in which he speaks, or if he prophesies to them, or teaches them, which we are to understand by the word "doctrine," then they would be edified. With things that have no life, like the great organ or the piano, if every tone were exactly the same, what edification could there be? No one would understand what was being played. "And even things without life giving sound, whether pipe or harp, except they give a distinction in the sounds, how shall it be known what is piped or harped?" If the trumpet give an uncertain sound, if the trumpeter goes out ahead of the army, but gives forth notes that nobody can understand, the soldiers are unable to respond. "For if the trumpet give an uncertain sound, who shall prepare himself to the battle?" Just in the same way, if a man stands up in a congregation and gives out sounds that have no meaning to the people, there is no edification. Here is a good rule: "So likewise ye, except ye utter by the tongue words easy to be understood, how shall it be known what is spoken? for ye shall speak into the air." In this I think the apostle not only rebukes the vanity of ministers who delight to use the pulpit as a place to display their education and culture, but also the use of language that is far above the heads of the people to whom they are ministering. Charles H. Spurgeon said: "I am afraid that many of my ministerial brethren must imagine that when Scripture tells them to 'Feed My sheep,' it means 'Feed My giraffes,' for they put the food so high that people would have to be giraffes to reach it." Scripture says, "Feed My sheep." Always put the food down where the sheep can get it. It should be the ambition of the preacher of the Word to use language so simple and so plain that everybody can understand. A few months ago a lady brought to me a little boy about ten years of age, and she said, "I want my little grandson to meet you. I hope you won't be offended about what he said. I had been telling him about you and he wanted to hear you. He said to me, 'Why, grandma, he is not a great preacher; I could understand every word he said'." I replied, "Well, my dear madam, I consider that a great compliment." I

hope you will always pray that when I stand up
to minister the Word, I may do it in such a way
that the youngest child, as well as the oldest saint,
may understand every word; because if we do
not, we are just speaking into the air.

The apostle says there are many different
voices in the world, and all of them have some
signification, but if the person listening does not
understand the signification, they go for nothing.
So if I speak in a tongue that others do not understand, I shall be as a barbarian to them and they
shall be barbarians to me. He says, Since you
are so zealous of spiritual gifts, seek that you
may excel to the edifying of the Church. Try to
get from God that which will be the greatest
blessing to the people to whom you minister.
"Wherefore let him that speaketh in a tongue
pray that he may interpret. For if I pray in a
tongue, my spirit prayeth, but my understanding
is unfruitful." I may have within me a great urge
and a great sense of need, and I might express it
in sounds, but my understanding is not praying,
and the apostle repudiates anything like that.
Suppose I am able to pray in Latin, but do not
understand Latin. People went through long
prayers in Latin in the early days. The spirit
may have been praying, yet the understanding
was unfruitful. The Reformation brought people back to use the common language of the coun-

tries in which they lived in addressing God and in the worship of God, so that the understanding might go with the spirit. "What is it, then? I will pray with the spirit." Certainly I should pray with the spirit; my inmost being must be aroused; but "I will pray with the understanding also; I will sing with the spirit, and I will sing with the understanding also" (verse 15).

What he has said of preaching or public ministry of the Word is just as true of singing. Therefore the importance of singing hymns that express Scriptural truth. There are many songs which we sing because we like the tunes; but sometimes the words are not in accordance with Scripture at all. Some people think that songs must be suitable if the words are from the Bible. Take the book of Psalms, which were written before redemption was accomplished. David sang, "Turn away Thy wrath from me." I won't sing that. Why? Because divine wrath has been turned from me. It fell upon my blessed Substitute, and I know I won't come into judgment, for I am saved from judgment. There are many lovely things in the Psalms in which all our hearts may go out in worship and praise, but we are to sing from the standpoint of people who have already been redeemed. There should not be any question as to our relation with God. If we do not understand this, we shall always be in confusion.

"Else, when thou shalt bless with the spirit, how shall he that occupieth the room of the unlearned say Amen at thy giving of thanks, seeing he understandeth not what thou sayest?" (ver. 16). In the early Church when a man gave thanks the rest were to say Amen. But they must understand then what he is saying; otherwise one might verily give thanks well, but the others would not be edified.

"I thank my God, I speak with tongues more than ye all." He did not boast of this, but stated a fact. "Yet in the Church I had rather speak five words with my understanding, that by my voice I might teach others also, than ten thousand words in a tongue." Now you get the distinction between the two. I would rather, he said, speak five words in a language they can understand, than ten thousand words in a tongue. When he went out to the barbarians he was glad to talk to them in a tongue, but when he came into the assembly he would not speak to them in a tongue. I know some dear people who, I am sorry to say, would rather speak five words in an absolutely unknown tongue than ten thousand words in good, plain English. If they could only feel the thrill of some power taking hold of them, and speak in some weird language that no one could understand! Yet it is only selfishness. It is the selfish desire to have something that other people

do not have. The apostle says, I do not want **to**
attract attention to myself or my gift. "Brethren,
be not children in understanding." The folk that
are running after these things are like children.
"Howbeit in malice be ye children." Have the
sweet, kindly spirit of children toward one another. "But in understanding be men." Then he
goes back to the book of the prophet Isaiah. He
shows how the prophet had to reprove Israel:
"With men of other tongues and other lips will
I speak to this people; and yet for all that will
they not hear Me, saith the Lord." God said, "I
will send Gentiles to speak to them." And **for**
more than nineteen hundred years, He has proclaimed the gospel to the Jews through the converted Gentiles. "For all that will they not hear
Me, saith the Lord." One may have the ability
to speak so as to reach the conscience, but that
would not necessarily bring them to Christ.
"Wherefore tongues are for a sign, not to them
that believe, but to them that believe not," a sign
that the Spirit of God is working in power.

"But prophesying serveth not for them that
believe not, but for them which believe." Then
he says in effect: if therefore the whole congregation come together in one place and everybody is
able to speak with tongues, one and another rising
and speaking in strange languages, and there are
unsaved people sitting about, "if there come in

those that are unlearned and unbelievers, will they not say that ye are mad?" People would say just that. They would go away saying, "What a lot of lunatics they were! I could not understand a word." "But if all prophesy, and there come in one that believeth not, or one unlearned, he is convinced of all, he is judged of all: and thus are the secrets of his heart made manifest; and so falling down on his face he will worship God and report that God is in you of a truth." When the servants of God proclaim His truth in the power of the Spirit, we may expect the careless to be awakened, and the anxious to be led into assurance and to know that God is speaking through human lips to their souls.

GODLY ORDER IN THE ASSEMBLY OF THE SAINTS

✓ ✓ ✓

"How is it then, brethren? When ye come together, every one of you hath a psalm, hath a doctrine, hath a tongue, hath a revelation, hath an interpretation. Let all things be done unto edifying. If any man speak in an unknown tongue, let it be by two, or at the most by three, and that by course; and let one interpret. But if there be no interpreter, let him keep silence in the church; and let him speak to himself, and to God. Let the prophets speak two or three, and let the other judge. If anything be revealed to another that sitteth by, let the first hold his peace. For ye may all prophesy one by one, that all may learn, and all may be comforted. And the spirits of the prophets are subject to the prophets. For God is not the author of confusion, but of peace, as in all churches of the saints. Let your women keep silence in the churches; for it is not permitted unto them to speak; but they are commanded to be under obedience, as also saith the law. And if they will learn anything, let them ask their husbands at home: for it is a shame for women to speak in the church. What? came the Word of God out from you? or came it unto you only? If any man think himself to be a prophet, or spiritual, let him acknowledge that the things that I write unto you are the commandments of the Lord. But if any man be ignorant, let him be ignorant. Wherefore, brethren, covet to prophesy, and forbid not to speak with tongues. Let all things be done decently and in order" (1 Cor. 14: 26-40).

WE are now to consider the practical working out of all this in the public assemblies of the people of God. Instinctively, we feel, I think, as we come to these verses, that they speak of conditions, of order in the early churches, of which we know very little today. This ought surely to lead us to search and try our ways, and to see how far we have departed from the simplicity of primitive Christianity.

I do not mean to imply that there is not a certain amount of liberty given in Scripture to adapt ourselves and the order of our meetings to the times in which we live and the recognized customs prevailing among different races and nations, because it is clear that we are not under restraint as to this. We are told in this very passage to "let all things be done decently and in order." This might be rendered "respectably and by arrangement" (ver. 40). The Holy Spirit is the Spirit of liberty, and He does not seek to press everyone into one mold. He is the Spirit of a sound mind, and He expects us to use God-given common-sense in carrying on the work of the Lord, and in the conduct of our assemblies.

But in these closing verses of this chapter He lays down certain principles which should govern us as we are gathered together for worship and the ministry of the Word. It is God who gathers

His people around His blessed Son, our Risen Lord, who says, "Where two or three are gathered together in My name, there am I in the midst" (Matt. 18:20). While these words had reference originally, as the context shows, to a prayer-meeting, they really apply to all assemblies of the saints of God, whether they come together for worship, for ministry, or for intercession. On such occasions all should be subject to the Holy Spirit's direction.

You get the practical application of this in the verses that follow: "How is it then, brethren? When ye come together, every one of you hath a psalm, hath a doctrine, hath a tongue, hath a revelation, hath an interpretation. Let all things be done unto edifying." Because of the liberty they had in Christ, those early Christians were in the habit of participating in the meetings as their own feelings prompted them. One would sing a psalm, another would speak in a tongue, another would interpret, another had a doctrine, someone would have a fresh revelation from God; and it resulted in sad confusion. The apostle shows that all things should be done in an orderly and godly manner and with the edification of the whole company in view, not the personal enjoyment of some gifted individual.

"If any man speak in a tongue, let it be by two, or at the most by three, and that by course," not

several at one time, and let there be an interpreter. "But if there be no interpreter, let
him keep silence in the Church; and let
him speak to himself, and to God." One might
say, "But it is the Lord who has given me the
gift of tongues, so I must speak out in meeting."
But this does not necessarily follow, for Paul
says, "The spirits of the prophets are subject to
the prophets." It is plain that even if one has
such a gift, if he could not interpret, he must remain silent in the church. This shows that a
tongue is a definite language, which might be
interpreted if another understood it, so that all
might understand and be edified.

And in regard to prophesying, let them speak
two or three, not a large number in one service,
and let the others judge; that is, in the sense of
discerning; they are to weigh all carefully before
God and compare it with the Word. None of us
has a right to say, "This is the truth of God and
I demand a hearing." Our Lord Himself urged
the people to search the Scriptures. The preacher
is to speak, the people are to listen, and then to
compare what they hear with the Word. But if
another would speak, let the first hold his peace;
that is, wait until the other is through. Everything is to be done in an orderly way. "Ye may
all prophesy one by one." But not more than
three in one meeting, lest there be confusion in-

stead of spiritual edification. "For God is not
the author of confusion, but of peace."

And then in the next few verses we have something over which there has been a great deal of
controversy in the Church of God, but there
should not be. If one would speak in tongues,
but there is no interpreter, he is to keep silent.
If a prophet is speaking and another would follow, let the first keep silent. Now the next
verse: "Let your women keep silence in the
churches." Surely, "keep silence" means exactly
the same here as in the other instances. But by
"churches" he does not mean buildings. He is
not telling us that no woman could give a testimony or offer prayer in a religious building. The
word for church is properly "assembly;" and
what he is saying is this: "When you are gathered
together in your regular church service, let the
women keep silent in the assembly, for they are
commanded to be under obedience, as also saith
the law." Now we need to remember this is by
the Holy Spirit as truly as any other part of the
epistle. He said it through Paul, the inspired
apostle. Some have objected that Paul was an
old bachelor and did not like women! He was
the inspired servant of God and wrote as directed
by the Holy Spirit. Now this does not touch the
question raised in the eleventh chapter, where
women, providing they had their heads covered,

were permitted to pray and prophesy in some other
sphere. But here the reference is to the official
meeting of the Church when all are gathered together as a worshiping company. If at such a
time the women hear something they do not
understand, do not let them interrupt the meeting by inquiring aloud nor by seeking to teach.
Let them ask their husbands at home. "Well," a
lady said to me, "that is not meant for me; I
have no husband." The word for "husband" is
elsewhere rendered "man." Let them ask their
men at home. Neither men nor women were to
interrupt in a public assembly, but let them dis-
cuss things at home if there is something they do
not understand. In these days, it is often the
men that do not understand and they ask the
women at home! It should be noted that in those
early days only a few women, comparatively,
could read or write. You have to take into consideration the time when the letter was written,
when slavery and debasement of women were
common. But I think the principle is clear
enough. And then, lest there should be any misunderstanding, the apostle asks, "Came the Word
of God out from you? Or came it unto you only?"
Well, the Word of God came to us. Very well,
then. We are not to decide what we are going
to accept or reject. God Himself speaks with
authority. We are to do as He commands. "If

any man think himself to be a prophet, or spiritual, let him acknowledge that the things that I
write unto you are the commandments of the
Lord." What things? Why, the things we have
just been reading in this passage. They are the
commandments of the Lord. But if any one
objects to this, Paul puts him down among those
who are ill-taught. "If any man be ignorant,"
just let him take the place of ignorance and say
he does not understand, but do not let him pretend to be wiser than those who obey the injunc-
tion of the Lord.

He concludes this section with these words:
"Wherefore, brethren, covet to prophesy, and forbid not to speak with tongues." So if there is
anybody attending the meetings of the Church
who can talk in a language he has never learned,
let there be an interpreter so that people may
understand; but do not try to pass off something
that cannot be interpreted. The apostle is speaking of definite languages.

And so from chapter 10 to the close of chapter
14, the Spirit has given us the divine order for
the assembly of God, and he adds the words we
have referred to already, "Let all things be done
decently," that is, "respectably," "and in order,"
or, "by arrangement;" that is, such as the Word
of God authorizes, not substituting an order
which it condemns.

I realize that this is a section over which there has been a great deal of controversy, but it is one that the Spirit of God has given for the edification of the whole Church, and we shall always find our greatest blessing as we are subject to His direction. Sometimes we think that we can improve upon what God has commanded, but we may be sure of this: that His ways are always best. This is not only true in the assembly of God, but in all details of every individual life.

Women have a wide sphere for service and testimony outside of the worship meeting of the assembly. The home is pre-eminently woman's sphere. In social gatherings too she has abundant opportunity to witness for Christ. No one is more peculiarly adapted to work among children and to help her own sex than a godly well-instructed woman. In visitation work, in the sick-room and elsewhere, her services are invaluable. If God has restricted her so that it is not for her to usurp the place of pastor or teacher in the public assembly, it is not to slight her gifts, nor to ignore the value of her services elsewhere. The true test of love for Christ is obedience to His Word. He knows best what each one of us should do in order to glorify Him. Our happiness should consist in acting in accordance with His revealed Word. This honors God and glorifies the Head of the Church, our blessed Lord.

A Priscilla may teach an Apollos, a Mary Magdalene may be the risen Lord's messenger to His faint-hearted disciples, a regenerated woman of Samaria may evangelize the men of her city, a Dorcas may serve by ministering to the comfort of the poor, a Phoebe may be a deaconess of the assembly, but a woman, no matter how gifted and godly, is not to take the place of the man in the assembly of God, but to set an example of lowly subjection to the revealed will of God, assured that He values devoted obedience above any possible form of activity, however much it may be approved by those who have never learned to let God's Word be the supreme authority.

THE GOSPEL AND THE WITNESSES TO THE RESURRECTION

✦ ✦ ✦

"Moreover, brethren, I declare unto you the gospel which I preached unto you, which also ye have received, and wherein ye stand; by which also ye are saved, if ye keep in memory what I preached unto you, unless ye have believed in vain. For I delivered unto you first of all that which I also received, how that Christ died for our sins according to the scriptures; and that He was buried, and that He rose again the third day according to the scriptures: and that He was seen of Cephas, then of the twelve: after that, He was seen of above five hundred brethren at once; of whom the greater part remain unto this present, but some are fallen asleep. After that, He was seen of James; then of all the apostles. And last of all He was seen of me also, as of one born out of due time. For I am the least of the apostles, that am not meet to be called an apostle, because I persecuted the church of God. But by the grace of God I am what I am: and His grace which was bestowed upon me was not in vain; but I labored more abundantly than they all: yet not I, but the grace of God which was with me. Therefore whether it were I or they, so we preach, and so ye believed" (1 Cor. 15: 1-11).

✦ ✦ ✦

IT is evident that there was a small party in the Corinthian assembly who had imbibed Sadducean notions and were seeking to foist them upon believers as the truth of God. They denied the reality of a physical resurrection. We

need not suppose that they went so far as to deny
spiritual survival after death, but they were like
many today who refuse to accept the teaching of
Scripture that the physical body of Christ came
forth from the tomb in resurrection, and hence
that the bodies of all men will eventually be
raised.

Paul meets this serious error in this great
resurrection section. As we ponder it and enter
into its wonderful teaching, we are almost thankful that the error was permitted to arise so early
in order that it might be met by the pen of inspiration. How much we would have lost had
there been no occasion to write this magnificent
chapter!

In preparing to combat, yes, to annihilate the
false teaching, the apostle first gives a re-statement of the evangel. He shows that there is no
gospel to preach to dying men if the resurrection be denied. "Jesus and the resurrection,"
we know, summarized the proclamation, not only
of Paul, but of the twelve. Festus wondered at
the strange "superstition" about "One Jesus
which was dead, whom Paul affirmed to be alive."
Yes, Jesus—the One who died, lives again, and
lives in a material body, though glorified, and so
marvellously changed as compared with what it
was before the cross. But it bears the print of
the nails still. On the throne the risen Christ

appears "as a Lamb that had been slain."

In verses 1 to 11 we have the re-statement of the gospel, and the witnesses of the resurrection, which alone give validity to that message of redeeming grace.

"Moreover, brethren," he says, "I declare unto you the gospel." This gospel, this good news for lost sinners, he had preached and they had received. It was the gospel of grace, and in this they stood; for we need to remember that our standing is in grace as truly as our salvation is by grace. Through this gospel they were saved, providing their faith was genuine. He is not intimating in verse 2 that some who had believed the gospel might be lost at last, but rather that continuance in the faith was the evidence of reality. This is important. It is always true that "he that endureth to the end, the same shall be saved." It is quite possible to give a mere mental assent to the truth of the gospel and by baptism and lip profession to take the place of a Christian, when actually there has been no work of grace in the soul. This is to "believe in vain." It is a mere empty faith which accomplishes nothing so far as the salvation of the individual is concerned. Real faith will be emphasized by godly living, and "He who hath begun a good work" in the believer "will perfect it until the day of Jesus Christ."

In verses 3 and 4 he gives us the basic truths of the gospel, as he had preached it in Corinth and elsewhere. First, "Christ died for our sins according to the Scriptures." There are three things to be noticed here: "Christ died." That is a fact of history, and in itself might not mean anything more than the death of a martyr. But, second, "for our sins" is a definite doctrinal statement and explains the reason for that death. It was an expiatory sacrifice. "He gave Himself a ransom for all." He took the sinner's place and bore the sinner's judgment. He died that we might never die. Third, this was "according to the Scriptures." Throughout the Old Testament, in type and actual prophetic declaration, we find the sacrificial, atoning death of Christ everywhere before us. All the sacrifices of former dispensations pictured His one offering of Himself upon the cross. The prophets looked forward to that great event as the supreme fact of revelation. Psalms 22 and 69 Isaiah 53, Zechariah 12 and 13, and many other scriptures, set this forth. God had declared in Lev. 17: 11, "The life of the flesh is in the blood, and I have given it to you upon the altar to make an atonement for your souls." Yet we know that it was not possible that the blood of bulls and of goats should put away sin. Only through the propitiatory death of Christ could this be accomplished, and, thank

God, it has indeed taken place, and all in accordance with the Scriptures.

Then, observe, "He was buried." This suggests the reality of His death. It was not, as Mrs. Eddy has intimated in her blasphemous chapter on Atonement, His *seeming* death, but He was actually dead, and because He was dead they buried His precious body in Joseph's new tomb. But, thank God,

> "Death could not keep its prey,
> He tore the bars away."

And so we come to the last point of this declaration of the gospel: "He rose again the third day, according to the Scriptures." The resurrection of Christ was the Father's expression of satisfaction in the work His Son so blessedly accomplished on the cross, when He gave Himself a ransom for our sins. The sin question settled, God raised Him from the dead and set Him at His own right hand in the highest glory, exalted to be a Prince and a Saviour.

We need to remember that apart from His physical resurrection there was no proof that God had accepted His work as an atonement for our sins. But having been delivered up to death for our offences, He has been raised again for our justification. Some prefer to render this, "Be-

cause of our justification." His death so fully
met all the righteous claims of God's throne
against our sins that now God has declared, by
bringing Him back from the dead, that there is no
longer a barrier to our complete justification.

The physical resurrection of our Lord Jesus
Christ is fundamental. There is no room for
human theories here. It is not merely a question
of survival after death. It will not do to say, as
one has done, that "the body of Jesus sleeps in a
Syrian tomb, but His soul goes marching on."
This is to deny His resurrection altogether. His
soul was never dead. His body died, and it was
His body that was raised again.

Note that the resurrection of Christ is ascribed
to each Person of the Trinity. All had part in
that glorious work. The Lord Jesus said, "Destroy this temple, and in three days I will raise
it up....He spake of the temple of His body"
(John 2: 19, 21). He was raised up from the
dead by the glory of the Father (Rom. 6: 4; see
also Heb. 13: 20). And His resurrection is attrib-
uted to the Holy Spirit (Rom. 8:11). There is no
contradiction. All is blessed harmony. The entire Godhead was concerned in the resurrection.

And His resurrection, as His death, was also
according to the Scriptures. In Lev. 23 we see
this pictured in the Feast of the Firstfruits on
the morrow after the Passover Sabbath. In Ps.

16: 10 and Isa. 53: 10 we see that for Him the
path of life lay through death, but that after
death He was to see His seed and prolong His
days. In Ps. 110 we see Him as the Risen One
taking His seat at God's right hand in heaven.

We have the witnesses to the resurrection in
verses 5 to 8. God would give positive testimony
regarding this great fact to those who are appointed to go out and proclaim the message of
salvation through the crucified and risen Christ
throughout the world.

His many visible appearances to so large a
number of reputable witnesses, the fact that His
dead body could never be located anywhere, the
manifestations of the Holy Spirit's power, and the
confident assurance and new bravery of His
apostles, together with the way God set His seal
upon their ministry in miracles of healing and
the salvation of thousands, all alike proved that
Jesus had vanquished death and come forth from
Joseph's new rock-hewn tomb to die no more.
That tomb is still empty and ever shall be. The
body that once lay in that inner crypt, enswathed
in the linen cloths, came out of its cerements like
a butterly leaving the chrysalis shell when God's
appointed hour had struck (John 20: 4-8).

It was not simply the survival of the spirit after
the death of the body, for although that might
prove immortality, it would not be resurrection.

What Scripture plainly declares is that *the body that hung on the cross is the body that was raised from the grave.* It still bore the print of the nails and the wound in the side (John 20:27). Long years afterward, John the beloved saw in the midst of the throne "a Lamb as it had been slain." The marks of His passion will be upon His body forever (Rev. 5:6).

> "Thy wounds, Thy wounds, Lord Jesus,
> Those deep, dark wounds, they tell
> The sacrifice that frees us
> From sin and death and hell.
>
> "They bound Thee once forever
> To all who own Thy grace;
> No power those bonds shall sever,
> No time those scars efface."

And He has said, "Because I live, ye shall live also." He is "the firstfruits of them that slept" (1 Cor. 15:20). His literal bodily resurrection is the pledge that eventually "all that are in the graves shall hear His voice, and shall come forth" (John 5:28, 29), some to life eternal, and others, alas, to everlasting woe.

It is true that a great change had come over His body in resurrection. He could enter a room when all doors were locked. He could appear and disappear at will. And so we are told in regard to ourselves that what is sown in burial is not the body that shall be (1 Cor. 15: 36-38). Nevertheless, there is positive identity. "*It* is sown...*it* is raised" (1 Cor. 15: 43, 44). *The body that died will live again,* but under altogether new and wonderful conditions.

Paul speaks of himself as having seen the risen Lord, and as one born out of due time. We are apt to think that this means that he was born much later than others, but the word he uses precludes any such thought. It really means, one born *before* the time. He is thinking of that glorious day when the risen, glorified Christ is to appear on earth once more, and His people Israel will look upon Him whom they have pierced, and as they recognize Him as their Lord and Saviour the nation will be born in a day. Paul had known that experience already. He first saw Christ in resurrection and, receiving Him as Saviour, became one of the new creation company.

He could never forget that he had once been an opponent of Christ and a persecutor of His Church. He felt that he was not fit to be called an apostle because of this, and yet he could rejoice in the infinite grace that had made him what he was—the messenger of that same Christ, whom he had once hated, to the Gentile world. As he went from country to country and from people to people, making known this glorious gospel, God

wrought in him in a mighty way, so that he could
say in all humility, "I labored more abundantly
than they all; yet not I, but the grace of God which
was with me." However, he would not stress the
work of the servant, but rather the message that
the servant carried to men. Whoever the preacher
might have been, when people believed the message they were saved.

Let me remind you again that apart from His
bodily resurrection we could have no proof that
God had accepted His propitiatory work, but that
the way into the holiest was now opened up for
all who would draw nigh, trusting His precious
blood as the only ground of redemption. In this
great resurrection chapter the inspired writer insists on the absolute necessity of Christ's rising
again in order that there might be validity to His
death as an atonement for sin. "If Christ be not
raised, your faith is vain; ye are yet in your
sins."

It is useless to laud Jesus as a teacher while
denying His bodily resurrection. He Himself
predicted it. He declared that He must be rejected and go into death and rise from the dead
the third day. His disciples could not understand
it at the time, but that empty tomb and the sub-
sequent appearance of their Lord in His resurrection body made all clear. Then they remembered His words. And after His ascension to

heaven in that same body, and the descent of the Holy Spirit, they went everywhere declaring His resurrection from the dead. Apart from this they would have had no gospel to preach, and apart from this there is no message for sin-laden, condemned humanity today. The proclamation that has brought life and blessing to untold millions through all the Christian centuries is that embodied in Romans 10: 9, 10: "That if thou shalt confess with thy mouth the Lord Jesus, and shalt believe in thine heart that God hath raised Him from the dead, thou shalt be saved. For with the heart man believeth unto righteousness; and with the mouth confession is made unto salvation."

Believe what? Confess what? That He who died for our sins has been raised again for our justification, and now sits enthroned at God's right hand in His literal, glorified body, exalted to be a Prince and a Saviour. This is the basis of all gospel testimony and the only sure foundation upon which our salvation rests.

He has said, "Because I live, ye shall live also." We rest upon His Word and rejoice in hope of the glory of God.

CHRIST'S RESURRECTION, THE PLEDGE OF OURS

✓ ✓ ✓

"Now if Christ be preached that He rose from the dead, how say some among you that there is no resurrection of the dead? But if there be no resurrection of the dead, then is Christ not risen: and if Christ be not risen, then is our preaching vain, and your faith is also vain. Yea, and we are found false witnesses of God; because we have testified of God that He raised up Christ: whom He raised not up, if so be that the dead rise not. For if the dead rise not, then is not Christ raised: and if Christ be not raised, your faith is vain; ye are yet in your sins. Then they also which are fallen asleep in Christ are perished. If in this life only we have hope in Christ, we are of all men most miserable. But now is Christ risen from the dead, and become the first-fruits of them that slept" (1 Cor. 15:12-20).

✓ ✓ ✓

IN these verses the Holy Spirit develops for us and vigorously defends one of the great fundamental truths of Christian testimony. As we have noticed already, there were some in the Corinthian assembly who were raising questions as to the bodily resurrection of the saints. I do not suppose that they thought for one moment that people cease to exist when they die. One can hardly think of any real Christian believing that, but they doubtless thought, being influenced largely by the pagan philosophies with which they were familiar before their conversion, that the spirit lived on in another world, but as far as the body was concerned when death came and it was laid away in the tomb, that was the end of it. They never expected to meet their loved ones again in physical form or to take again a material body. The apostle meets that as a definite error and shows what serious consequences such a view would necessarily involve. He asks, "If Christ be preached that He rose from the dead, how say some among you that there is no resurrection of the dead?" This is the very foundation of Christianity. Everywhere the apostles went they preached Jesus and the resurrection. Our faith rests upon that.

The two great truths that Scripture teaches are that He was delivered up to death because of our sins, and that He was raised again as the token of God the Father's satisfaction in the work that His Son accomplished. Thus as the risen One He ever lives, "to save them to the uttermost that come unto God by Him" (Heb. 7: 25). Some today have fallen into a similar error and teach that our Lord Jesus Christ never came out of the grave in His material body. They admit His existence in spirit, but deny His physical resurrection. But the great evidence that was given to the Christians of the earliest days that

the Lord Jesus had actually settled the sin ques-
ion, that redemption was completed, was the fact
that He came out of the tomb in the very body
that had gone into it, though changed in a most
wonderful way. Nevertheless His was a real
human body, and we know that it bore in the
palms of the hands the print of the nails. There
was still the mark where the Roman spear had
pierced His side, and if I read my Bible correctly, I believe the raised body of the Lord Jesus
will bear those marks for all eternity. In this
it will differ from the bodies of all the saints.

I do not think there is any reason to believe
that those who have been martyred for Christ's
sake will bear any evidence of suffering in their
bodies; there will be no scar, neither spot nor
blemish, nor any such thing. Our bodies will be
absolutely perfect when raised and glorified. Why
then should the body of our Lord Jesus bear those
scars that speak of His sufferings and of His
passion? Because these will be the visible evidences for all to contemplate throughout the ages
to come that the very same Jesus who died for
our sins upon the cross has been raised in the
power of an endless life. The apostle John had a
vision of heaven long years after the ascension
of our Lord, and when he described the glorious
central throne and other thrones surrounding it
he said. "I beheld, and lo, in the midst of the

throne and of the living ones, and in the midst of
the elders, stood a Lamb as it had been slain"
(Rev. 5: 6). That is, the glorified body of the
Lord Jesus Christ had upon it the evidences that
He was the One who had once been slain, who
had been sacrificed on Calvary for our redemption. One of our poets has written:

> "I shall know Him, I shall know Him,
> As redeemed by His side I shall stand,
> I shall know Him, I shall know Him,
> By the print of the nails in His hand."

Yes, He lives in heaven in the very body in which
He once walked this earth, but that body is now
changed and glorified. Christian testimony begins with this, and if one is seeking the way of
life, if he inquires, "What must I do to be saved?"
the answer comes in unmistakable clearness, "If
thou shalt confess with thy mouth Jesus as Lord,
and shalt believe in thine heart that God hath
raised Him from the dead, thou shalt be saved"
(Rom. 10: 9, *R. V.*). Therefore, we have no right
to think of any man as a Christian who denies
the physical resurrection of our Lord Jesus
Christ.

"For if the dead rise not, then is not Christ
raised." What if Christ be not raised? Some
say, "If He is living in Heaven, is that not sufficient?" No! "If Christ be not raised, your faith is

vain; ye are yet in your sins." If our Lord Jesus
Christ did not come forth triumphant from that
tomb, then we have no gospel to preach to lost
men. If the body of Jesus still sleeps in the tomb,
then you and I are absolutely hopeless, there is
no salvation for us. The fact that He rose from
the dead is the proof that the offering-up of Himself upon the cross satisfied the claims of divine
righteousness, and met every requirement of infinite holiness. God Himself raised Him from
the dead in token of His satisfaction in His work,
and now sets Him forth a Prince and a Saviour.
This was the message the apostles preached.

Paul says, "We preach Christ crucified," and
that should be true of every one of us. But that
was not all that he preached, for he preached
Christ raised from the dead and Christ exalted to
God's right hand, for he says: "Yea, and we are
found false witnesses of God; because we have
testified of God that He raised up Christ: whom
He raised not up, if so be that the dead rise not."

Somebody may ask, "Why do you say that if
Christ be not risen there is no way of knowing
that redemption is an accomplished fact?" You
see, when our Lord was here on earth, He told
His disciples that He was going to die. "The Son
of Man came not to be ministered unto, but to
minister, and to give His life a ransom for many"
(Matt. 20: 28). But He also told them, "The

Son of Man must be delivered into the hands of sinful men, and be crucified, and the third day rise again" (Luke 24:7). If that last statement of the Lord Jesus Christ has never been fulfilled, then He stands convicted of false testimony. He either was Himself deluded in thinking that He was the Saviour, the Redeemer who was to die for sinners and rise again, or else He was a deliberate deceiver. It is His resurrection, the fulfilment of His own prediction, that proves that He was the sacrifice for sin which He proclaimed Himself to be. Thank God, that testimony is true. We saw previously how God gave abundant witness to the resurrection of His beloved Son, how more than five hundred saw Him after He rose from the dead, and we remember the statement made by Horace Bushnell, "The resurrection of Jesus Christ is absolutely the best attested fact in ancient history." You cannot think of any other incident in ancient history that has anything like the number of witnesses to its truth as we have to the resurrection of the Lord Jesus Christ.

My sins nailed Him to the cross. He, the sinless One, took my place and died under the judgment of God, but after the sin question was settled, after He had poured out His life, having died for us, three days were permitted to elapse to prove the reality of His death, then God brought

Him back from the dead to declare His acceptance of the work of His Son. The resurrection is the testimony that God is satisfied and now can open His arms in love to every poor sinner in all the world and proclaim a full, free and eternal salvation for all who believe, through the work that His Son has accomplished.

"If Christ be not raised, your faith is vain; ye are yet in your sins." The only way that I know that my sins are gone is because He who made Himself responsible for them, who died for them, now sits enthroned at God's right hand, and there are no sins on Him there.

I have often tried to illustrate it thus: Let my two hands speak of two persons. Let my left hand speak of my blessed Lord Jesus Christ and my right hand speak of myself, a sinful man. My Bible has a red cover; we will let it speak of my crimson sins, of my scarlet guilt, and as this red-covered Book lies on this right hand, let it be a picture of myself with those crimson sins all resting upon my soul. What am I going to do about it? I cannot cleanse my own heart. "If I wash myself with snow water and make myself never so clean," says Job, "yet shalt Thou plunge me in the ditch and mine own clothes shall abhor me" (Job 9:30, 31). I cannot cleanse my heart, I cannot put away my sins. But see, here is the blessed Lord Jesus Christ, illustrated by this left

hand of mine. There is no scarlet Book resting
upon that hand because He was the sinless One,
He knew no sin of thought or word or deed, He
was absolutely the Holy One. But in grace He
went to that cross of shame and was nailed upon
the tree on Calvary's hill, and when He hung
there, "Jehovah laid on Him the iniquity of us
all." I transfer this red Book to the hand that
represents Jesus. That crimson load that rested
on me was transferred to Him when He hung on
the cross, for then He was bearing the load of our
sins. That explains the darkness that enwrapped
His soul, the cry of anguish, "My God, My God,
why hast Thou forsaken Me?"

> "The Holy One who knew no sin,
>   God made Him sin for us;
> The Saviour died our souls to win,
>   Upon the shameful cross."

Having borne sin's judgment He descended to
the grave and lay there for three days and three
nights. During that interval no one in all the
world knew whether His work was satisfactory,
no one knew whether He had really settled the
sin question. "We *thought*," said the troubled
disciples, "that it had been He which should have
redeemed Israel" (Luke 24:21). They had no
way of knowing whether it was true or not until,
when the first day of the week came, He rose in

triumph from the grave, and broke the bands of death asunder and now that hand, which represents Christ, has no red load upon it, for I have hidden that which stands for that load in this desk. There are no sins upon the risen Christ, for He has left them all behind in His open grave and has ascended to God's right hand without them. The Irishman was right when he said, "What a wonderful salvation! If anybody will have to be kept out of heaven because of my sins, it will have to be Jesus; but, blessed be God, they cannot keep Him out, He is there already." The resurrection is the proof that God is satisfied. I am not now in my sins, I know that Christ has put them all away, His resurrection tells me that since I have put my trust in Him I shall never again have to face that question.

The apostle concludes this section with these words, "If Christ be not raised, your faith is vain; ye are yet in your sins. Then they also which are fallen asleep in Christ are perished." If Jesus has never been raised from the dead, then we are in a hopeless state, those who have trusted in Him are trusting in a bruised reed, we who are counting solely upon this risen Lord and upon the work He did have believed in vain. "If in this life only we have hope in Christ, we are of all men," not exactly, "most miserable"—for I suppose there are other very miserable men living for the devil—but what he really says, I believe, is, "We are of all men most to be pitied," for we have staked everything on the redemptive work of the Lord Jesus Christ. Because of our faith in Him we have given up the world and its pleasures and follies, we have become strangers and pilgrims in this scene, and now if there is no risen Christ, if this is all a mistake, we are going to lose both worlds. We gladly gave up this world because we thought we saw another above our heads, but that is only a dream, a fantasy, if Christ be not risen, and so "we are of all men most to be pitied." The unconverted man can at least enjoy this present world, but the converted man says, "There is nothing here for my heart, it has been won by that One who has gone over yonder, and for His name's sake I have surrendered the things that other men live for down here." But what a blunder, what a mistake, if Christ be not risen! I am simply following a will-o'-th'-wisp that will land me at last in darkness and despair.

However, the apostle does not close this section with any such dreary suggestion. He says, "But now *is* Christ risen from the dead, and become the firstfruits of them that slept." There is no question about it. We know that He who died has been raised again. He Himself said, "I lay down My life that I may take it again." He was put to death in the flesh but quickened by the Spirit. "The God of peace...brought again from the dead our Lord Jesus, that great Shepherd of the sheep" (Heb. 13:20). Christ *is* risen, and His resurrection is the earnest of ours. He has become "the firstfruits of them that slept." Every Israelite understood that figure. The days of planting and the days of cultivation had gone by, the summer was ending, the harvest days just beginning, and the Israelite went out in his field and saw a fast ripening sheaf. He plucked it and presented it to the Lord in the temple or at the Tabernacle gate as the firstfruits, the earnest of the coming harvest, and by-and-by when a few more days or weeks had gone by, he went back to that field and the ripened grain was everywhere, but the great harvest was like the sheaf of the firstfruits, it was the same in character, and so our Lord Jesus is the firstfruits of resurrection, "the firstfruits of them that slept." By-and-by will come the day when all His own will be called forth from the tombs. That will be the glorious harvest and in that day every other one will be like the firstfruits. We shall be like Him, our blessed, glorious Lord; we too shall have resurrection bodies, we too shall be forever triumphant over death, and throughout an eternity of bliss we shall glorify the One who has redeemed us to Himself.

THE PAGEANT OF RESURRECTION

✓ ✓ ✓

"For since by man came death, by man came also the resurrection of the dead. For as in Adam all die, even so in Christ shall all be made alive. But every man in his own order: Christ the firstfruits; afterward they that are Christ's at His coming. Then cometh the end, when He shall have delivered up the kingdom to God, even the Father; when He shall have put down all rule and all authority and power. For He must reign, till He hath put all enemies under His feet. The last enemy that shall be destroyed is death. For He hath put all things under His feet. But when He saith all things are put under Him, it is manifest that He is excepted, which did put all things under Him. And when all things shall be subdued unto Him, then shall the Son also Himself be subject unto Him that put all things under Him, that God may be all in all" (1 Cor. 15: 21-28).

✓ ✓ ✓

FOLLOWING the apostle's argument that the resurrection of our Lord Jesus Christ is the basis of our hope for eternity, he makes it plain that this is not a debatable question, it is not something about which those professing the name of Christ may have different opinions. It is a fundamental fact, "Now *is* Christ risen from the dead, and become the firstfruits of them that slept." He has come out of the grave as a sample of the great harvest which is yet coming forth from the tomb at His return.

"For since by man came death, by man came also the resurrection of the dead." It was Adam as federal head of the race who plunged our entire humanity into death and judgment by his sin. But the Second Man, the Lord from heaven, has gone down into death; He has triumphed over it; He has robbed it of all its terror; and He has come forth a victor. And now through Him comes the resurrection of the dead, whether of course the resurrection of the righteous dead or the wicked dead, all shall come forth from the tomb through Him. The emphasis here is upon the fact that it is the Man Christ Jesus who calls the dead to life, and that is what we should expect, for God sets the one over against the other. The first man plunged the race into ruin, the Second Man brings redemption. In our emphasis upon the deity of the Lord Jesus we must never belittle or in any way lose sight of the perfection of His humanity. He is as truly Man as if He had never been God, and He is as truly God as if He had never become Man.

"There is one Mediator between God and men, the Man Christ Jesus; who gave Himself a ransom for all" (1 Tim. 2: 5, 6); and it is the Son of Man whose voice shall eventually be heard by all the dead; first by the righteous dead, the saved

dead, when He comes again to call His own to be
with Himself, and then at last by the unsaved
dead when they are summoned from the tomb to
judgment, for Scripture knows nothing of a
general resurrection.   It distinctly teaches two
resurrections.   Our Lord speaks of those who
shall be rewarded in "the resurrection of the
just," and we read that there "shall be a resurrection both of the just and of the unjust."   The
Lord Jesus Christ Himself said, "Marvel not at
this: for the hour is coming, in the which all that
are in the graves shall hear His voice, and shall
come forth; they that have done good, unto the
resurrection of life."   That is the first resurrection.   "They that have done evil, unto the resurrection of damnation."   That is the other one.
In Revelation 20: 6 we are told, "Blessed and holy
is he that hath part in the first resurrection: on
such the second death hath no power, but they
shall be priests of God and of Christ, and shall
reign with Him a thousand years."   "But the rest
of the dead lived not again until the thousand
years were finished" (Rev. 20: 5).

In this chapter the apostle of course has specially
in mind the resurrection of the righteous, because
he began the chapter by saying, "I declare unto
you the gospel which I preached unto you, which
also ye have received, and wherein ye stand."
And that gospel is that "Christ died for our sins

according to the Scriptures; and that He was buried, and that He rose again the third day according to the Scriptures," and He is coming again to complete the work that He began. So we read in verse 22, "As in Adam all die, even so in Christ shall all be made alive." The term, "in Adam," included all who received their natural life from Adam. As we have pointed out, he was the head of a race and we are all his children by natural birth. Every person in the world is in Adam by natural birth, and over all of Adam's race hangs the death sentence. "As in Adam all die, even so in Christ shall all be made alive." Just as the term, "in Adam," takes in an entire race, so the term, "in Christ," takes in a race, but naturally a narrower, a smaller, group than is included "in Adam," for we are all in Adam by nature, but only a limited number are in Christ by grace.

In speaking of some relatives of his Paul calls them his "kinsmen who also were in Christ before me." They may not have been in Adam before him; I do not know whether they were older than he; but he says they were "in Christ" before he was. I often wonder if that was not one reason why Paul had that remarkable experience on the Damascus turnpike. They had probably been praying for him, and in answer to their prayers God broke him down and saved him. **We** are "in Christ" only through a second birth, through beccming members of a new creation. Just as we receive our natural life from Adam we received divine life from the risen glorified Christ, and we are then said to be "in Christ." And so it is the resurrection of the just that Paul has in view.

"In Christ shall all be made alive. But every man in his own order." The word "order" was a military term in those days, and was used to describe the different companies of soldiers. We would say, "Every one after his own cohort." "Christ the firstfruits; afterward they that are Christ's at His coming." When He returns, when He descends in glory to the upper air, He will give that quickening shout of which we read both in the latter part of this chapter and in 1 Thess. 4: "And the dead in Christ shall rise first: then we which are alive and remain shall be caught up together with them in the clouds, to meet the Lord in the air: and so shall we ever be with the Lord" (1 Thess. 4: 16, 17).

"Then cometh the end." I do not know that we need that italicized word, "cometh," for that does not represent anything in the original. It is, "Then the end." "They that are Christ's at His coming.....then the end," when the resurrection will be completed, when the glorious kingdom reign of our Lord Jesus will have come to an end, "when He shall have delivered up the kingdom to God, even the Father, when He shall have put down all rule and all authority and power. For He must reign, till He hath put all enemies under His feet." Our Lord Jesus Christ is now sitting at the Father's right hand until this earth shall be made His footstool, and when He descends, He will take the kingdom and will reign for a thousand wonderful years. He will bring in that age when righteousness shall cover the earth as the waters cover the sea, when "the earth shall be filled with the knowledge of the glory of the Lord" (Hab. 2:14). During the thousand years the Lord will exercise righteous government and righteous judgment in this scene. It comes to a close with the passing away of the material universe as we know it.

Then comes the day of judgment, when the wicked, raised from their graves, will appear at the Great White Throne and sentence be given according to their works. When the mediatorial kingdom is ended all will be handed back to the Father, that God may be all in all. Christ may be likened to the receiver of this world. Suppose a business in San Francisco is owned by a firm of three persons in New York City. They send a manager out to take charge of the business, but this manager proves to be dishonest and incompetent, and the business is in inextricable diffi-

culties. One member says, "You allow me to go
out there and act as receiver, and I will try to
straighten everything up and put the business on
its feet." He goes out there, takes charge of
everything, goes over all the books, and finds out
where the crookedness has been.   It may take
him months, perhaps years, before he straightens
things out, but after everything is cleared, every
bill paid, and there are no longer any liabilities,
he goes back to New York, presents his account,
and hands it all back to the firm. Does he cease
to have an interest in it? No; for he is a member of the firm; but the firm takes complete charge
and he no longer exercises administration media-
torially.   This universe was put under the domin-
ion of Adam. God created him in innocence and
put him in charge, and said to him, "I have given
you authority over it all."   But through his being deceived by Satan, through incompetency and
dishonesty, the whole thing was thrown into tur-
moil.   And so our blessed Lord Jesus, one of the
Eternal Trinity, is coming back to this world and
will take charge of things, and when everything
has been subjected to God and all the wicked and
utterly impenitent have been dealt with, He will
hand it back to the Father that God may be all
in all. Shall we lose our Saviour then? No, He
will remain the same blessed, loving Jesus that
He has ever been since His incarnation, but the

kingdom will be delivered up to the Father, and God (the Father, Son, and Holy Spirit) will maintain it in righteousness for all eternity.

"The last enemy that shall be destroyed is death." Death will hold within its grasp all the wicked dead up to the end of the millennium, but God will not permit that condition to last for ever. Death will be destroyed. Satan himself will be banished to the lake of fire, and the wicked will share his doom because they refused God's grace. When the Lord Jesus has thus put all things under the feet of God the Father, He Himself voluntarily occupies the place of the Father's beloved Son and the Servant of the redeemed. He will serve us through all the ages to come, for love delights to wait upon the objects of its affection.

There is a beautiful picture in the Old Testament. We read when a man who had been sold into slavery fulfilled his time, he could go out free. If his master had given him a wife, the wife and children would remain in bondage but he could go free. But if that servant should say, "I love my master, my wife, and my children; I will not go free," then they were to put him through a peculiar ceremony. They were to place his ear against the door and pierce it through with an awl, and he would then serve his master forever. What a striking picture that is of the place our blessed Lord Jesus has taken voluntarily in order to be identified with us for eternity! He came into this world as the servant, He took a servant's place, and having completed His service He could have gone back free at any time to the Father's house, but He chose not to do so. There were those down here upon whom His love was set, "Christ loved the Church, and gave Himself for it" (Eph. 5: 25), and so we can think of Him saying to the Father, "I love my Master, my Bride, my children; I will not go out free." And so He could say, "Mine ear hast Thou bored." He bears the mark of eternal subjection because of His love to us. I have often pictured that Hebrew servant sitting in his little cabin home on his master's plantation. Mother is getting the meal and the children are playing about. One little tot climbs up on his knee and says, "Father, what is that ugly hole in your ear? I do not like that." And I think the wife hears it and says, "Oh, my darling, don't speak that way; to me that is the most beautiful thing about your father. We were in bondage and he could have gone out free and left us behind, but he wouldn't do it. He loved me and gave himself for me; he loved you, my dear children, and because of his love for us he chose to remain a perpetual servant. That mark tells of his undying love." So will it be with our blessed Lord Jesus, the subject One for all eternity, and as we look upon those wounds which will never be effaced, we shall say, "There we have the evidence of His unchanging love." What a Saviour!

> " 'Man of sorrows,' what a name
> For the Son of God who came
> Ruined sinners to reclaim!
> Hallelujah! what a Saviour!
>
> "When He comes, our glorious King,
> All His ransomed home to bring,
> Then anew this song we'll sing,
> Hallelujah! what a Saviour!"

We shall be the joy of His heart and He the joy of ours for an eternity of bliss. And mark how everything hangs upon the cross. That is why we delight to look back and remember His suffering there for us. Others may think of His beauty as a lowly Nazarene, or of His glorious transfiguration upon the mount, but to every redeemed soul He looks most beautiful as we think of Him wearing His crown of thorns, bleeding, suffering, dying for us.

BAPTIZED FOR THE DEAD

✦ ✦ ✦

"Else what shall they do which are baptized for the dead, if the dead rise not at all? why are they then baptized for the dead? And why stand we in jeopardy every hour? I protest by your rejoicing which I have in Christ Jesus our Lord, I die daily. If after the manner of men I have fought with beasts at Ephesus, what advantageth it me if the dead rise not? let us eat and drink; for to morrow we die. Be not deceived: evil communications corrupt good manners. Awake to righteousness, and sin not; for some have not the knowledge of God: I speak this to your shame" (1 Cor. 15:29-34).

✦ ✦ ✦

THE outstanding expression in this particular portion found nowhere else in Scripture is "Baptized for the dead." Exactly what does it mean? Down through the centuries a number of different interpretations have been suggested. One of the most common among orthodox believers is that we are to understand by the expression, "Baptized for the dead," that we as Christians are baptized for or in honor of our Lord Jesus Christ who died. He died, went down into death, and we have been identified with Him, and in our baptism we confess our death with Him, therefore, "Baptized for the dead" really means, "Baptized for Christ who died." Certainly that interpretation is not repugnant to Christian consciences. It is absolutely true that intelligent believers are baptized into the death of Jesus Christ, for that, in fact, is the exact meaning of the ordinance of baptism. But is this what is meant here?

In baptism we confess that we were sinners, that we deserved to die, that our Lord Jesus Christ died in our room and stead, and now we are saying, as it were, before the world, before all men, "I take my place with the Christ who died; I desire henceforth to be recognized as one identified with Him in His death, in His burial, and in His resurrection." Looked at in this way the ordinance is wonderfully precious. I never can understand the state of soul of Christian men who would try in any way to belittle or set aside Christian baptism. I know many precious souls have been brought to Christ simply by witnessing the carrying out of this ordinance. There is something so solemn about it as it definitely sets before us Christ's death on our behalf and our identification with Him, that it cannot but speak to every one who has ears to hear. So I fully accept that view, but do not believe that it explains the expression in the text, "Else what shall they do which are baptized for the dead, if the dead rise not at all."

Another suggested explanation that has found favor with many is that baptism for the dead means that we ourselves who are baptized confess that we are dead, that we have died with Christ, and that therefore our baptism is one for or of the dead as taking that place, although in this world we no longer belong to the world. We have died, and we bury the dead, and so we are buried because we have died to the old life. Undoubtedly baptism teaches that. We who were once living unto the world, we who were once living to the flesh, have now, in the cross of Christ, died to all that; as having died, the ordinance of baptism speaks of a burial. We are through with the old life. But I do not think that explains the expression in the text.

From the very earliest days there has been another suggested explanation, a rather grotesque one. It has been taken up in our own day and spread abroad as though it were the very gospel of God, by those commonly known as "'Latter Day Saints," or Mormons. Personally, I belong to the Former Day saints, I am not interested in any "Latter Day Saints" movement. It is my joy to be linked with the saints of all ages unto whom Christ Jesus has been made wisdom, righteousness, sanctification, and redemption. But the view held by these Mormons and a few others is that the apostle means that baptism in itself is a saving ordinance, that apart from it none will ever be saved, and since a great many have died without having the opportunity of being baptized, somebody else must be baptized for them if they are going to be saved. And so they say that the apostle is referring to living Christians being baptized vicariously on behalf of people who have died unbaptized. This is a very common thing among the so-called "Latter Day Saints." In fact, they have many temples in which they carry out the ceremony of baptism for the dead, and people are urged to be baptized, some over and over and over again, for dead people who were never baptized in this life.

When in Salt Lake City some years ago, a young Mormon elder told me he believed that the members of the Mormon church were saving more souls through being baptized for the dead than Jesus Christ ever saved through dying on Calvary's cross. He mentioned a very wealthy lady who had come out from the East a good many years ago and had been baptized in Salt Lake City over 30,000 times. Every time she was baptized she paid a sum of money into the Church, so you can see that baptism for the dead is rather a good thing from the financial standpoint. She was using her entire fortune redeeming people from death and destruction through being baptized for the dead! She had been baptized for all

the friends and relatives about whom she knew
anything at all who had died, and then she had
gone into history and literature and sought out
thousands of names and had been baptized for
every one of them. She had been baptized for
Alexander the Great, for Nebuchadnezzar, for
Julius Cæsar, for Napoleon Bonaparte, for Cleo-
patra, and thousands of other historical characters, in order that she might be the means of
their salvation; and it was concerning this lady
especially that this youthful elder said to me with
a very solemn face, "I believe in the day of judgment it will be proven that this lady through being baptized for the dead has saved more souls
than Jesus Christ!" That blasphemous theory
finds no place whatever in the Word of God. In
the first place the Word of God never teaches that
baptism is essential to salvation. Nowhere in
Scripture are we told that if people die unbaptized, they are lost.

It is quite true that it is perfectly right and
proper, that people who are saved should be baptized, and we find this ordinance linked with faith
because it is the confession of the faith that
we have. But when Scripture says, for instance,
"Go ye into all the world, and preach the gospel
to every creature. He that believeth and is baptized shall be saved," it never adds, "He that is
not baptized shall be damned," but, "He that *be-*

lieveth not shall be damned." We have the remarkable example of the first soul ever saved
after Christ was nailed to the cross, the thief who
hung there beside Him, who was saved that day
without any possibility of being baptized. With
hands and feet nailed to the tree he could do
nothing, he could not carry out any ordinance or
do anything by which to earn salvation, but he
was saved alone by the finished work of the One
who hung on the central cross. And every man
who is ever saved will be saved through what
Jesus did when He died on that tree. So we put
away the Mormon conception. There is a fourth
view which certain Christians have held throughout the centuries, and that is that some of these
Corinthians imagined that baptism was essential
to salvation and therefore were being baptized
vicariously for others who had died in heathenism, and so the apostle refers to it without saying whether it is true or not. But we can be
sure that Paul would not refer to it in the way he
does without telling them that it was contrary
to the mind of God that living people should be
baptized for the benefit of dead people.

I have spoken of four suggested interpretations of these words, and I come now to what I
believe is the exact meaning of the text. First,
let me say that the expression, "Baptized for the
dead," means literally in the Greek text, "Bap-

tized in place of, or over, the dead ones, or those
who have died." The word "dead" is in the plural,
it is not a singular noun; therefore it cannot refer
to the Lord Jesus Christ; it is not, "Baptized
because of Christ." Neither the preposition nor
the noun will permit of that interpretation, but
the actual rendering would have to be, "Baptized
in place of dead ones." It is not, "baptized on
behalf, or for the benefit, of dead ones." The
preposition does not suggest that. In the earlier
part of the chapter the apostle reproves those who
denied the physical resurrection of the Lord Jesus
Christ, and says, "If Christ be not raised, your
faith is vain; ye are yet in your sins" (ver. 17).
Everything for a believer depends upon the resurrection of our Lord Jesus Christ. He was delivered up to death for our offenses, He was raised
again for our justification, and if He be not
raised, manifestly redemption has never been accomplished, the sin question has never been settled, they who have fallen asleep in Christ are
perished, they have found that their profession
has gone for nought, for there is no redemption
if Christ be not raised, and it naturally follows
that if that be the case, we are making a tremendous mistake for, "If the dead be not raised,
your faith is vain; ye are yet in your sins," and
therefore Christ is powerless to save. Think of
the millions of people who have been willing to

stake everything for eternity upon this Christ
who cannot save if the dead rise not, but if Christ
be not risen, they have blundered terribly. We
might better go on and enjoy this world, for death
ends all if that theory be true.

Verses 20 to 28 form a parenthesis in which the
apostle turns aside from his argument to give us
an outline concerning the pageant of the resurrection, and then goes on and develops it. You will
find that in verse 29 he picks up the thread of the
argument again from verse 19, saying, "If in this
life only we have hope in Christ, we are of all men
most to be pitied. Else what shall they do who
are baptized in place of the dead, if the dead rise
not at all? why are they then baptized for the
dead?" This may be translated, "What shall they
do which are baptized in the place of the dead
ones if no dead ever rise? Why are they then
baptized in the place of the dead ones?" Do you
not see that the argument is clear and luminous?
Those who have fallen asleep in Christ have
perished if Christ has not been raised again, and
yet every day other people are being baptized in
their places, others are professing faith in Christ,
others are availing themselves of the ordinance of
baptism, they are filling up the places made vacant on earth by those who have died professing
Christ. But if Christ be not risen, then those
who have died are lost, they have gained nothing

by their profession. Why then should we go on
filling up the ranks all down the centuries and
putting other people in the place of danger if
there is nothing to be gained by it? This is a
military figure. A regiment of soldiers goes into
battle, and after the battle is over they count the
men and find perhaps that seventy-five have been
slain. Immediately they begin to recruit others
in place of the dead, not to do the dead any good,
but to take their places. Seventy-five other men
are drawn into that regiment, are recruited in
place of the dead, they don the uniform and go
forth to take part in other conflicts. But if they
are fighting a losing battle, if there is no possibility of ever winning, if they are just wasting
their lives, why are they then recruited for the
dead? What is the use of their taking the places
of those who have died? It is the height of folly
if they know there is nothing but certain defeat
and destruction awaiting them.

Think of Christian people as a mighty army.
Down through the centuries, for nineteen hundred
years, the Church has been in conflict with the
powers of sin and death and hell, and throughout
the ages one generation of Christians has fallen
and another has taken its place, and the public way
of manifesting the fact that they have thus enlist-
ed in the army of the Lord is through baptism.
But what a foolish thing if Christ be not risen and

if the dead rise not! What are they gaining by being baptized in place of the dead? Would it not have been better to have wound up the history of Christianity in the first centuries and said, "The whole movement is a failure, there is no risen Christ, there is no possibility for salvation here in this life"? A man may accept the philosophy of Christianity and keep it to himself. Possibly his neighbors would never suspect his belief and he would not be subject to martyrdom, but if he really believes in the Lord Jesus Christ he says, "I must make it known," and the right way is through baptism, through confessing Christ in that way as the One who died and rose again. The moment a man was baptized in Paul's day, and many centuries afterwards, he put himself in the way of possible martyrdom. His neighbors said, "That man is a Christian." "How do you know?" "He has been baptized, confessing the name of the Lord Jesus Christ." Paul was risking his life every hour, for there were enemies of Christianity on every hand. But if Christ be not risen, why should he, why should I and my fellow-laborers stand in the place of jeopardy? Paul says, "I protest by your rejoicing which I have in Christ Jesus our Lord, I die daily." I am putting myself in the place of death every day, I am exposed to death, and I am ready to die for Jesus Christ. Paul knew He had risen for he had seen

Him in the glory as He appeared to him that day
when he fell stricken on the Damascus road, and
Paul became the outstanding defender of Christianity. He says, "I am set for the defence of
the gospel," and for the name of Christ he took
his life in his hands and died daily.

"If after the manner of men I have fought with
beasts at Ephesus, what advantageth it me, if
the dead rise not? Let us eat and drink; for
tomorrow we die." What does Paul mean? He
is referring to that time when he was almost torn
asunder by beast-like men in that riot at Ephesus. He saw that angry mob pressing upon him
as they shouted, "Great is Diana of the
Ephesians" (Acts 19: 28) and he thought of
that great throng ready to destroy him, and
likened them unto beasts. But, he says, it is all
right no matter what they do to me, Christ is
real for He is risen again, and I know Him as
the risen One and am ready to die for His name's
sake. "But what advantageth it me, if the dead
rise not?" Why should I live like this, why
should any Christian give up the world and live
a life of self-denial and devotion to the One whom
this world has rejected, if the dead rise not? Why
not accept the philosophy of the worldling? In
Isaiah 22: 12, 13 God reproves the careless worldlings, "And in that day did the Lord God of hosts
call to weeping, and to mourning, and to bald-

ness, and to girding with sackcloth: and behold, joy and gladness, slaying oxen, and killing sheep, eating flesh, and drinking wine: let us eat and drink; for tomorrow we shall die." They did not respond to His call and humble themselves before Him, but went on in the ways of the world. "Eat and drink; for tomorrow we shall die." Here are the words from which the apostle quotes. If Christ has not been raised, if there is no reality in Christianity, then get all the enjoyment out of the world that you can. The worldling says, "Let's have a good time while we live, for we are going to be a long time dead." If death ends everything, why not go on and get what you can out of this life? But there is a better world beyond the grave, there is a Saviour who died to put away our sins and who lives triumphant in glory waiting to receive to Himself those who trust Him. So we say, "You can have your feasts, your fame, your frivolity, your wealth, Christ is more to me than all of these." The Christian, you see, is a man who has heard the drum-beat of another country and so does not keep step with the drum-beat of this world.

"Be not deceived," says the apostle, "evil communications corrupt good manners." People say, "It does not make any difference whether Jesus died and rose; we can be just as good without this assurance." But when they deny the death

and the resurrection of our Lord Jesus Christ,
you find that they will throw the reins upon their
lusts and live for the world and please themselves. So to us the word comes home, "Awake
to righteousness, and sin not." You are linked
with a risen Christ and you are in this world to
glorify Him. Let that risen One control your
heart and life, and yours will be a holy life devoted to the glory of God. "Some have not the
knowledge of God: I speak this to your shame."

A number of years ago I was at the burial of
an aged saint. For a great many years he had
been a bright witness for Christ in the part of
the city where he lived and had brought up his
family in the fear of God. One of his children
was a missionary in the Philippine Islands. He
had grandchildren who attended the church services, but had not as yet confessed the Lord. As
I closed the funeral service and we were about
to take our last look at that face until the coming
of our Lord Jesus and our gathering unto Him, I
felt led to step to the casket and say, "Just wait
a minute before we take our farewell look at the
face of our beloved brother. He has been a witness for Christ in this city for many years, his
place will not easily be filled, he will be greatly
missed by Christians. I wonder whether anyone
at this funeral service would like by the grace
of God to seek to prepare to take his place. Is

there anybody here who has heard the voice of
God speaking to you and perhaps you have never
yet come to Christ, but right here you will close
with the Lord, you will take Him as your Saviour
and be ready to be baptized for the dead? This
one has gone, there is a vacant place in the ranks;
will you take his place?" I waited a moment, and
then a fine, tall, young man, his grandson, arose
from his seat and came forward. He faced the
audience and said, "Today I accept my grand-
father's Saviour, and I want you to pray that I
may be able in some measure to take his place;"
and then he knelt at that casket and gave himself to the Lord, and the next Sunday night I
baptized him for the dead. It is simply the filling
up of the ranks, taking the places of those who
have gone before. Christian baptism always emphasizes that it is a public testimony, a testimony
that one has turned from the world, trusted
Christ, and will now seek to live for His glory.
And so one generation has been baptized for the
dead of the past generation, and that one for the
past, and so on, clear back to the very beginning
of Christianity.

LECTURE XXXVI.

HOW ARE THE DEAD RAISED UP?

✓ ✓ ✓

"But some man will say, How are the dead raised up? and with what body do they come? Thou fool, that which thou sowest is not quickened, except it die: and that which thou sowest, thou sowest not that body that shall be, but bare grain, it may chance of wheat, or of some other grain: but God giveth it a body as it hath pleased Him, and to every seed his own body. All flesh is not the same flesh: but there is one kind of flesh of men, another flesh of beasts, another of fishes, and another of birds. There are also celestial bodies and bodies terrestrial: but the glory of the celestial is one, and the glory of the terrestrial is another. There is one glory of the sun, and another glory of the moon, and another glory of the stars: for one star differeth from another star in glory. So also is the resurrection of the dead. It is sown in corruption; it is raised in incorruption: it is sown in dishonor; it is raised in glory: it is sown in weakness; it is raised in power: it is sown a natural body; it is raised a spiritual body. There is a natural body, and there is a spiritual body. And so it is written, The first man Adam was made a living soul; the last Adam was made a quickening spirit. Howbeit that was not first which is spiritual, but that which is natural; and afterward that which is spiritual. The first man is of the earth, earthy: the second Man is the Lord from heaven. As is the earthy, such are they also that are earthy: and as is the heavenly, such are they also that are heavenly. And as we have borne the image of the earthy, we shall also bear the image of the heavenly" (1 Cor. 15: 35-49).

WE have come in our study to the latter part of this great chapter. Having settled the question of the resurrection of our Lord Jesus Christ, the apostle takes up another problem that has perplexed and exercised the minds of many. If there is to be a resurrection of the dead, in what body will they arise? In answering this he gives us a special divine revelation, and we should remember that apart from revelation this is a matter of which we can know nothing. We are just as ignorant today of what comes after death as those philosophers were five hundred years before Christ whose discussions and dialogues on life, death, and immortality have been embalmed for us in the dialogues of Plato. Men still read of Socrates, Glaucas, Plato, Aristotle, and all the rest of them, and know no more today than they did then, for if God has not spoken all is mere speculation at the best. But He has spoken, He has given us His sure Word, and we may have the certainty of the knowledge that, "All Scripture is given by inspiration of God, and is profitable for doctrine, for reproof, for correction, for instruction in righteousness" (2 Tim. 3:16). Let us hear then what God Himself, the Creator of all, the God of the resurrection, has to say on this subject.

In the eighth chapter of Romans the apostle Paul comes to the close of his wonderful exposi-

tion of our threefold salvation: salvation from
the guilt of sin, salvation from the power of sin,
and salvation from the presence of sin; and he
looks on to the time when we who believe shall
receive the redemption of the body. We have
already received the redemption of our souls, we
are already saved from the guilt of sin and the
judgment due to sin, but we are still in poor
failing human bodies. Christians get sick just
as other people do, and Christians die just as
other folk die. Every little while somebody rises
up with a new gospel to tell us that we may have
the redemption of the body in this life, and that
no Christian need ever be sick if we will just
claim the Lord as our healer. But no matter how
fervently they believe it, no matter how faithfully
they teach it, they all take cold if they sit in a
draft, they all get indigestion when they eat
things that do not agree with them, they all get
sick and die eventually, unless they get run over
by an automobile and die by accident. They are
just as truly subject to sickness and death as
other people are. All the great faith healers of
the past are dead, and all of those of the present
will die soon unless the Lord Jesus should come
in our lifetime and we should be changed and
caught up to meet Him without passing through
death. Those under the Adamic sentence all die.
But, thank God, there is redemption for the body.

The hour is coming when our Lord Jesus Christ shall return from Heaven and shall transform these bodies of our humiliation and make them like unto the body of His glory. And this is just as true of the decayed bodies of those who have died as it is of those who are living when our blessed Saviour returns. But this at once presents a difficulty.

The natural mind says, "I can understand how He can touch this mortal body of mine and quicken it into immortality if I should be living when He returns, but if I should die before He comes, and my body go back to the dust from which it came, and that dust be scattered to the four winds of the heavens, I cannot understand how it could be raised again. I may have a body in resurrection, but it will surely be another body; I shall not actually be raised from the dead." Scripture answers that objection in the passage we have just read, "Some man will say, How are the dead raised up? and with what body do they come?" In other words, In what way are they brought from the tomb, and what kind of a body will they have in the resurrection? The apostle says, Take a lesson from nature, "thou simple one." The word "fool" here is rather strong; he is not insulting his readers by calling them fools in the sense in which we use the word, but the Greek word means, "unthinking one." It

you would only stop to think, you would realize
that there are many analogies in nature to the
resurrection. We can think of some apart from
these given in Scripture. Take the caterpillar
crawling along the leaves. Suddenly a strange
alteration comes over it and it spins a cocoon
around itself. Its whole appearance is changed
and it dies to its old life altogether. It stays in
that cocoon a while and eventually it emerges,
and out comes, not a caterpillar but, a beautiful
butterfly, a lovely creature which is able to soar
up into the air, and no longer crawls upon the
ground, the grass or the leaves. It is a wonderful picture of what the resurrection may be.

The apostle uses the illustration of a farmer
sowing grain. He sows it, to use the words that
are so often used at funeral services, "in the sure
and certain hope of a glorious resurrection." The
bare grain is sown by the farmer who believes
that wnen it falls in the ground and seems to rot
away that will not be the end of it. It will come
forth into a fuller life than it has known before.
But when the resurrection of that grain takes
place, he does not see grain such as he has sown
coming up from the ground; he first sees a blade
of green, and by-and-by quite a stalk arises and
then a head of wheat, oats or barley. "Thou
simple one, that which thou sowest is not quickened, except it die: and that which thou sowest,

thou sowest not that body that shall be, but bare grain, it may chance of wheat, or of some other grain: but God giveth it a body as it hath pleased Him, and to every seed his own body." There is no mistake made. If wheat is sown, it is wheat that rises from that grain; if he sows oats then oats will rise; if barley is sown, barley arises from that grave. There is absolute identity and yet a wonderful change. That beautiful head of grain is much more lovely to look upon than the simple little seed that went into the ground. And so with the resurrection body; there will be absolute identification in some way to the body that died. How much of that grain is in the seed of wheat? Get down to the root of the wheat-stalk and you will still find the little shell out of which this stalk has come. Just so will it be in the resurrection. God will not have to use every part of this body. I do not possess today a particle of the body that I had a few years ago. When I was a boy in school, they said that the body changes every seven years. Now they say it changes every three years. I am not conscious of that change except, of course, that I know that my nails and hair grow and have to be cut. In just the same way my entire body is changing continually. There is not a bit of this body today that I had three-and-a-half years ago, and yet I know that I am I. I say to you, "You are looking

so much better than you were when I last saw
you," or maybe you are looking a little worse;
and you do not say, "Well, that is because you
never saw me before if you haven't seen me for
three-and-a-half years." No, you are the same
person, and the body is your body, and you know
it is, and yet there is not a cell in it that was
there three-and-a-half years ago. And so we say
that there is identity, but not necessarily the
using of the entire body that is put into the grave
when the Lord raises us in resurrection.

The next thing the apostle stresses is that there
are different kinds of flesh. We do not understand the differences, and yet we know that they
are there, and that we never pass from one to
another.

"There is one kind of flesh of men." Men are
made to live upon the earth, and that is the only
way they are comfortable. There is another
kind of flesh, that of beasts, and they can live
even in the earth. Think, for instance, of the
bear or the raccoon, who as winter approaches
go into a burrow or a hollow tree, and become
dormant for the period of several months until
spring comes again, and then they emerge. That
would be impossible for a man, but it is not for
beasts. The beast is adapted to this environment; its body is different to that of a human
being.

And there is another flesh, that of fish, and it is adapted to an environment that neither beasts nor men can live in. They may enter into that environment for a limited period, but would drown if they had to be kept under water continually. The fish is at home there; he is so constituted by God that when he is taken out of the water, he dies. One of the great German writers has well said, "If fish are philosophers, if they are capable of thinking, I am absolutely certain that every philosophical fish is quite sure that it is impossible for any creature to live out of water." It knows that when drawn out of the water it finds itself gasping and will soon die.

Then there is the flesh of birds, and the bird is suited to fly in the air, differing altogether from mankind or beasts or fish. And so, if there are differences here on earth, why need you wonder about the difference between bodies suited to Heaven and bodies suited to this lower scene?

"There are also celestial bodies," that is, heavenly bodies, "and bodies terrestrial," earthly bodies. Our Lord Jesus came into this world and took a terrestrial body, but after having made satisfaction for our sins on the cross, He came forth in resurrection in a celestial body, and in that body He ascended through the heavens into the very presence of God where "He ever liveth to make intercession" for us. His celestial body

is the pattern of what ours shall be; we shall
have bodies in resurrection that are not subject
to the laws that control us now. When we turn
to Scripture and hear our blessed Lord talking
with the Sadducees who denied that there was
any resurrection, we get a little better understanding of this. They came and said, "Here was
a woman who had a husband, and he died, and
the brother of that man married the woman, and
he died, and there were no children. Then another brother married her, and this went on until
she had been married seven times, and they had
all died. Last of all the woman died also. Whose
wife shall she be in the resurrection?" They
thought they had put a puzzling question. But
the Lord Jesus simply said, "You do err, not
knowing the Scriptures, nor the power of God.
They that are accounted worthy to attain to that
age (that is, the coming glorious age of the kingdom and the resurrection) neither marry, nor are
given in marriage...for they are like unto the
angels, being children of the resurrection." The
angels are sexless. They do not propagate their
kind. Each is an individual creation; and believers, in the resurrection, will be like unto the
angels. That means that in resurrection we are
not going to be men and women as we are now,
but we will simply be redeemed people with no
sex distinctions whatsoever, because the day will

have gone by when the human race is to be propagated as now.

Then again in this epistle where the apostle is reproving believers for making a great fuss about questions of foods, some that are clean and some that are unclean, he says, "Meats for the belly, and the belly for meats: but God shall destroy both it and them" (chap. 6:13). What is he telling us here? As long as we are in this world, our bodies have to be nourished by food, and so this body has a digestive tract by means of which we are able to take from our food those elements that repair the waste, and build up our physical constitutions. But in the resurrection that will not be so, and therefore the whole digestive tract as we now know it, is to be destroyed. It is not that you will not be able to eat, for Jesus took a piece of broiled fish and some honeycomb after His resurrection, but it was not necessary that there should be any digestive tract to dispose of it. We shall have bodies that are unchanging. All the changes of time will have come to an end and our bodies will be like to the glorified body of the Lord Jesus Christ.

But even when we have our celestial bodies there will be differences in the glories that we shall enjoy. So the apostle turns to contemplate the material celestial orbs, the sun, the moon, and the stars. Notice how they differ in glory.

"There is one glory of the sun, and another glory
of the moon, and another glory of the stars: for
one star differeth from another star in glory."
We read elsewhere, "They that turn many to
righteousness shall shine as the stars forever and
ever" (Dan. 12: 3). And when we get our resurrected bodies, they will be bodies of light like that
body in which our blessed Lord was manifested
on the Mount of Transfiguration, and as Saul of
Tarsus saw Him when he said, "I saw a light
from heaven, above the brightness of the sun"
(Acts 26: 13).

In that day there will be differences in glory
according to the measure of our devotedness to
Christ down here, for he says, "So also is the
resurrection of the dead." We are all saved by
the same grace and through that same grace we
will be raised and changed at the coming of the
Lord. But we will not all be rewarded in the
same way, for reward is for faithful service, and
I am afraid many of us are going to lose a great
deal at the judgment-seat of Christ because we
have not been more true and real in all our ways
down here. The day is soon coming when you
and I would give worlds, if we possessed them, if
we had only let God have His way absolutely in
our lives. The greatest joy, the greatest blessing that can come into any life is whole-hearted
surrender to the will of God, no matter what it

may seem to mean, no matter how difficult it may seem at the time. The things that many of us have dreaded are the things that brought us the greatest blessing as we have sought to walk with our gracious God and Father. In that day when the Lord looks over our lives, when He goes over everything with us, when He says, "Well done, thou good and faithful servant...enter thou into the joy of thy Lord," how we shall rejoice to have His approbation, and how we shall wish that we had been more devoted. There is not one soul with Christ today who looks back on his earthly life and says, "I wish I had not been quite so out-and-out for God; I wish I had been less self-denying; I wish I had been more concerned about my own comforts." But I fancy there are many who say, "If I had my life to live over again, no matter what suffering, what rendings of the heart-strings it might mean, I would never hesitate a moment to let God have His will in everything in my life." It is not a question of whether or not we get to Heaven. All who are saved by grace will be there, but there will be a difference in our rewards.

"So also is the resurrection of the dead. It is sown in corruption; it is raised in incorruption: it is sown in dishonor; it is raised in glory: it is sown in weakness; it is raised in power: it is sown a natural body; it is raised a spiritual body.

There is a natural body, and there is a spiritual body." Observe the impersonal pronoun all through these verses. Thus you will see there is identification between the bodies that die and the bodies that rise, and yet there are differences in appearance. There is a natural body and there is a spiritual body. Could you have identification brought out more clearly than that? The body that is sown is the one that is raised, and yet it is changed. It will be incorruptible. Death occurs only a few hours before corruption begins; but the new body will be incorruptible; it will be a glorified body. Just what that means may be seen from what the disciples beheld on the Mount of Transfiguration. They saw the blessed Lord Jesus shining in that glory and they beheld Moses and Elijah, we read, in the same glory with Jesus. Moses, a man who had died, and yet was there in the glorified body. Elijah, a man caught up to Heaven without dying, and he was in the glorified body.

And then we read that "It is raised in power." How weak this poor body is! The spirit often is willing, but the flesh is weak. We find ourselves hindered by the body, but the day is coming when instead of being a hindrance to the spirit the body will be like wings to that spirit, and we will be able to go to the uttermost parts of the universe on the business of the Lord easier than we could cross the street today.

"It is raised a spiritual body." Do not misunderstand that. A spiritual body is not a body made of spirit. God is a Spirit and is not said to have a body. He took a body when the Lord Jesus Christ became incarnate. "In Him dwelleth all the fulness of the Godhead bodily"—or, "in a body" (Col. 2: 9). You and I are spirits each dwelling in a body.

But I am not all spirit; I am also soul. "I pray God your whole spirit and soul and body be preserved blameless unto the coming of our Lord Jesus Christ" (1 Thess. 5:23). The soul is the seat of my emotional nature, the seat of all my natural instincts; as a man, it is my human self; but the spirit is the highest part of my nature to which God can make Himself known. "The Spirit itself beareth witness with our spirit, that we are the children of God" (Rom. 8: 16). As a Christian I ought to be constantly under the control of the spirit, I ought to live according to the highest part of my nature; but every little while I find that instead of being controlled by the spirit part of me I am controlled by my soul, and I am more or less a creature of emotions. I am easily influenced this way or that emotionally, and often to my detriment and that of others. And this is called here "the natural body." The word translated "natural" is simply the Greek adjective from the word "soul," that is, a *soulish* body. This

body is the suited vehicle for the expression of
the emotions of my soul. The spirit is often willing to do certain things but the flesh is weak.
The body being a soulish body is a hindrance to
the spirit. But in resurrection I shall have a
body that is spiritual, that is, a body suited to
and dominated by the spirit. There will be
nothing then to hinder the full expression of the
spirit, and I shall be absolutely subject to God
who is a Spirit.

And so it is written, "The first man Adam was
made a living soul; the Last Adam was made a
quickening Spirit." Adam was the head of the
old creation; God formed him out of the dust of
the ground. If you do not believe that, wait a
while, and your body will go back to the dust
and prove that Scripture is right. God breathed
into this man Adam, and he became a living soul
and he is the progenitor of the race. But the
Last Adam is our Lord Jesus. He is the risen
One and so has become a quickening Spirit. He
breathed on His disciples and said, "Receive ye
the Holy Spirit," and we are linked with Him.
He is the Last Adam, the Lord from Heaven, and
we are going to have bodies like He now has.
As linked with Adam I have a body like his, but
in resurrection I shall have a body like that of
the blessed Lord Himself.

"Howbeit that was not first which is spiritual,

but that which is natural; and afterward that
which is spiritual. The first man is of the earth,
earthy: the Second Man is the Lord from heaven."
The first man was of the dust, dusty—or of the
dirt, dirty. That is what man is by his relationship with Adam. The Second Man is the Lord
from Heaven, our blessed glorified Saviour. The
very word "Adam" means "red clay." "As is
the earthy, such are they also that are earthy:
and as is the heavenly, such are they also that
are heavenly. And as we have borne the image
of the earthy, we shall also bear the image of
the heavenly." As we have borne the image of
the earthy, and as we have looked like our first
father, and had the appearance of the natural
man in this world, so we shall bear the image of
the Saviour. I think this helps to explain a
passage which has bewildered people: "When He
shall appear, we shall be like Him; for we shall
see Him as He is" (1 John 3: 2).

A lady said to me one day, "If we are all going
to be like Him we will all look alike, and how are
we ever going to know each other?" That is not
what it says. We have borne the image of the
earthy; we are like Adam, but we do not all look
the same. The wonder of it is that if it were
possible for the one billion eight hundred million
men and women of the world to pass before you,
you would never find two that are exactly alike.

Sometimes we find two people so nearly alike that we can hardly tell them apart, but there is always some little difference. The infinite variety in creation is amazing when you think that there is so little to work with: only one nose, one mouth, two ears, two eyes, one chin, two cheeks, and one forehead! And yet the Creator has made over one billion eight hundred million different specimens in each generation, and each generation diverse from every other. I do not know much about music, but I am always dumbfounded when I think how much can be made from seven tones. I cannot understand it. I should have thought all the music would have been written years ago, and that nobody could by any possibility make up another air. But there are symphonies that can be written that men have never dreamed of. So with the human family, there is infinite variety and yet we are all like the first man Adam.

And now in the resurrection body there will be infinite variety too, and yet all shall be like Him in that we shall have incorruptible bodies and yet every one different. We shall know each other yonder as we have never known each other down here. What a wonderful hope is this that Scripture puts before believers!

THE RAPTURE OF THE SAINTS

✝ ✝ ✝

"Behold, I show you a mystery; We shall not all sleep, but we shall all be changed, in a moment, in the twinkling of an eye, at the last trump: for the trumpet shall sound, and the dead shall be raised incorruptible, and we shall be changed. For this corruptible must put on incorruption, and this mortal must put on immortality. So when this corruptible shall have put on incorruption, and this mortal shall have put on immortality, then shall be brought to pass the saying that is written, Death is swallowed up in victory. O death, where is thy sting? O grave, where is thy victory? The sting of death is sin; and the strength of sin is the law. But thanks be to God, which giveth us the victory through our Lord Jesus Christ. Therefore, my beloved brethren, be ye stedfast, unmoveable, always abounding in the work of the Lord, forasmuch as ye know that your labor is not in vain in the Lord" (1 Cor. 15: 51-58).

✝ ✝ ✝

WITH these words the apostle Paul brings to a close his great treatise on the resurrection, first dealing with that of Christ and then with that of the saints. In this particular section he shows us that while all will have part in the glorious event at the resurrection of the saints, yet some will not pass through death, but will be changed instead of being raised.

522

We noticed in the closing verses of the previous portion the statement that, "Flesh and blood cannot inherit the kingdom of God." The kingdom of God refers, of course, to that future reign when the authority of God will be manifested in Heaven and over all the earth. The kingdom of God will consist of two spheres. Our Lord Jesus says, "Then shall the righteous shine forth as the sun in the kingdom of their Father" (Matt. 13:43). Those are the heavenly saints in the kingdom day. Then we also read of people brought into this blessing here on earth during the kingdom. They, of course, will be in bodies of flesh and blood. The apostle is here considering the heavenly side of the kingdom when he says, "Flesh and blood cannot inherit the kingdom of God." As we have remarked before, those that are "accounted worthy to attain to that age and the resurrection from the dead, neither marry, nor are given in marriage: but are as the angels of God in heaven" because they are the children of the resurrection. That will be the heavenly aspect of the kingdom. Observe, the apostle does not say, "Neither flesh *nor* blood," but says, "Flesh *and* blood." That is, our bodies in their present condition as sustained by blood are not suited for Heaven, for the coming glorious kingdom, and therefore we must be changed How will this change take place?

"Behold, I show you a mystery." We have often pointed out that a mystery in the New Testament is not something mysterious and difficult to understand. The Greek word is almost anglicized here, and does not mean something strange and hard to comprehend, but a mystery is something revealed only to the initiated. Some of you have been initiated into some secret society, and have not discovered anything very mysterious, but you have found that there are certain things on the inside that folk like myself on the outside do not know anything about. That is the real use of the word here. It is a secret not known to the generality of the people, but made known to the initiated, and all God's beloved people are looked upon by Him as His initiated ones. The only lodge I have ever joined is "The Grand Army of the Redeemed." I was initiated into that by being born again, and then the Holy Spirit conducted me from chair to chair and revealed the mysteries as you have them here in the Word of God.

There are a number of these sacred secrets which were kept from the people of God in past dispensations, but are made known now in the glorious dispensation of the Holy Spirit. One of them is this mystery of the first resurrection and the rapture of the living saints. "Behold, I show you a mystery; we shall not all sleep, but we

shall all be changed." This is a very remarkable
statement. We often hear it said that, "There is
nothing more certain than death and taxes."
Taxes seem to be quite certain, but I am glad to
say that death is *not* absolutely certain for the
Christian. "Well," some one says, "doesn't the
Word say, 'It is appointed unto man once to die'?"
That is the divine appointment for man as such,
but there will be a generation of God's redeemed
people who will be exempt from that. "We shall
not all sleep." He uses the word "sleep" in place
of "die," for death to the believer is the putting
of the tired, weary, worn body to sleep until the
Lord Jesus comes to waken it again. It is only
the body that sleeps. The real man, the spirit
and soul, is absent from the body and present
with the Lord, taken home to be with Christ,
which is far better, so that the bodies of our
friends in Christ who have died are sleeping, but
they themselves are with Christ, wonderfully
happy in His presence. The apostle Paul gives
us an idea of their state and condition when he
speaks of being "caught up to the third heaven."
That is the immediate dwelling-place of God. The
first heaven is the atmospheric heaven; the second is the stellar or the starry heaven, and the
third is God's dwelling-place.

The apostle had the experience of being caught
up into the third heaven, and he was so enrap-

tured that he could not tell whether he was in the body or out of the body. That teaches us several things. First, if Paul was in the body, his body was no clog upon him, and when we are in the presence of the Lord in the body our bodies will be no hindrance to us as they often are now. But if Paul was taken out of the body, then he did not miss his body. He was just as conscious out of as he could be in it. Some say that it is impossible to live out of the body, but it is no more impossible than it is for the works of a watch to go on running without the case. The body dies, it is put to sleep, but the believer lives on, "Absent from the body, present with the Lord" (2 Cor. 5:8). In the first resurrection the body is raised in glory, and the spirit comes to dwell in the body again. That is the state of the believer when Christ calls us forth from the tomb.

How many have questioned these words, "We shall not all sleep." It is a remarkable fact that in the Douay Version, which is read by a large section of the professed Church of Christ, this passage reads, "We shall all rise again, but we shall not all be changed." How it ever got into the text perplexes people, but that is exactly what is written in the Vatican manuscript. But older ones read like the translation we have here, "We shall not all sleep, but we shall all be changed."

The manuscript of the fourth century, from which
the Douay Version was translated, shows how unbelievers had already come in; some scribe tam-
pered with the text, and if it were not that we
have older manuscripts giving it as here we might
be perplexed about it. But "we shall not all
sleep," and there may be some of us in this generation who will be living when our Lord Jesus
Christ returns. But whether living or dead we
shall all be changed.

Every one of us must undergo the glorious
change in order to have part in the heavenly side
of the kingdom, and that shall take place instantly, in a moment, in the twinkling of an eye.
I cannot think of anything much faster than that.
It does not say, "In the *winking* of an eye," but
"in the *twinkling* of an eye." As quickly as a
gleam of light shines in the eye, so quickly shall
we be changed at the coming of the Lord Jesus
Christ. I have often tried to think of what that
would mean. There are dear children of God
lying on hospital beds, weak and suffering, enduring days of pain and nights of anguish, and they
are crying in the distress of their souls, "O Lord,
how long?" One moment enduring excruciating
pain, and the next rising to meet the Lord in the
air in a body that can never suffer again. Then
there are some of God's people whose minds have
failed because of the stress of things, perhaps

shut away in some sanitarium, possibly melan-
choly and in gloom, maybe imagining that God
has forsaken them and that there is no hope for
them. The poor brain has given way completely,
and yet the next moment with intelligence such
as the angels have, as they find themselves in
their glorified bodies looking into the face of the
Lord Jesus Christ. What a marvelous hope it is!
No wonder the apostle calls it this "blessed hope."
"We shall all be changed, in a moment, in the
twinkling of an eye."

When will that be? "At the last trump." How
may we understand that? There are those who
have attempted to link this trump with the trumpet of the seventh angel in Revelation. In that
book you have a series of seven trumpets, and
when they are blown, various judgments are
poured out upon the earth, and when the seventh
is blown, the kingdom of God is ushered in. Some
have thought the apostle is referring to that
trumpet, thus indicating that the Church of
God would be here on earth going through all
the tribulation and distress, only to be saved
out of it when the seventh trumpet is blown.
But the book of Revelation was not written until
approximately thirty years after the writing
of this epistle, so that there is no possible way
by which there could be a connection between
these trumpets. And when we turn to the First

Epistle to the Thessalonians we find that this trumpet is called, "The trump of God" (1 Thess. 4:16). It is not the trumpet of an angel. Why is the trump of God here called "the last trump?" That expression was very familiar to the people who lived in Paul's day. It was in common use in connection with the Roman Army.

When a Roman camp was about to be broken up, whether in the middle of the night or in the day, a trumpet was sounded. The first blast meant, "Strike tents and prepare to depart." The second meant, "Fall into line," and when what was called "the last trump" sounded it meant, "March away." The apostle uses that figure, and says that when the last trump of this age of grace sounds, then we shall be called away to be forever with the Lord. We have heard the first. Many of you remember when you were just part and parcel of the world, you were living with the world and like the world, and you were settling down here, but you heard the gospel trumpet awakening you out of your sleep. And then I trust you have heard the second trumpet calling you to take your places in fellowship with God's beloved people as soldiers in this scene. And now what wait we for? For the last trump, when we shall be summoned, not to march away nor yet to fly away, but when we "shall be caught up together...to meet the Lord in the air" (1

Thess. 4:17). When will it take place? It is an undated event in the ways of God with men. It may take place today, it may be tonight; but whether at midnight or in the morn or in the daytime it will make no difference to us for we have been redeemed with the precious blood of Christ. "The trumpet shall sound, and the dead shall be raised incorruptible." I do not need to dwell on that.

"And we—who are living—shall be changed. For this corruptible must put on incorruption, and this mortal must put on immortality." You will notice that you have the two groups. "This corruptible"—that refers to the dead—"must put on incorruption." The dead whose bodies have corrupted away will be raised in incorruptible bodies. But the living, "This mortal," those that are alive but subject to death if time goes on, "shall put on immortality." This is the promise that we have in Romans 8:10, where we read, "If Christ be in you, the body is dead." A little word is omitted there which may be added to make it more clear. "The body is *still* dead because of sin." You may be a believer, but your body is still under the Adamic sentence, "Dying thou shalt die." But the spirit is alive and is the pledge of the new life yet to be. "But if the Spirit of Him that raised up Jesus from the dead dwell in you, He that raised up Christ from the dead

shall also quicken your mortal bodies by His
Spirit that dwelleth in you" (Rom. 8: 11). I
know that some have taught that the indwelling
Spirit gives new life to the mortal body right
here and now. But that is what the apostle
denies in the tenth verse, "If Christ be in you,
the body is still dead because of sin." But if the
Spirit—the Spirit of life—dwells in you, some
day He shall quicken into newness of life your
mortal body by the Spirit that dwelleth within
you. When will that be? At the coming of our
Lord Jesus Christ and our gathering together
unto Him.

Then we read, "This mortal must put on
"immortality." Notice the terms "mortal" and
"immortal." These refer to the body; never to
the spirit or soul. The everlasting existence of
man is taught in Scripture, but immortality is a
blessing that will be revealed when our Lord
comes.

"When this corruptible shall have put on incorruption, and this mortal shall have put on immortality, then shall be brought to pass the saying that is written, Death is swallowed up in victory." And now he goes back and quotes from
the book of the prophet Hosea, chap. 13: 14,
"Death is swallowed up in victory. O death, where
is thy sting? O grave, where is thy victory?"
Death comes in and takes from us our nearest

and dearest, and our hearts are pained because of the separation. But if we know Christ, and if our loved ones were in Christ, the sting of death is gone, and we are looking on to a glorious reunion when Jesus comes again. What a wonderful event it will be when saints who have been separated here on earth will recognize one another as we are caught up to meet the Lord in the air. Then we can sing, "O death, where is thy sting? O grave, where is thy victory?" That which makes death terrible to the unsaved is sin; "The sting of death is sin;" but if we know that sin has been put away, that sin has been purged by the precious atoning blood of Christ, then that sting of death is gone.

"The strength of sin is the law." Do you believe that? I wonder whether some of you have not thought that the law is the strength of holiness. You have imagined that the way to be holy was to be under the law, and you have tried to obtain sanctification by keeping the law. It says here, "The strength of sin is the law," not, "The strength of holiness is the law." What does he mean? The law simply stirs up everything in the human heart that is opposed to God, and instead of producing holiness the result is greater transgression. That is what the apostle puts before the Galatians and the Romans. The law never produces holiness. It is the heart occupied with the Lord Jesus Christ that produces holiness. When you have seen that the law condemns, but that Christ has borne the condemnation for you, then you can look away to Him, and as you are occupied with Him you will be a holy man or woman. You cannot make yourself holy by rules and regulations. Not even God's law given at Sinai has the ability to make men holy, but the living glorified Christ can change people into His image as they are taken up with Him, so that they become holy.

Paul concludes this section by saying, "Thanks be to God, which giveth us the victory through our Lord Jesus Christ." Death may seem for the moment to triumph. It looked like triumph when death came into your home. I felt it was a triumph of death when it came years ago into our home and took one after another whom I loved most tenderly, but as I look on to the glorious future and realize that death is to be swallowed up in victory at the coming of the Lord Jesus Christ, I can already claim by faith that conquest over it and exclaim, "Thanks be to God, which giveth us the victory through our Lord Jesus Christ." So the verse with which the section closes comes home to every one of us, "Therefore"—because these things are true—"my beloved brethren, be ye stedfast, unmoveable, always abounding in the work of the Lord, for-

asmuch as ye know that your labor is not in vain
in the Lord." They tell me that occupation with
these precious truths that have to do with the
coming of the Lord Jesus Christ may have a
tendency to make people heady and theoretical,
and no longer useful in the Church of God here
on earth, but I do not know anything that should
so grip the soul and put one to work for God as
the knowledge of the truth we have just been
considering.

THE FIRST DAY OF THE WEEK

✓ ✓ ✓

"Now concerning the collection for the saints, as I have given order to the churches of Galatia, even so do ye. Upon the first day of the week let every one of you lay by him in store, as God hath prospered him that there be no gatherings when I come. And when I come, whomsoever ye shall approve by your letters, them will I send to bring your liberality unto Jerusalem. And if it be meet that I go also, they shall go with me. Now I will come unto you, when I shall pass through Macedonia: for I do pass through Macedonia. And it may be that I will abide, yea, and winter with you, that ye may bring me on my journey whithersoever I go. For I will not see you now by the way; but I trust to tarry a while with you, if the Lord permit. But I will tarry at Ephesus until Pentecost. For a great door and effectual is opened unto me, and there are many adversaries. Now if Timotheus come, see that he may be with you without fear: for he worketh the work of the Lord, as I also do. Let no man therefore despise him: but conduct him forth in peace, that he may come unto me: for I look for him with the brethren. As touching our brother Apollos, I greatly desired him to come unto you with the brethren: but his will was not at all to come at this time; but he will come when he shall have convenient time" (1 Cor. 16: 1-12).

✓ ✓ ✓

MANY have wondered why such a seemingly prosaic portion of Holy Scripture as this should be preserved for us down through the ages, and have asked what special spiritual help it gives, what lesson it has for the people of God since the days when the apostle wrote it. We can quite understand that there were certain personal things that would be of interest to the Corinthians, but what difference would it make to us whether this portion of Scripture should be lost or not? It is just these personal touches in the letters of the apostle Paul and other apostolic writers that prove that these epistles are not forgeries. Any one trying to write a forged letter to pass off upon people as the Word of God, would certainly leave out just such details as we have here, but these are things that come bubbling up from the warm heart of the actual writer of the letter who was in touch with all these people to whom and of whom he speaks. I want to note briefly several things in connection with the persons mentioned, before dwelling more at length on the topic of this address.

The Christianity of Paul was a very practical thing. One occasion for the writing of the first part of this chapter was that there had been a prolonged famine in the land of Palestine and in other parts of Syria, as a result of which many of the Jewish believers were suffering greatly. The apostle, moving around among the Gentile Christians in Europe, where conditions were very different, laid the responsibility upon them of ministering to the needs of their Hebrew breth-

ren in Christ. That is something that Christians
have sought to imitate all down through the centuries since. It is a most practical way of showing the unity of the Church of Christ and of
manifesting the compassion of our Lord toward
those in need. It is this that was pressed so
earnestly upon the Corinthian Church—their responsibility to help their Jewish brethren. They
could not say, "Oh, well, these folks in another
land are not intimately related to us. If they
have not been provident enough to lay aside during the years of plenty, why should we share
our possessions with them?"

Christianity demands that we recognize the
fact that we are members one of another, and if
one member suffers all the members suffer. In
fact it is more than that: Christianity demands
that we show deep interest even in men and
women of the world who are not one with us in
Christ, for we are told, "As we have therefore
opportunity, let us do good unto all men,
especially unto them who are of the household of
faith" (Gal. 6: 10). And this has characterized
the true Church of God wherever there has been
a cry of need. When nations, peoples or cities
are in distress, Christian people are the first to
put their hands into their pockets and share with
those who are in need. I wish that those who
spurn the Church, those who ridicule the mes-

sage of the gospel, would bear this in mind. I wonder, if it depended upon utter unbelievers, how much interest would have been taken in past years in famine refugees in India, in China, or in those who suffered as a result of the World War in Europe and elsewhere. The Red Cross is first of all a product of Christianity. That red cross is the blood-stained cross of our Lord Jesus Christ. It is these practical ministries that show that believers have the same love that animated our Saviour when He came from Heaven to give Himself for a lost world. So Christians are to look out those in need and seek to make things easier for them.

The apostle is very careful that everything should be done in a manner that would commend itself to the consciences of others. He never went out on his own responsibility accumulating large sums of money, supposedly for the poor, without being accountable to any one, lest he might have been laid open to suspicion, and people might have said, "He uses this to feather his own nest." No; it is as though he says, "I do not want to be responsible for your money: I want you to make your offerings in my absence." "Upon the first day of the week let every one of you lay by him in store, as God hath prospered him, that there be no gatherings when I come." He wished nothing to do with it, but allowed them to appoint the men that they trusted to take charge of this fund and carry it to Jerusalem. He told them that, if they wished, he would go with them, but he would not take the responsibility of handling the funds. That is a very good principle. Many a professed servant of Christ has gotten into difficulty through soliciting and obtaining money for which he gave no proper accounting. We can all take a leaf out of Paul's book when it comes to handling funds.

He was laying out his work for the coming season, for he was not one to trust to haphazard openings. He was coming to the Corinthians when he passed through Macedonia and he said that he might winter with them. First he would visit Ephesus, and then later he was going to Jerusalem, and he was anxious to be there by the Feast of Pentecost, the time when years before the Holy Spirit descended and the Church was formed. He wanted to be there on that specific occasion for it would give him a remarkable opportunity of reaching the thousands of Jews who would come up from all over the world to keep the feast, and he would be enabled to meet them and to present the gospel to them. Then too, many Christians would be there with whom he could have happy fellowship.

"For a great door and effectual is opened unto me, and there are many adversaries." God had opened a door for the testimony, and of course there were those that opposed him. No servant of God who is in the current of the divine will ever has to hunt for open doors for testimony. He simply needs to be obedient to the Lord. The trouble is we are not all willing to let the Lord guide us. He has told us that it is "He that openeth, and no man shutteth; and shutteth, and no man openeth" (Rev. 3:7). The business of the servant of Christ is to be in His will and say, "Here, Lord, I am at Thy bidding. Open doors or close them as Thou wilt. If Thou wilt have me go, I will go; if Thou wilt have me refrain from going, I am under Thy command and Thy control." If the Lord opens the door, never mind the adversary. "A great door and effectual is opened unto me, and there are many adversaries." The adversaries did not frighten Paul. He went forward, "Strong in the Lord, and in the power of His might" (Eph. 6:10), knowing that, "Greater is He that is in you, than he that is in the world" (1 John 4:4).

Then in verse 10 notice his kindly interest in his younger fellow-servants: "Now if Timotheus come, see that he may be with you without fear: for he worketh the work of the Lord, as I also do." This is our friend, Timothy, and I take it that he was a bit troubled with what our psychologists call an Inferiority Complex. He was not constantly shoving himself forward; he rather under-rated than over-rated his ability, and Paul realized that because he was so humble and lowly there were some who might belittle him and set him to one side. Paul says, "He is my companion in the gospel; he does the same kind of work that I am doing, so help him forward."

And then I think there is something to be learned from the way he speaks of Apollos. "As touching our brother Apollos, I greatly desired him to come unto you with the brethren: but his will was not at all to come at this time; but he will come when he shall have convenient time." Some folk have an idea that the apostles were the first bishops of the Church, that they had all authority in their spheres, and that the apostle Paul was an archbishop of western Asia and eastern Europe. If that were the case, he could command the other brethren to go as he directed. He would have said to Timothy, "You go here," and to Apollos, "You go yonder," and they would have gone. But there is nothing like that here. Paul did not occupy any such place; he did not lord it over other servants of Christ. He was himself a servant subject to the Lord Jesus and recognized that the others were in exactly the same position. He would say a good word for Timothy, but he would not command him. Here he suggests to Apollos that it might be well to go to Corinth and minister to the brethren there; he had been there before and they had been greatly benefited by his ministry. But Apollos said, "I do not have any leading of the Lord to go there; at some later day I may." And Paul says, "Very well, it is not for me to tell you where to go; you are the Lord's servant."

All these things help us to understand the conditions that prevailed in the early Church. There was no great hierarchy lording it over the rest, but just the various local assemblies of believers and the servants of Christ, as gifted by the Lord, acting as subject to Him. I would not like to tear this chapter out of my Bible. It helps me to understand God's way of guiding His servants in their ministry for Him.

We come back now to that which he especially wants to stress, "Concerning the collection for the saints, as I have given order to the churches of Galatia, even so do ye. Upon the first day of the week let every one of you lay by him in store, as God hath prospered him, that there be no gatherings when I come." I want to trace out with you the place that the first day of the week had in the early Christian Church, and that which it should have in the Church of God today. Let us turn back to the Old Testament, to Leviticus 23. There we have the seven great outstanding Hebrew festivals, the feasts of the Lord, the different occasions on which the people of Israel came together in a special way, beginning with the Passover and finishing with the Feast of Tabernacles. In Leviticus 23: 10, 11 we read: "Speak unto the children of Israel, and say unto them, When ye be come into the land which I give unto you, and shall reap the harvest thereof, then ye shall bring a sheaf of the firstfruits of your harvest unto the priest: and he shall wave the sheaf before the Lord, to be accepted for you: on the morrow after the sabbath the priest shall wave it." When was the Sabbath? The third verse says, "Six days shall work be done: but the seventh day is the sabbath of rest, an holy convocation; ye shall do no work therein: it is the sabbath of the Lord in all your dwellings." The Sabbath then was the seventh day. The feast of the firstfruits took place on "the morrow after the Sabbath," which was the first day of the week. And what was this feast of firstfruits? It was the feast that immediately followed the Passover.

What was the Passover? We have had its typical significance in the fifth chapter of our epistle. The apostle says, "Christ our passover is sacrificed for us: therefore let us keep the feast, not with old leaven, neither with the leaven of malice and wickedness; but with the unleavened bread of sincerity and truth" (chap. 5: 7, 8).

The Passover was the recurring memorial feast of the death of the lamb, the shedding of the blood, and the sprinkling of the blood upon the door-posts and the lintels in Egypt, by which the people were delivered from judgment. For God had said, "When I see the blood, I will pass over you" (Ex. 12:13). The Passover speaks of the death of Christ.

Following the Passover you have the sheaf of firstfruits presented before the Lord. Of what does it speak? It tells of grain that has fallen into the ground in death, but has come forth in new life. Jesus said, "Except a corn of wheat fall into the ground and die, it abideth alone: but if it die, it bringeth forth much fruit" (John 12:24). He was the corn of wheat who fell into the ground in death; He has come up in resurrection. The feast of the firstfruits speaks of this. The apostle has already explained it for us in chapter 15:23: "But every man in his own order: Christ the firstfruits; afterward they that are Christ's at His coming." On the first day of the week the sheaf of firstfruits was presented before the Lord, and this is a type of the resurrection of Christ. In the last chapter of Matthew's Gospel, verse one, we read, "In the end of the Sabbath" —the word is plural and should be translated "Sabbaths"—"as it began to dawn toward the first day of the week, came Mary Magdalene and the other Mary to see the sepulchre." And what had happened? The blessed Lord had risen in power on that first day of the week, that morning after the Sabbath, and from that time on the first day of the week had a very special place in the thoughts and in the hearts and minds of followers of our Lord Jesus.

Psalm 118 prophetically sets forth the rejection of Christ and then His resurrection. We read there in verse 22: "The stone which the builders refused"—that is, His rejection, His crucifixion—"is become the head of the corner"—that is His resurrection. That was what made Him the Head of the corner. "This is the Lord's doing; it is marvelous in our eyes" (Ps. 118: 23). Men crucified Him; God raised Him from the dead, and made Him the Head of the corner.

The psalm continues, "This is the day which the Lord hath made; we will rejoice and be glad in it." What day? The day when Christ was made the Head of the corner. It was the day of His glorious resurrection, the day of the presentation of the firstfruits, the first day of the week. You see what an honored place the first day of the week has in God's Word.

Then going back once more to Leviticus 23, we read in verses 15, 16: "And ye shall count unto you from the morrow after the sabbath, from the day that ye brought the sheaf of the wave-offering; seven sabbaths shall be complete: even unto the morrow after the seventh sabbath shall ye number fifty days; and ye shall offer a new meat-offering unto the Lord." This would be another first day of the week. What was this feast? It was Pentecost. And now, on the morrow after the seventh sabbath following the Passover, which typified the death of our Lord Jesus Christ, while the disciples were gathered together in Jerusalem, "suddenly there came a sound from heaven as of a rushing mighty wind, and it filled all the house where they were sitting. And there appeared unto them cloven tongues like as of fire, and it sat upon each of them. And they were all filled with the Holy Ghost, and began to speak with other tongues, as the Spirit gave them utterance" (Acts 2: 2-4).

The day of Pentecost had fully come, and the Lord received to Himself a new meal offering in those that had been redeemed by His precious blood. It was on the first day of the week that the Holy Ghost came from Heaven to baptize believers into one Body, and so, from this time on, the first day of the week has always had its special place in the Church of God.

In Acts 20 we read of Paul coming to Troas and remaining there a week with the brethren. In verse seven we read: "And upon the first day of the week, when the disciples came together

to break bread, Paul preached unto them, ready
to depart on the morrow; and continued his
speech until midnight." It does not say that on
the first day of the week the disciples came together to hear Paul preach, but it says, "Upon
the first day of the week, when the disciples came
together to break bread." That is what they
were accustomed to do on that day. They came
together to participate in what we call the Communion Service, to take part in the breaking of
bread and the drinking of the cup which speaks
of the precious body of our Lord Jesus given up
to death and of His blood poured out for our redemption. And when they thus came together
that night they found they had a wonderful visitor ready to minister the Word to them. Many
of them were slaves and had to work during the
day, and so they came together at night. Paul
participated with them in the meeting and
preached the Word to them, and the service went
on until midnight.

When you go back to the earliest records which
have come down from those whom we call "the
apostolic fathers," those who wrote shortly after
the New Testament was completed, we learn it
was the custom of the believers to gather together on the first day of the week for worship
and for the ministry of the Word, and, above all,
to partake of what they called the Eucharist, the

Thanksgiving. They thought of the Lord's Supper as the Feast of Thanksgiving, when Christians came together to give thanks to the Lord Jesus for the suffering and sorrow that He went through for our redemption. One of these early fathers has written something like this: "Upon the first day of the week, the day that we Christians call the Lord's Day, the day after the Jewish Sabbath, we come together to break bread," etc. There have been those who have tried to tell us that we are all wrong in recognizing the first day of the week as a special day for worship and praise, that we should Judaize and go back to the law of Moses for our special day. But all that has been set aside in the old economy, for in the new dispensation we find God gives special honor to this new day, the first day of the week. On this day they came together to break bread. The Holy Ghost descended on this day, Christ arose from the dead on this day, and on this day they made their offerings for the work of the Lord.

The apostle tells them to lay aside at home as God hath prospered them, so that when they come together they may give to the Lord. They were to go over what they had received during the week, and see how God had blessed them, and give the Lord a part. Of course I take it that no Christian would give less than a Jew did, and he gave a tenth to God. So God would have a tenth at least, and more if they could afford it. When they came together to break bread they gave their offering to meet the needs of the Lord's work, and to care for the needy.

Yes, we can thank God for preserving to us, all down through the centuries, the privilege of gathering together on the first day of the week. How we ought to praise Him that we live in a land that, in some sense at least, recognizes the sanctity of the day so that we can come together to worship and praise Him. How much we would lose were we to be denied this privilege!

LECTURE XXXIX.

QUIT YOU LIKE MEN

✓ ✓ ✓

"Watch ye, stand fast in the faith, quit you like men, be strong. Let all your things be done with charity. I beseech you, brethren, (ye know the house of Stephanas, that it is the firstfruits of Achaia, and that they have addicted themselves to the ministry of the saints), that ye submit yourselves unto such, and to every one that helpeth with us, and laboreth. I am glad of the coming of Stephanas and Fortunatus and Achaicus: for that which was lacking on your part they have supplied. For they have refreshed my spirit and yours: therefore acknowledge ye them that are such. The churches of Asia salute you. Aquila and Priscilla salute you much in the Lord, with the church that is in their house. All the brethren greet you. Greet ye one another with an holy kiss. The salutation of me Paul with mine own hand. If any man love not the Lord Jesus Christ, let him be Anathema Maran-atha. The grace of our Lord Jesus Christ be with you. My love be with you all in Christ Jesus. Amen" (1 Cor. 16: 13-24).

✓ ✓ ✓

THERE is something delightfully personal in most of the closing messages of the apostle Paul to the various churches. He was a very human man as well as a very spiritual one. The late Dr. C. I. Scofield used to say that when we are first converted we have to be changed from natural to spiritual, but after being saved awhile we need another conversion to become natural again—in a different sense, of course. So many of us allow ourselves to become rather stilted and unnatural in our desire to be spiritual, and we lose that sweet, gracious warmth that should characterize us as Christian men and women.

Paul was a man with a tender heart. He made very real friendships and never went back on a friend. He may have grieved over some of them who forsook him, but he continued to pray for them even when they turned away from him. And those with whom he could continue to have happy fellowship were a real joy to him. I want you to notice the various personal references in this portion. For the moment we will pass over verses 13, 14.

In chapter 1, when some of them were making too much of leaders and saying, "I am of Paul," or "I am of Apollos," or "I am of Cephas," and others again were making Christ the head of a party and saying, "I am of Christ," he had said, "I am so glad that I did not baptize any of you lest you should say I had baptized in my own name." He was not setting baptism at naught in the slightest degree. Sometimes we find people who make these words the basis of their notion that Paul was making light of Christian baptism. But these Corinthians were making so

much of human leaders that he would not have
people going about boasting that they were baptized by Paul and therefore considering that they
had a different standing from others. He was
very glad, under the circumstances, that as far
as he could remember, he had baptized only
Crispus and Gaius and the household of
Stephanas.

And now he tells us something about that
household of Stephanas. They were not little infants, but he says, "I beseech you, brethren, (ye
know the house of Stephanas, that it is the firstfruits of Achaia, and that they have addicted
themselves to the ministry of the saints)." The
very first home to be opened up to the gospel,
when he went to Corinth, was that of Stephanas.
He and his family were brought to Christ and
evidently were in a position to help others, for
from that time on they "addicted themselves to
the ministry of the saints." The word translated
"addicted" is exactly the same word that is elsewhere translated "ordained." So one could say
that the household of Stephanas had "ordained
themselves to the ministry of the saints." What
a blessed ordination! Instead of constantly looking for other people to do things for them, they
said, "We are going in to do for others; we will
try to be a blessing to others; we will set ourselves apart to help God's beloved people." And

so the apostle says, "Submit yourselves unto such, and to every one that helpeth with us, and laboreth." You see, like Epaphroditus, they made themselves of no reputation that they might bless other people.

Stephanas himself had evidently launched out into evangelistic work, and he with others had come to meet Paul. Paul wrote this letter from Philippi and he says, "I am glad of the coming of Stephanas and Fortunatus and Achaicus: for that which was lacking on your part they have supplied." I take it that he means, "I knew you wanted to send me something to help me with my expenses but have not done so, but now these brethren have come and brought an offering and I appreciate it very much." When he was in Corinth the first time, he would not take anything from them because they were all heathen, and when they were newly come out of heathenism he did not want any one to say, "Paul is just here for what he can make out of us." He says, "I robbed other churches, taking wages of them, to do you service" (2 Cor. 11: 8). Others gave the money that enabled him to meet part of his expenses, and what he lacked he earned by tent-making.

He did not have such a great regard for the "cloth," you know, that he could not soil his hands. He went into business with Priscilla and

Aquila. But now that he has left Corinth, he is glad to receive from the Corinthian church a missionary offering to help him in his work. We at home are glad to send our money to those laboring in heathen lands to help make the gospel known. In return, we read, "The churches of Asia salute you, Aquila and Priscilla salute you much in the Lord, with the church that is in their house." Aquila and Priscilla used to live in Corinth, and Paul stayed with them when he was there, but now they are away and naturally send their greetings back to the home church.

"Greet ye one another with an holy kiss." There is such a thing as a Judas kiss, or, it might be, an insincere hand-shake. It means the same thing. Someone says to another, "Well, I am so glad to see you," and then she has hardly turned her back before she says, "Hateful old cat; I wish she would stay away!" Or, another says, "Good morning, brother, so pleased to meet you," and then he turns around and says, "I haven't any use for him." That is an unholy greeting. In the ancient times women kissed women and men kissed men. Women still kiss one another when they meet, but be sure it is a holy kiss. Do not profess to love her when deep in your heart there is resentment and unkindness. As brethren greet each other let it be in sincerity. Let the heart that is behind it be right. Said

Jehu, "Is thine heart right, as my heart is with thy heart?" And when Jehonadab said, "It is," we read that Jehu "took him up to him into the chariot" (2 Kings 10:15). We need to get rid of hypocrisy; we have a lot of pretension to fellowship that is not real. "I would have you," says the apostle, "to be sincere," that is, to be genuine in all things.

I will drop the rest of the chapter for the moment and go back to verses 13, 14. Here is Paul's closing exhortation, "Watch ye, stand fast in the faith, quit you like men, be strong. Let all your things be done with charity," or, "with love." How we need to heed this. "Watch ye." As long as we are in this world we are in the place of danger, we are surrounded by pitfalls and snares on every hand. "Watch ye and pray, lest ye enter into temptation" (Mark 14:38), said our Lord Jesus Christ. We dare not trust ourselves and we cannot trust the world through which we journey.

> "Are there no foes for me to face?
>   Must I not stem the flood?
> Is this vile world a friend to grace,
>   To help me on to God?
>
> "Since I must fight if I would reign,
>   Increase my courage, Lord!
> I'll bear the toil, endure the pain,
>   Supported by Thy Word."

It is one of the first principles of soldiery to keep a sharp lookout for the enemy, and so we must be on the watch for the enemy of our souls.

"Stand fast in the faith." There are too many people who blow hot and blow cold; they are one thing in one company and quite different in another. But the servant of Christ, the child of God, should be one who realizes that there has been committed to him the greatest of all possible responsibilities and therefore he is to "stand fast in the faith." As the apostle elsewhere writes to Timothy, "That good deposit that was committed unto thee, keep by the Holy Ghost which dwelleth in us" (2 Tim. 1:14). It is only in the power of the Holy Spirit that we can keep the faith.

And then we have the words, "Quit you like men." He reproved these Corinthians in the early part of the letter because some of them were acting like babies; some were divided into little sectarian groups, and he said, "When you talk like this, it is childishness." "I have fed you with milk, and not with meat: for hitherto ye were not able to bear it." Whenever you see Christians fussing, quarreling about their own rights, complaining because they are not properly recognized, because people do not greet them as they think they should, because they do not get enough applause for what they do, put it down as the "baby" spirit coming out. They have not yet reached spiritual maturity. The man in Christ is indifferent to praise or to blame. If I belong to Christ, I am here to serve Him. If I have His approbation, that is the thing that counts. "Quit you like men." May God deliver us from our babyishness. In some churches half the time of the minister is spent trying to keep weak Christians quiet over little slights. If you are living for God, people cannot slight you because you will not let them. It will not make any difference to you. "Quit you like men, be strong."

Someone says, "That is just my trouble. I know I ought to be strong, but I am so weak." Of course you cannot be strong in your own strength. We read: "Be strong in the Lord, and in the power of His might" (Eph. 6: 10). And the more you realize your own weakness, and the more you throw yourself upon Him, the more you will be able to stand in the evil day, for His strength is made perfect in our weakness.

And then again, you are not to be strong in your own human spirit, but to be strong by the Spirit of the Lord. Turn to Ephesians 3: 16, 17. The apostle prays, "That He would grant you according to the riches of His glory, to be strengthened with might by His Spirit in the inner man; that Christ may dwell in your hearts by faith." The Holy Spirit is the Spirit of Christ, and He has come to dwell in you if you are a believer. If He is controlling the life, dominating your will, it is not a question of your ability to stand, it is a question of His. You are simply yielded to Him, and as you are yielded to Him you are enabled to be strong and to stand for His glory.

But then, you need spiritual nourishment, and so you become strong through the Word. Writing to young men, the apostle John says, "I have written unto you, young men, because you are strong" (1 John 2:14). How did they get that strength? "And the Word of God abideth in you." You show me a weak, wobbling believer, and I will show you a Christian not giving very much time to meditation upon the Word of God. Show me one who is a strong, devoted, earnest Christian, seeking only the glory of the Lord Jesus Christ, and I will show you one who is living on the Book. As you eat the Word, as you feed upon the truth, you get strength that you cannot obtain in any other way. People go around lamenting their weakness and their leanness. I get so tired of people coming and saying, "Do pray for me that I may be a stronger Christian." What is the use of praying for you? You might say, "Do pray that I may get stronger physically." "What kind of food do you eat?" I ask. "Not any." And I would say, "Then there is no use praying for you." What you need as a Christian is a good meal of spiritual nourishment, and you can get it only in the Book. You may do all the praying you like to be a strong Christian, and your prayer will never be answered until you begin to answer it yourself by feeding upon the Word of God.

But do not stop there, for we also become strong through obedience. Turn back to the Old Testament to a very blessed scripture, Joshua 1: 7: "Only be thou strong and very courageous, that thou mayest observe to do according to all the law, which Moses My servant commanded thee: turn not from it to the right hand or to the left, that thou mayest prosper whithersoever thou goest." *"To do"*—notice that. That is where we lack. We know, but we do not *do*. "This book of the law shall not depart out of thy mouth; but thou shalt meditate therein day and night, that thou mayest observe to do according to all that is written therein: for then thou shalt make thy way prosperous, and then thou shalt have good success" (Josh. 1: 8). They had only the five books of Moses when God gave that command. You have a whole Bible with its sixty-six books. Apply this to the entire Bible. "Let it not depart out of your mouth. Meditate therein day and night, that you may observe to do according to all that is written therein: *for then* you shall make your way prosperous, *and then* you shall have good success." I suppose you want to make a success of your life, young man or young woman. Here then is the divinely-appointed way to do it.

And so, if you want strength, this is how you get it. Live in fellowship with Christ, walk in the Spirit, feed upon His Word, obey His Word, and then when the hour of trial comes, you will not be weak-kneed, you will not be vacillating, you will not be carried about like a leaf before the wind. You will have strength to stand, and you will be able to glorify God even in the fire. It is the testing that is the proof.

> "It is easy enough to be pleasant,
>   When life flows on like a song,
> But the man worth while is the man with a smile
>   When everything goes dead wrong."

The Christian who is really worthwhile is the man who can be bereft of everything—he can lose his good clothes, his money, his home, his health—and after everything is gone he can say, "The Lord gave, and the Lord hath taken away; blessed be the name of the Lord" (Job 1:21). That is the kind of Christian God would have me be, strong in the hour of trial, and strong too in the hour of temptation.

I am afraid a good many of us keep from fall-

ing into various sins because they never come
very close to us, and then we look with contempt
upon people who go down when stress comes. If
you had been exposed to the same temptation
that that poor failing brother or sister was exposed to, you might have gone down just as he
or she did. You would have, if not kept by the
mighty power of God. It is only by living in
fellowship with God that you will be kept from
yielding. The colored brother said, "It is a queer
thing about me, I can resist everything but
temptation." A good many of us are like that.
Go through the Book of God and you will find
that the men who could resist in the hour of
temptation were the men who knew God before
the test came. David was not in fellowship with
God when that awful temptation came, or he
never would have gone down. Joseph was tempted under far more adverse circumstances and he
stood fast, exclaiming, "How then can I do this
great wickedness, and sin against God?" (Gen.
39: 9). Our blessed Lord could say, "I have set
Jehovah always before Me: because He is at My
right hand, I shall not be moved." The man who
resists temptation is the man strong in the Lord
before temptation comes. But there is always
danger that the strong will be contemptuous of
the weak. So he adds, "Let all your things be
done with charity." Be very exact with your-

self, but very generous in your judgment of other people; be very, very strict with yourself, but very gracious in dealing with those who are weak. Remember what they have to contend with. Perhaps they do not know the Lord as well as you do, so seek by grace to manifest the love of Christ to them.

We now come to the end of the chapter. In verse 22 we have a very solemn word before the apostle closes this letter. I wonder whether there are those listening to me who do not love the Lord Jesus Christ. May I just ask you to pause and face this question, *Do you love the Lord Jesus Christ?* What is your heart's answer? Can you say, "I do," or to be perfectly honest, do you have to say, "No; I do not love Him?" May the Spirit of God give you to realize the solemnity of the warning, "If any man love not the Lord Jesus Christ, let him be Anathema Maran-atha." What strange expressions! I think the Holy Spirit of God providentially allowed our translators to leave those two peculiar words untranslated. One of them is a Greek word, "Anathema," and it means, "Accursed, devoted to judgment." The other word, "Maran-atha" is a Syriac word, and means, "The Lord cometh." If you translated the entire passage, it would read like this, "If any man love not the Lord Jesus Christ, let him be devoted to judgment

at the coming of the Lord." What a solemn word
that is! O unsaved one, may God give you to
realize the dangerous position in which you stand.

"If any man love not the Lord Jesus Christ, he
will be devoted to judgment at the coming of the
Lord." The Lord has not yet returned, and
though you do not love Him, you may love Him.
You cannot stir up any love in your own heart
but you may trust Him, the One who loves you,
the One who gave Himself for you, the One who
died on the cross for your sins. Open your heart
to Him, receive Him, bow at His feet in repentance, hide nothing, confess your sins, your sins
of hypocrisy, of dishonesty, of immorality, of
selfishness, of covetousness, whatever wickedness
it my be. Tell Him all about it. Do not say, "O
Lord, I am not much of a sinner; I never did many
things that are wrong; I pray Thee forgive me,"
but get into the company of David who when his
conscience was awakened said, "O Lord, pardon
mine iniquity; for it is great" (Ps. 25:11). You
would almost have expected him to say, "It isn't
very great, so pardon it." No; he says, "It is great."
It is such great iniquity that only a great God can
pardon and a great Saviour can deliver. "If with
all your heart ye truly seek Him, He will be
found of you." If you will turn to Him honestly
facing your sin, acknowledging your guilt, trusting Him as your Saviour, and then confess Him

before men, He will put love in your heart and you will be able to say, "I love Him, my Saviour, my Redeemer," and you will not be devoted to judgment, you will be saved from judgment, and so will be able to enter into the blessedness of this closing benediction:

"The grace of our Lord Jesus Christ be with you." And then the apostle adds so humanly, "My love be with you all in Christ Jesus." Thank you, Paul; we are glad to get this message from you, and when we get Home to Heaven, we will look you up and will talk it over together. Till then we will seek to carry out the truth we have found in this Epistle.